# THE RABBIS' BIBLE

## VOLUME ONE: TORAH

*by Solomon Simon and Morrison David Bial*
with the editorial assistance of Hannah Grad Goodman
woodcuts by Irwin Rosenhouse

**BEHRMAN HOUSE,** Inc.
Publishers          New York

*In honor of my father Eruchim Ben-Zion,*
*and my mother Mere,*
*who embodied the spirit of God's word*
*in their daily lives.*

SHLOMO SIMON

*In honor of my parents, Jacob and Carrie Bial*

MORRISON DAVID BIAL

HONOR YOUR FATHER AND YOUR MOTHER
EVEN AS YOU HONOR GOD,
FOR ALL THREE HAVE BEEN PARTNERS
IN YOUR CREATION

ZOHAR III 93a

5   6   7   8   84   83   82   81

© Copyright 1966, by Behrman House, Inc., 1261 Broadway, New York, N.Y. 10001

Library of Congress Catalog Card Number: 66-20409

Standard Book Number: 87441-020-7

MANUFACTURED IN THE UNITED STATES OF AMERICA

# PREFACE

THE BIBLE is a world in itself and this edition of the Pentateuch is intended as a textbook companion and guide to it, a book for the young and adult study group. An abridged version of the Humash is arranged as a continuous text across the tops of the pages with a continuing keyed commentary at the bottoms. That commentary explores the vast literature of Biblical interpretation including the two Talmuds, the Midrashim, the medieval and modern Jewish commentators, as well as legend and folklore. Together the Biblical text and commentary weave three thousand years of Jewish wisdom and tradition into a single strand, each reinforcing and interpreting the other.

The Bible never tells a story for its own sake nor quotes a piece of poetry for its poetic beauty alone; each verse was meant to teach a lesson, point a moral, record an important folk memory or event in the history of the Jewish people. With that in mind, we have included law, history, ritual, and ceremony—everything of value in ethical precept. The text avoids archaism but does no violence to the Biblical context by undue colloquialism.

A Teacher's Resource book has been prepared to make the study of Bible a still more meaningful experience by presenting the more profound meanings and subtle philosophies embodied in what is often a hyperbolic and symbolic Scriptural text. And rather than apologetics, what is offered is interpretation rich in ancient lore and replete with modern scholarship, so that throughout, the student, the teacher and the reader will find new insight and understanding of the relevance in the Torah:

> *Turn it, turn it again and again, for everything is in it. Contemplate it, grow gray and old over it, for there is no greater good.*
>
> PIRKÉ AVOT 5:25

**NOTE**

Biblical and place names are spelled as in the Jewish Publication Society (1917) translation. Otherwise the modern Sephardic pronunciation is used for Hebrew transliteration.

Occasionally verses have been rearranged slightly to provide for an even flow of the narrative. So too, the legal sections have been selected from the various chapters of a single book and rearranged. The Rabbis held: *"Én mukdam u-m'uḥar ba-Torah*—There is no early or late in the Torah."

# CONTENTS

## GENESIS

## EXODUS

# LEVITICUS

# NUMBERS

# DEUTERONOMY

# 1. GENESIS [1-3]

### GOD CREATES THE WORLD

IN THE BEGINNING, [1] God created [2] the heaven and the earth. [3] Now the earth was unformed and void, and darkness was upon the surface of the deep; and the spirit of God moved over the face of the waters.

And God said, "Let there be light!" [4] And there was light.

And God saw that the light was good; and God divided the light from the darkness. God called the light Day, and the darkness He called Night. And there was evening and there was morning, one day.

---

[1] IN THE BEGINNING: Our Rabbis said: When a king builds a palace, he consults an architect's plans.

When God created the universe, He, too, worked from a plan—the Torah. Before the heaven and earth were formed, the Torah existed, written in black fire on white fire. God looked into the Torah and created the world.

בְּרֵאשִׁית בָּרָא אֱלֹהִים אֵת הַשָּׁמַיִם וְאֵת הָאָרֶץ.

And God said, "Let there be a space in the midst of the waters, dividing them." And it was so.

And God called the open space Heaven. And there was evening and there was morning, a second day.

Then God said, "Let the waters beneath the heaven be gathered into one place, that the dry land may appear." And it was so.

And God called the dry land Earth, and the gathered waters He called Seas. And God saw that it was good.

Then God said, "Let the earth put forth grass, seed-bearing plants, and many kinds of fruit trees."

And it was so. The earth brought forth grass, plants that yield seed, and trees [5] bearing fruit in which was seed; and God saw that it was good.

---

[2] THE PLAN OF CREATION: Why did God say of this world that "it was good"? Because it was not the first that had been created. He had made others, but they had not pleased Him.

Why not? Because they had been made without the Torah—in other words, without plan and order. Furthermore, their creatures were not able to choose between good and evil, to rise or to fall. Our world, however, is based on the Torah, which gives it plan and purpose. Moreover, it allows man freedom of choice: he can decide whether or not he will obey God's laws. God's hope is that man will rise to the greatness for which he was created.

[3] JUSTICE VERSUS MERCY: The world could not exist if God had created it only in accordance with strict law and justice. At man's first transgression, the world would have had to be destroyed, either by fire or by water. On the other hand, if God ruled by compassion alone, the world would be filled with evil and wickedness, as in the days of Sodom and Gomorrah. Therefore, God joined mercy with justice, and with both He ruled the world.

To what may this be compared? To a king who possessed precious goblets of glass. If he poured hot water into them, they would shatter; cold water, they would crack. When he mixed the two, the goblets could hold the water. In the same way, God combined justice with mercy, that man might endure.

וַיַּרְא אֱלֹהִים כִּי טוֹב.

And there was evening and there was morning, a third day.

And God said, "Let there be lights in the heaven to separate the day from the night; and let them be for signs, and for seasons, and for days and years. And let them give light upon the earth." And it was so.

And God made the two great lights: the greater light to rule the day, and the lesser light to rule the night; and the stars. And God set them in the heaven to give light upon the earth; and God saw that it was good. And there was evening and there was morning, a fourth day.

---

[4] LET THERE BE LIGHT: First, light was created; then the world. Compare this, said our Sages, to the situation of a king who wished to build a palace while it was yet dark, and lit lanterns to work by.

But what was the source of the light which existed although there was neither sun nor moon? Rabbi Sh'muel explains: "God wrapped Himself in a white garment of holiness, and its radiance shone from one end of the world to the other."

Rabbi Eleazar, however, said, "The light on the first day was not like that of the sun, the moon and the stars which were created on the fourth day, but was so brilliant that man would have been able to see from one end of the world to the other." Why did God take this light away? "Because He foresaw the sinful generation of the deluge, and the rebellious people of the tower of Babel." When will the light be restored? "In the end of days, when all the world will be just and righteous and man will use the gift for good."

[5] THE TREES AND THE AXE: On the third day were created the grass, and herbs, and the mighty cedars of Lebanon, and other great trees. The trees rose high into the air, and stood tall and proud.

And God created iron the same day. At this the trees began to tremble. "Woe to us," they wept. "The time will come when we shall be felled by axes made of iron."

God replied, "If you will live together in peace, and if there will be no traitor among you, disaster will not befall you; for without wood for axe-handles, the iron will not be able to harm you."

וַיַּעַשׂ אֱלֹהִים אֶת שְׁנֵי הַמְּאֹרוֹת הַגְּדֹלִים: אֶת הַמָּאוֹר הַגָּדֹל לְמֶמְשֶׁלֶת הַיּוֹם
וְאֶת הַמָּאוֹר הַקָּטֹן לְמֶמְשֶׁלֶת הַלַּיְלָה וְאֶת הַכּוֹכָבִים.

Then God said, "Let the waters be filled with living creatures, and let birds fly above the earth in the open space of the sky." And God created the great sea-beasts, and every crawling creature, so that the waters swarmed, and various kinds of winged birds; and God saw that it was good.

And God blessed them, saying, "Be fruitful and multiply, and fill the waters in the seas, and let the birds increase on the earth." And there was evening and there was morning, a fifth day.

Now God said, "Let the earth bring forth the many kinds of living creatures, cattle, and creeping thing, and beast." And it was so.

And God made the various kinds of beast, and the cattle, and every creeping thing upon the earth; and God saw that it was good.

And God said, "I will make man [6]

---

[6] MAN CREATED LAST: Why was man created last of all the creatures? Several explanations are given by our Sages.

For one, let man beware, lest he become arrogant and haughty; for it can be said of him, "The gnat, the fly and even the mosquito are older than you."

Again, man was created last that everything might be ready for him. God was as a host who set a table with every delicacy and then welcomed the guest to his place.

Third, man was created on Friday afternoon that he might immediately greet Sabbath, the Queen.

[7] WHY WAS MAN CREATED SINGLY? Why did God create only one man? So that no one can boast, "I am of nobler lineage," our Sages explain. All mankind is descended from the same man. All are equal before God.

Hence, the families of nations cannot quarrel, saying, "We are greater than other peoples." Rather, as the prophet Malachi put it, "Have we not all one Father?" (2:10).

Because mankind descended from one man, the Rabbis make the point that he who destroys one life is as though he had slain an entire creation, whereas he who saves one life is as if he had saved all mankind.

כֹּל הַמְאַבֵּד נֶפֶשׁ אַחַת כְּאִלּוּ אִבֵּד עוֹלָם מָלֵא, וְכָל הַמְקַיֵּם נֶפֶשׁ אַחַת כְּאִלּוּ קִיֵּם עוֹלָם מָלֵא.

in My image, and in My likeness. Let him rule over the fish of the sea, and over the birds in the air, and over the cattle, and over all the earth, and over every thing that creeps upon the earth." And God created man in His own image; in the image of God He created him. [7] And God saw that everything He had made was very good. And there was evening and there was morning, the sixth day.

The heaven and earth were finished, and all the host within them. And on the seventh day God ended His work which He had made, and He rested on the seventh day. [8] And God blessed the seventh day, and made it holy; because on it He rested from all His work of creation which He had made.

This is the story of the heaven and of the earth when they were created.

## THE PLANTING OF THE GARDEN OF EDEN

WHEN THE LORD GOD formed man from the dust of the earth, [9] and breathed into his nostrils the breath of life, man became a living being. [10] Then the Lord God planted a garden in Eden to the East, and there He put the man whom He had formed. Out of the earth the Lord God made every sort of tree to grow, pleasant to the sight, and good

---

ᴇᏽ [8] GOD ENDED HIS WORK: The Rabbis asked, "If God rested on the seventh day, how is it that He ended His work on it?"

To this they replied, "He created rest on the Sabbath, which is not merely the absence of work. Through rest man refreshes his spirit and renews his sense of life. The Sabbath, therefore, is a time for joy and reflection, for repose and tranquillity."

ᴇᏽ [9] MAN WAS CREATED OF DUST: Our Sages said, "God formed Adam of dust from *all over* the world: yellow clay and white sand, black loam and red soil, that the earth may not declare to any race or color of man that he does not belong here; that this soil is not his home."

ᴇᏽ [10] THE ONE ADAM: Since there was only one Adam, one might expect all men to be alike, yet this is not so. A human being stamps many coins and all are the same; but God in His glory and greatness stamps each man with the stamp of Adam, yet not one is like another.

וַיְכֻלּוּ הַשָּׁמַיִם וְהָאָרֶץ וְכָל צְבָאָם. וַיְכַל אֱלֹהִים בַּיּוֹם הַשְּׁבִיעִי מְלַאכְתּוֹ אֲשֶׁר עָשָׂה, וַיִּשְׁבֹּת בַּיּוֹם הַשְּׁבִיעִי.

for food. The Tree of Life was in the midst of the Garden, and also the Tree of Knowledge of good and evil.

And the Lord God took the man, and put him into the Garden of Eden to tend it and to look after it. And the Lord God commanded the man, "Of every tree in the Garden you are free to eat, but from the Tree of Knowledge of good and evil [11] you shall not eat; for on the day that you eat of it you shall surely die."

## THE CREATION OF THE WOMAN

THE LORD GOD brought to the man every beast of the field, and every bird of the air, to see what he would call them. And whatever he would call each living creature, that was to be its name.

And the man gave names to all cattle, and to the birds of the air, and to every beast; but for Adam himself no helper was found who was like him. And the Lord God said, "It is not good that man should be alone; I will make a helper for him."

And the Lord God caused a deep sleep to fall upon the man; and when he slept, He took one of his ribs, and closed up the flesh. And the rib, which the Lord God had taken from the man, He fashioned into a woman, and brought her to the man. [12] And the man said, "This is now bone of my bones, and flesh of my flesh; she shall be called

---

◄§  [11] THE TREE OF LIFE AND THE TREE OF KNOWLEDGE: The Bible speaks of two trees: the Tree of Life and the Tree of Knowledge. Why are they mentioned together?

The Tree of Life was tall, and shaded the entire Garden. The Tree of Knowledge, though shorter, surrounded the other. No one could touch the Tree of Life until he had penetrated the Tree of Knowledge.

◄§  [12] GOD BRINGS EVE TO ADAM: There is a Midrash that God Himself sanctified the union of Adam and Eve, for the lifelong relationship between a man and a woman is sacred to Him. He Himself took Eve by the hand and brought her to Adam. He said to the angels, "Come, let us prepare the wedding ceremony."

The angels surrounded the canopy, and God pronounced the blessing upon the bridal couple. The angels played upon musical instruments and danced to entertain the bride and groom.

וַיֹּאמֶר יְיָ אֱלֹהִים: לֹא טוֹב הֱיוֹת הָאָדָם לְבַדּוֹ, אֶעֱשֶׂה לוֹ עֵזֶר כְּנֶגְדּוֹ.

Woman, because she was taken out of Man." Therefore shall a man leave his father and his mother, and shall cleave unto his wife, and they shall be one flesh.

And God blessed them, and He said to them, "Be fruitful and multiply, and fill the earth, and master it; and rule over the fish of the sea, over the birds of the air, and over every living thing."

And they both were naked, the man and his wife, and felt no shame.

### THE SERPENT

NOW THE SERPENT was the most cunning of all the creatures that the Lord God had made. And he said to the woman, "Has God said that you shall not eat from any tree in the Garden?"

And the woman said to the serpent, "From the fruit of the trees of the Garden we may eat; only of the fruit of the tree which is in the midst of the Garden God has said: You shall not eat of it, nor touch it, lest you die."

And the serpent said to the woman, "You surely would not die; for God knows that on the day you eat of it, your eyes shall be opened, and you shall be like God and know good from evil."

When the woman saw that the tree was good for food, and that it was a delight to the eyes, she took of its fruit, and ate. [13] She also gave some to her husband, and he ate. And the eyes of both of them were opened, and they realized that they were naked. So they sewed fig-leaves together, and made themselves coverings.

Toward the cool of the day, they heard the voice of the Lord God in the Garden. And Adam and Eve hid themselves from the Lord God among the trees.

### THE PUNISHMENT FOR THE FIRST SIN

THE LORD GOD called to the man, "Where are you?"

---

[13] THE TREE OF KNOWLEDGE: How was it that Eve broke God's command so soon? To keep her from temptation, Adam had told her that God forbade them even to touch the Tree of Knowledge. In adding to God's words, Adam brought trouble upon them.

Of all the creatures, the serpent was the superior. He stood upright on two feet, and his height equaled the camel's. As king of the animals, he was jealous of Adam. Carefully, he planned the conversation that was to bring about the downfall of man. "Is it true,

וַיֹּאמֶר לָהֶם אֱלֹהִים: פְּרוּ וּרְבוּ וּמִלְאוּ אֶת הָאָרֶץ וְכִבְשֻׁהָ וּרְדוּ בִּדְגַת הַיָּם
וּבְעוֹף הַשָּׁמַיִם וּבְכָל חַיָּה הָרוֹמֶשֶׂת עַל הָאָרֶץ.

And he replied, "I heard Thy voice in the Garden, and because I was naked I hid myself."

And He said, "Who told you that you were naked? Have you eaten from the tree of which I forbade you to eat?" And the man said, "The woman whom Thou gavest me, she gave me of the tree, and I ate."

Then the Lord God said to the woman, "What is this you have done?" And the woman said, "The serpent tricked me, and I ate."

The Lord God said to the serpent, "Cursed shall you be among all the beasts of the field; upon your belly shall you go. And there shall be hatred between you and the woman, and between your children and her children."

To the woman He said, "In pain shall you bring forth children; and your husband shall rule over you."

And to Adam God said, "Because you have listened to the voice of your wife and have eaten from the tree from which I forbade you to eat, cursed be the earth because of you. Thorns and thistles shall it bring forth for you. By the sweat of your brow you shall earn your living, until you return to the ground, for dust you are and unto dust you shall return."

And the man called his wife's name Eve [Life], because she was the mother of all living.

And the Lord God made for Adam and his wife garments of skins and clothed them.

So the Lord God expelled man from the Garden of Eden. He drove the man out, and He placed the cherubim at the east of the Garden of Eden with flaming, whirling sword, to bar the way to the Tree of Life.

---

Eve," he began, "that Adam has said you may eat of every tree in the Garden?"

"We may not so much as touch the Tree of Knowledge," Eve replied, "lest we be stricken."

At this, the serpent pushed her against the Tree. "You see," he said, "nothing has happened! Neither will you die if you eat of the fruit. God Himself ate from this Tree before He created the world. If you eat from it, you, too, will be able to create worlds."

"My master, Adam, did not speak the truth," Eve thought to herself. Thereupon she succumbed to the serpent and ate of the fruit of the Tree of Knowledge.

בְּזֵעַת אַפֶּיךָ תֹּאכַל לֶחֶם עַד שׁוּבְךָ אֶל הָאֲדָמָה כִּי מִמֶּנָּה לֻקָּחְתָּ, כִּי עָפָר אַתָּה וְאֶל עָפָר תָּשׁוּב.

# 2. GENESIS [4-11]

CAIN AND ABEL

AND EVE GAVE birth to Cain; and she later gave birth to his brother Abel.

Abel was a shepherd, and Cain was a tiller of the soil. And in the course of time, Cain brought from the fruit of the earth an offering to the Lord. And Abel also brought an offering to the Lord from the choicest of the first-born of his flock.

The Lord took notice of Abel and his offering, but of Cain and his offering He took no notice. And Cain became very angry, and his face fell.

Then the Lord said to Cain, "Why are you angry, and why is your face fallen? If you do right, you shall be happy, but if you do not do right, sin lies in wait at the door."

And it came to pass when Cain and Abel were in the field, that Cain turned on his brother Abel and slew him. [1]

---

[1] CAIN AND ABEL: The slaying of Abel by Cain was not entirely unforewarned. As youths the two brothers had often quarreled. To

וַיְהִי הֶבֶל רוֹעֵה צֹאן וְקַיִן הָיָה עוֹבֵד אֲדָמָה.

Then the Lord said to Cain, "Where is your brother Abel?" And Cain answered, "I do not know; am I my brother's keeper?" [2]

And He said, "What have you done? The voice of your brother's blood cries to Me from the earth. [3] The earth has opened its mouth to receive your brother's blood from your hand. When you till the soil, it shall never again give you its full strength. A fugitive and a wanderer shall you be on the earth."

And Cain said to the Lord, "My punishment is greater than I can bear."

And the Lord said to him, "Therefore anyone who kills Cain shall suffer vengeance sevenfold." And the Lord put a mark on Cain, lest anyone who met him should kill him.

---

keep them apart, Adam, their father, gave them different occupations. Cain, the elder, became a farmer; Abel, a shepherd.

Real strife broke out when the brothers offered sacrifices to God. Abel selected the best of his flocks, but Cain offered that which was left from his own meal. God did not accept this halfhearted service.

Cain considered himself wronged, and the brothers quarreled. "Let us separate, and divide our possessions between us," Cain suggested. Abel agreed.

"You will take the cattle and sheep," Cain continued, "and I shall take the land." Abel accepted this, too.

However, when Abel took his herd to pasture the next morning, he was confronted by Cain, who demanded, "Get off my land! The earth is mine!"

"Your garment is wool," Abel countered. "Take it off! It is mine!" And the brothers came to blows again.

Abel fled, but Cain pursued and overtook him. The struggle began anew, but Abel overpowered his brother and threw him to the ground. The terrified Cain now began to plead. "Are we not brothers? If you kill me, what will you say to our father?"

Abel responded to his brother's pleading and released him. But as Abel walked away, Cain rose, seized a stone and hurled it at Abel and slew him.

וַיֹּאמֶר יְיָ אֶל קַיִן: אֵי הֶבֶל אָחִיךָ? וַיֹּאמֶר: לֹא יָדַעְתִּי, הֲשֹׁמֵר אָחִי אָנֹכִי?

## THE GENERATIONS FROM ADAM TO NOAH

WHEN GOD CREATED man, in the likeness of God made He him. Male and female created He them, and blessed them. These are Adam's descendants:

Adam was the father of Seth;

Seth fathered Enosh;

Enosh fathered Kenan;

Kenan fathered Mahalalel;

Mahalalel fathered Jared;

Jared fathered Enoch;

Enoch fathered Methuselah;

Methuselah fathered Lamech;

And Lamech had a son, and called him Noah;

And Noah lived to be five hundred years old; and he was the father of Shem, Ham, and Japheth.

## THE STORY OF THE FLOOD

THE EARTH WAS filled with corruption and violence. And the Lord saw that the wickedness of the man on the earth was great. And the Lord regretted that He had made man on the earth, and it grieved Him deeply. Therefore the Lord said, "I will blot out mankind that I have created from the face of the earth; both man and beast, and creeping thing and birds of the air, for I regret that I have made them."

---

⋘ [2] AM I MY BROTHER'S KEEPER? "Am I responsible?" was Cain's challenge to God. "If two gladiators fight before a king and one is killed, is not the king to blame that he did not stop the contest? Are not You at fault, O God, because You did not command me to halt?"

"I made you in My image," God replied, "with a brain and a soul. Were I to direct your every act, you would be no more than a puppet. You have a will of your own, and are responsible for your actions."

⋘ [3] THE VOICE OF YOUR BROTHER'S BLOOD: This brief line raises two questions: Does blood have a voice? And, why does the Hebrew use the plural, d'mé, "bloods"?

When Abel was slain, the Rabbis explained, all the children who would have been born to him, and their children, and theirs after them to the end of time, came and wept before the Lord because they would not know life.

בְּיוֹם בְּרֹא אֱלֹהִים אָדָם, בִּדְמוּת אֱלֹהִים עָשָׂה אוֹתוֹ, זָכָר וּנְקֵבָה בְּרָאָם, וַיְבָרֶךְ אוֹתָם.

But Noah found favor in the eyes of the Lord, because Noah was righteous and wholehearted. [4] Noah walked with God.

And God said to Noah, [5] "The end of all living things is come before Me, for the earth is filled with violence through them; and I will destroy them from the earth. [6] Make yourself an ark of gopher wood. Make the ark with rooms, and cover it with pitch inside and out.

"I will bring a flood upon the earth, to destroy every creature with the breath of life in it; everything on the earth shall perish. But I will make My cove-

---

[4] NOAH WAS A GOOD AND JUST MAN: We know that Abraham was a righteous man, but long before he lived, Noah too was said to be righteous and good. "How did one recognize the just and good man," the Rabbis asked, "in the days before the Torah and its commandments had been given to Moses? What is required of the non-Jew?"

We are told that the sons of Noah received seven commandments which, if obeyed, would earn them God's love. The commandments forbade idolatry, murder, theft, unchastity, severe cruelty to animals, or profaning the Name of God; and required that they settle disputes by law, not by force.

[5] NOAH, THE INVENTOR: According to legend, Noah was a benefactor to mankind because he introduced the plow, the hoe, the scythe and the sickle. Until his time, man had to tend the land with his bare hands. Since the soil was not properly prepared, no one could be sure what would grow. If he sowed wheat, oats might sprout, because the wheat seeds had been planted so shallowly that the wind often blew them away and brought seeds of oats or rye or weeds. The sprouts might be choked by weeds; crops could not be harvested properly.

After Noah taught mankind the use of tools, the earth could be plowed to the proper depth; plants were hoed, grew abundantly and were easily harvested. The yield increased a hundredfold; the world prospered, and there was food for the generations of men.

וְנֹחַ מָצָא חֵן בְּעֵינֵי יְיָ. נֹחַ אִישׁ צַדִּיק תָּמִים הָיָה בְּדֹרוֹתָיו, אֶת הָאֱלֹהִים הִתְהַלֶּךְ נֹחַ.

nant with you; and you shall go into the ark, you, and your sons, and your wife, and your sons' wives.

"Of all living creatures, two of every kind you shall bring in the ark, to keep them alive. They shall be male and female of each kind, of the bird, of the cattle, and of every creeping thing on the ground, two of every kind shall come with you, to keep them alive. Take also with you some of every kind of food that is eaten, and store it for food for you, and for them." And Noah did just as God had commanded him.

Noah, and his sons, and his wife, and his sons' wives went into the ark to escape the waters of the flood.

Then were all the fountains of the great deep released and the floodgates of heaven were opened. And it rained

---

≈§ [6] I WILL DESTROY THEM: Instead of being grateful for their prosperity, men became arrogant and rebellious. God patiently overlooked transgression and idolatry, but when men robbed the poor, the orphan and the widow, corrupted justice and shed innocent blood, God determined to punish them.

Because Noah was righteous, God told him of His distress at man's iniquity; nonetheless, He did not destroy the evildoers without warning, for God is merciful and long-suffering, slow to anger and abundant in goodness. He instructed Noah, "Make an ark of gopher wood, but do not hasten as you build it; perchance the people will repent and be saved."

Noah began by planting trees for the wood. "Why are you planting trees?" the people asked curiously.

"God has commanded me to build an ark," Noah replied, "for He will bring a flood upon the earth to destroy every living thing." The others laughed at him.

Year after year, Noah tended the trees, and the onlookers continued to ask, "Why do you do this labor?" Noah's answer was always the same: "God will bring a flood because men are wicked."

Season followed season for one-hundred and twenty-five years, and still the people jeered and laughed at Noah. When God saw that they did not repent, the flood began.

וּמִכָּל הַחַי, מִכָּל בָּשָׂר, שְׁנַיִם מִכֹּל תָּבִיא אֶל הַתֵּבָה לְהַחֲיוֹת אִתָּךְ, זָכָר וּנְקֵבָה יִהְיוּ.

forty days and forty nights. The flood continued for forty days on the earth. And the waters rose, and the ark floated upon the face of the waters. And the waters increased higher and higher, and all the high mountains were covered.

Every creature that moved upon the earth perished, bird, and cattle, and beast, and every swarming thing, and every man; everything in whose nostrils was the breath of life, died. Only Noah was left, and those who were with him in the ark.

And God remembered Noah, and all that were with him in the ark. And God caused a wind to pass over the earth, and the waters calmed; the fountains of the deep and the floodgates of heaven were closed, and the rain from heaven was stopped. And the waters became less and less upon the earth.

And at the end of forty days Noah opened the window he had made in the ark, and sent forth a raven. It went flying back and forth until the waters were dried up. Then he sent forth a dove to see if the waters had ceased

from the land. But the dove found no resting place for the sole of her foot, so she returned to him. And Noah put out his hand and took her, and brought her into the ark.

He waited another seven days, and again he sent the dove out of the ark. And the dove came back to him at evening; and there in her beak was a freshly-plucked olive leaf; [7] so Noah knew that the waters had subsided.

And he waited another seven days, and he sent forth the dove; and she did not return to him again.

It came to pass in the first month, on the first day of the month, Noah removed the covering of the ark and looked, and saw that the surface of the earth was dry.

And God said to Noah, "Come out of the ark, you, and your wife, and your sons, and your sons' wives. Bring out with you every living thing."

So Noah came out, and with him his sons, and his wife, and his sons' wives; and every creature.

And Noah built an altar to the Lord,

---

[7] WHY AN OLIVE LEAF? When the dove returned to the ark, she held an olive leaf in her beak. "Why the leaf of an olive tree?" our Sages pondered.

They answered, "Because the dove said: rather food which is provided by God, though it be bitter, than that of man, be it sweet as honey."

יִהְיוּ מְזוֹנוֹתַי מְרוֹרִים כְּזַיִת זֶה וּמְסוּרִים בְּיָדְךָ, וְאַל יִהְיוּ מְתוּקִים כִּדְבַשׁ וּמְסוּרִים בְּיַד בָּשָׂר וָדָם.

and made an offering on the altar. And the Lord said to Himself, "I will never again curse the earth because of man's evil. Neither will I again destroy every thing living, as I have done.

> "As long as the earth exists,
> Seedtime and harvest,
> Cold and heat,
> Summer and winter,
> Day and night,
> Shall not cease."

### THE RAINBOW

AND GOD SPOKE to Noah, and to his sons with him, saying, "I now establish My covenant with you, and with your children after you, and with every living creature that is with you: the birds, the cattle, and every beast with you; with all that came out of the ark. And I will establish My covenant that never again will there be a flood to destroy the earth."

And God said, "This is the sign of the covenant which I make between Me and you and every living creature that is with you, to endless generations: I have set My rainbow in the cloud, and it shall be a sign of a covenant between Me and the earth."

And the sons of Noah that went forth from the ark were Shem, Ham and Japheth. And sons were born to them after the flood, and from them the whole earth was populated.

### THE TOWER OF BABEL

NOW THE WHOLE earth had one language and the same words. And it came to pass, when they migrated from the east, that they found a plain in the land of Shinar, and they settled there.

And they said to one another, "Let us make bricks and bake them thoroughly."

And they said, "Come, let us build ourselves a city, and a tower with its top in heaven. [8] Thus we will make a name for ourselves, so that we may not be scattered abroad upon the face of the whole earth."

And the Lord saw the city and the

---

ɛ§ [8] THE TOWER OF BABEL: "Let us build a city," said King Nimrod, "and a tower so high that it will reach the heaven. We shall inscribe our names on its bricks and be remembered forever."

Thus Nimrod rebelled against God, the Rabbis pointed out. Men were so prosperous that they no longer put their trust in Him. Some said, "Why did God choose to dwell in heaven, while to us is given

עוֹד כָּל יְמֵי הָאָרֶץ, זֶרַע וְקָצִיר וְקֹר וָחֹם וְקַיִץ וָחֹרֶף וְיוֹם וָלַיְלָה לֹא יִשְׁבֹּתוּ.

tower which the children of man had built. And the Lord said, "They are one people, and they all have one language; yet this is what they begin to do. Now nothing which they decide to do will be impossible for them. Come, let us go down, and make a babble of their language that they will not understand one another's speech." [9]

So the Lord scattered them over the face of all the earth; and they had to cease building the city. That is why its name was Babel: because there the Lord made a babble of their language.

---

the earth? We will mount to heaven, dethrone Him, and dwell there."

Others cried, "Let us put our idols in heaven in His place."

"Let us go up to heaven," shouted another, "and war on Him with our bows and arrows!"

They decided to erect a tower that would reach the skies. Nimrod assembled six hundred thousand workers for the task.

The tower was built with great cunning. On the east side were steps by which to ascend; on the west, steps to go down. The structure grew to such a height that it took a year to reach the top, and a brick became more precious to the builders than a human being. If a man fell to his death, no one mourned; but if a brick dropped, the workmen wailed and tore their hair, because it would take a year to replace it.

Men lived on the tower all their lives. They married, bred children and reared them without setting foot on ground. Because Nimrod was more concerned with the tower than with those who built it, he sent up bricks rather than food; only when the men refused to work did he send up food enough, so that the tower would be finished.

[9] THEY COULD NOT UNDERSTAND ONE ANOTHER: God saw the tower, and became angry. He confounded the language of the builders so that they could not understand one another. If one asked for mortar, the other might hand him a brick, which the first, in his anger, would throw at his partner. As a result, the work stopped and the builders were scattered.

עַל כֵּן קָרָא שְׁמָהּ בָּבֶל, כִּי שָׁם בָּלַל יְיָ שְׂפַת כָּל הָאָרֶץ.

# 3. GENESIS [11–16]

FROM SHEM TO ABRAHAM

THESE ARE THE descendants of Shem, ancestor of all the children of Eber [the Hebrews].

Shem's son was Arpachshad;
Arpachshad's son was Shelah;
Shelah's son was Eber;

Eber's son was Peleg;
Peleg's son was Reu;
Reu's son was Serug;
Serug's son was Nahor;
Nahor's son was Terah;
Terah's sons were Abram, [1] Nahor, and Haran;
Haran was the father of Lot.

---

[1] THE BIRTH OF ABRAM: One evening as King Nimrod walked in his garden, a brilliant star appeared in the sky. Nimrod watched as it swung across the heavens, growing larger and larger until it seemed to swallow the four brightest stars. Then it plunged downward, to hover over a nearby house.

Nimrod summoned the royal astrologers and pointed out the star,

תֶּרַח הוֹלִיד אֶת אַבְרָם, אֶת נָחוֹר וְאֶת הָרָן.

Haran died during the lifetime of his father Terah. And Abram and Nahor each married: the name of Abram's wife was Sarai; and the name of Nahor's

---

gleaming steadily over a house beyond the park. As they all stared, the star lifted itself high, and disappeared into the heavens. "What does this portend?" Nimrod asked.

In the morning the wizards returned with their answer. "The star stood above the house of Terah, a maker of idols," they said. "Last night a son was born to Terah's wife. This boy will become so great that his fame will outshine that of the four greatest kings of our age."

Nimrod determined that the boy would not live. He sent for Terah, and said, "I want the boy who has been born to you. I will give you one hundred pieces of gold for him." Terah paled, for Nimrod's every word was law.

"Before I answer, O king, may I tell you what befell me yesterday?" Terah asked. "A man of wealth came to me and offered me a stable filled with oats and hay in return for my only horse. O king, shall I sell my horse for this great price?"

"Stupid man, of what use is fodder without a horse?" replied the king.

Terah bowed his head. "Of what value to me is all the gold in the world, if I have no son?"

In rage, Nimrod cried, "Sell me your son or both of you shall die!" Terah left in fear and trembling.

Terah's wife wept bitterly when she heard the story. It so chanced, however, that the infant son of a slave died in the night. Terah took its body to the palace, and Nimrod was satisfied that Abram, Terah's newborn son, was dead.

[1] ABRAM SEEKS GOD: Terah hid Abram in a cave high on a mountain. There the lad grew up alone, with none to teach or guide him. Yet he learned for himself the greatest truth of existence—of God who rules the world.

One night the boy had gazed up at the stars, and marveled, "How

שֵׁם אֵשֶׁת אַבְרָם שָׂרָי.

wife was Milcah. And Sarai was barren; she had no child. And Terah took his son Abram, his grandson Lot, and his daughter-in-law Sarai, and set out with

---

beautiful are the moon and stars! They must be gods." He bowed low before them, and worshiped.

The night passed, and the sun rose. "The warmth and light of the sun," Abram observed, "have driven away the moon and the stars. Surely the sun is god over all!" He bowed low to the sun.

Clouds came and hid the light of the sun; then a wind drove the clouds before it. Abram realized that all these were but part of the world and its wonders. "There must be a ruler over all the world," he pondered, "over the sun, the moon and the constellations, over all the creatures of the earth. I shall worship only the Creator and Ruler of the universe."

Abram bowed before the unseen God, and spoke a prayer in his heart. Suddenly a voice answered, saying, "Here am I, My son."

[1] ABRAM AND THE IDOL SHOP: One day Terah climbed the mountain, and there, to his delight, he found Abram alive and well. Terah brought him back to Ur.

A maker of idols, Terah carved images of wood and stone, which he sold in his shop. One day he went to market and left the boy to take care of the shop.

Soon a man came to buy an idol to protect his home, and Abram showed him an idol that was fierce of countenance. Greatly pleased, the man selected it as his god.

The lad could not contain himself. "How old are you?" he asked.

"I am fifty years of age, and have been a soldier for more than thirty years," was the answer.

Abram laughed. "You are fifty, whereas this idol was carved by my father only last week. And though you are a seasoned warrior, you seek protection from it!" Startled, the man left the shop.

An old woman entered next. "My house has been robbed, and my god was stolen from me. Sell me another," she said.

אָדוֹן יֵשׁ עֲלֵיהֶם – אֵלָיו אֶתְפַּלֵּל וְאֵלָיו אֶשְׁתַּחֲוֶה.

them from Ur of the Chaldees to go
into the land of Canaan. [2] But when
they came to the city of Haran, they
settled there. And Terah died in Haran.

ABRAM ARRIVES IN CANAAN

NOW THE LORD said to Abram, "Get you
up out of your country, and from your
kinsmen, and from your father's house,
and go to the land that I will show you.
And I will make of you a great nation,
and I will bless you and make your name
great, so that you will be a blessing.
And I will bless them that bless you, and

---

Abram smiled. "Your idol could not protect even himself, yet you
wish to buy another!" The woman ran out angrily.

[1] THE IDOL SMASHER: Abram looked at the rows of idols about him,
and picked up an axe. He smashed all but the largest of them, and
put the axe in its hands. When Terah returned, he found the shop
littered with fragments, while only the large idol remained whole.
"Who has done this?" he cried, appalled.

Abram was ready with an answer. "The idols were hungry, and
I brought them food. The big god seized your axe, killed them all,
and ate all the food himself."

Terah stared at the boy. "Abram, you are mocking me! You know
well that idols can neither move, nor eat, nor perform any act."

And then Abram said to his father, "Father, let your ears hear what
your tongue speaks."

[2] ABRAM LEAVES UR: Nimrod continued to persecute Terah and his
family, and the time came when Abram left, taking his father and
all his household with him.

The Rabbis asked, "Why did not God protect Abram so that he
need not leave?"

They answered that God wished him to spread His truths throughout the world. The Midrash says that Abram was like a vial of per-
fume: when he remained in Ur, it was as if the vial were tightly
sealed, and none knew its value or enjoyed its scent. When Abram
left, it was as though the vial were opened and its fragrance shared.

26

לֶךְ־לְךָ מֵאַרְצְךָ וּמִמּוֹלַדְתְּךָ וּמִבֵּית אָבִיךָ אֶל הָאָרֶץ אֲשֶׁר אַרְאֶךָּ.

any one that curses you I will curse; and in you shall all the families of the earth be blessed."

So Abram took his wife Sarai, and his nephew Lot, with all their possessions that they had accumulated, and the souls that they had acquired in Haran; [3] and they set out for the land of Canaan; and into the land of Canaan they came.

And Abram passed through the land as far as Shechem. [4] The Canaanites were then in the land.

And the Lord appeared to Abram and said, "To your children I will give this land."

And Abram built there an altar to the Lord, who appeared to him. And then Abram journeyed, going on his way to the Negev.

---

~§ [3] THE SOULS THEY HAD ACQUIRED: All the wise men of the earth together could not create a mosquito. Yet we read that Abram was "acquiring souls," (the Hebrew refers to "the souls he created"). How does one "create souls"?

He who brings a person near to God is as though he had created him, answers the Midrash.

Soon after Terah and his family settled in Haran, the Haranites heard tell of Abram and his good works. Because he was hospitable, gave freely to the needy, and executed righteousness, his name was blessed.

"All that you do, prospers," the Haranites told him. "Teach us, that we may do that which is right before God and man."

Thus Abram "created souls."

~§ [4] THE JOURNEY TO CANAAN: Why did Abram pass through Aramnaharaim, a good land and fertile, to settle elsewhere? Because he saw that its people depended on the richness of the land, and lived lives of idleness, with feasting and drinking throughout the day. "O Lord," Abram prayed, "may I be preserved from living as do these!"

When he came to Shechem, Abram saw that its people worked diligently, plowing and sowing, harvesting and threshing, and that each man shared in the labor. These Abram blessed; and he prayed, "O Lord, may my lot be as theirs!"

וְנִבְרְכוּ בְךָ כֹּל מִשְׁפְּחֹת הָאֲדָמָה.

## ABRAM PARTS FROM LOT

ABRAM WAS VERY rich in cattle, in silver and in gold. And Lot, who went with Abram, also had flocks and herds and tents, so that the land could not support them staying together. And quarrels arose between the herdmen of Abram's cattle and of Lot's cattle. [5]

Then Abram said to Lot, "I beg you, let there be no strife between you and me, nor between my herdmen and your herdmen; for we are kinsmen. Is not the whole land open to you? Separate yourself, please, from me. If you go to the left, then I will go to the right; or if you take the right, then I will go to the left."

Lot looked and saw that all the plain of the Jordan was well watered everywhere, like the garden of the Lord, like the land of Egypt. So Lot chose all the plain of the Jordan.

So they parted one from another. Abram dwelt in the land of Canaan, and Lot settled in the cities of the Plain, and moved his tent as far as Sodom. Now the men of Sodom were wicked and sinned against the Lord greatly.

And the Lord said to Abram, after Lot had parted from him, "Raise your eyes now, and look from the place where you are, to the north and to the south, to the east and to the west; for all the land that you see I will give to you and to your descendants forever. And I will make your descendants as the dust of

---

  [5] THE SHEPHERD'S QUARREL: Abram gave his shepherds a purse, saying, "Give this gold to the owners of the land, that our herds may not trespass when they graze." This his men did. Moreover, they muzzled the cattle so that they would not graze in fields through which they passed.

Lot's men, however, pastured their sheep without permission. Abram's shepherds said to them, "Why do you pasture on land which is not your master's?" The servants of Lot replied, "Did not God say to Abram: To you and to your descendants will I give all this land? Since Abram is childless, Lot will inherit his possessions. Therefore, this land on which the flocks graze really belongs to Lot."

When Abram heard of this he said to Lot, "Kinsman, let us separate and go each his way."

שָׂא־נָא עֵינֶיךָ וּרְאֵה מִן הַמָּקוֹם אֲשֶׁר אַתָּה שָׁם, צָפוֹנָה וָנֶגְבָּה וָקֵדְמָה וָיָמָּה, כִּי אֶת כָּל הָאָרֶץ אֲשֶׁר אַתָּה רוֹאֶה לְךָ אֶתְּנֶנָּה וּלְזַרְעֲךָ עַד עוֹלָם.

the earth; so only if one can count the dust of the earth shall your descendants be counted. Arise, walk throughout the land, [6] for I will give it to you."

And Abram moved his tent and went to dwell beside the oaks of Mamre, which are in Hebron. And there he built an altar to the Lord.

### ABRAM IN BATTLE WITH FOUR KINGS

THE KING OF Shinar, the king of Ellasar, the king of Elam, and the king of Goiim made war against the king of Sodom, and against the king of Gomorrah, the king of Admah, the king of Zeboiim, and the king of Bela—the four against the five. They joined in the valley of Siddim, which is the Salt Sea.

Now the valley of Siddim was full of slime pits. The kings of Sodom and Gomorrah fled, and they fell there; and the survivors fled to the mountains. The victors seized all the goods and provisions of Sodom and Gomorrah, and went their way. And they carried off Lot, the nephew of Abram, and his goods; for he was living in Sodom.

A fugitive came and told Abram.

And when Abram heard that his kinsman had been taken captive, he called out his trained men, born in his house, three hundred and eighteen men, and went in pursuit as far as Dan. He and his servants fell upon the enemy at night and defeated them, and pursued them as far as Hobah, which is on the left side of Damascus. And he recovered all the goods, and also brought back his kinsman Lot, and his goods, and the women and the people.

And Melchizedek, the king of Salem, brought forth bread and wine; and he was a priest of God Most High. And he blessed him and said, "Blessed be Abram of God Most High, Creator of heaven and earth. And blessed be God Most High, who has delivered your enemies into your hand." And he gave him a tenth of all.

The king of Sodom said to Abram, "Give me the people, and keep the goods for yourself."

But Abram said to the king of Sodom, "I have lifted my hand to the Lord, God Most High, Creator of heaven and earth, that I will not take anything that is yours, not a thread or a shoelace,

---

    &#8667; [6] WALK THROUGH THE LAND: Why did God tell Abram to walk through the land after He promised it to him? Only he who knows the land can possess it.

הֲרִימוֹתִי יָדִי אֶל יְיָ, אֵל עֶלְיוֹן, קוֹנֵה שָׁמַיִם וָאָרֶץ, אִם מִחוּט וְעַד שְׂרוֹךְ נַעַל וְאִם אֶקַּח מִכָּל אֲשֶׁר לָךְ.

lest you say: It was I who made Abram rich. Only let the men who went with me take their share."

## GOD'S COVENANT WITH ABRAM

AFTER THESE EVENTS, the word of the Lord came to Abram in a vision, saying, "Fear not, Abram, I am your shield. Your reward shall be very great."

And Abram said, "O Lord God, what canst Thou give me when I am childless, and my heir will be my steward, Eliezer of Damascus?"

And the word of the Lord came to him, saying, "This man shall not be your heir; but one born to you shall be your heir."

Then He took Abram outside and said, "Now look at the sky, and count the stars. Are you able to count them? So shall be your descendants." And Abram trusted in the Lord.

And it came to pass that, when the sun was going down, a deep sleep fell upon Abram; and a dread, like a great darkness, came over him. And God said to Abram, "Know that your descendants shall be strangers in a land that is not theirs, and shall be enslaved and oppressed for four hundred years. But I will judge that nation which they will serve; and afterward they shall come out with great wealth. But you shall go to your fathers in peace; you shall be buried in a good old age."

And when the sun went down and it was very dark, there appeared a smoking furnace and a flaming torch. [7] On that day the Lord made a covenant

---

৯৪ [7] A SMOKING FURNACE: Why did a great dread descend on Abraham, and why did he see a fiery furnace and a torch?

The future which God was promising him was not one of ease and wealth, but of stern obligation. The covenant demanded that Abraham and his descendants accept justice and righteousness as a way of life, and that they carry God's message to the world.

It is not easy to accept such a role. Because the future would be difficult, the vision came with darkness and dread. The furnace was the symbol of the suffering of the Jew; the torch, that he would be a light unto the nations.

Despite the burden that lay ahead, Abraham trusted in the Lord. Such true faith is in itself considered righteousness.

To this day the Jews live according to this vision and the covenant.

הַבֶּט־נָא הַשָּׁמַיְמָה וּסְפֹר הַכּוֹכָבִים, אִם תּוּכַל לִסְפֹּר אֹתָם, כֹּה יִהְיֶה זַרְעֶךָ.

with Abram, saying, "To your descendants do I give this land."

### ISHMAEL IS BORN

NOW ABRAM'S WIFE Sarai bore him no
children; and she had an Egyptian maid
whose name was Hagar. And Sarai took
Hagar, and gave her in marriage to her
husband Abram.

And Hagar bore a son to Abram;
and Abram named his son, whom Hagar
bore, Ishmael. And Abram was eighty-six
years old when Ishmael was born.

לְזַרְעֲךָ נָתַתִּי אֶת הָאָרֶץ הַזֹּאת.

# 4. GENESIS [17–21]

### NEW NAMES—ABRAHAM AND SARAH

WHEN ABRAM WAS ninety-nine years old, the Lord appeared to Abram and said to him, "I am *El Shaddai*; walk before Me, and be blameless. And I will establish My covenant between Me and you, and will make you great in number." And Abram bowed low as God spoke to him. "My covenant is with you, and you shall be the father of a multitude of nations. Therefore, your name shall no longer be called Abram, but it shall be Abraham. As for Sarai, your wife, you shall not call her Sarai, but Sarah. And moreover, I will bless her, and I will give you a son by her."

Then Abraham bowed low, but he laughed and he said to himself, "Can he who is one hundred years old become a father? Or can Sarah, who is ninety, bear a child?" So he said to God, "May Ishmael live before Thee!"

But God said, "Nevertheless, your wife Sarah shall bear you a son, and you shall name him Isaac; and I will establish My covenant with him as an everlasting covenant to his children after him. As for Ishmael, I have heard you;

וְלֹא יִקָּרֵא עוֹד אֶת שִׁמְךָ אַבְרָם וְהָיָה שִׁמְךָ אַבְרָהָם.

and indeed, I have blessed him, and will multiply him greatly. He shall be the father of twelve princes, and I will make him a great nation. But My covenant I will establish with Isaac, whom Sarah shall bear to you at this season in the next year.

"This is My covenant, which you shall keep, between Me and you and your descendants after you throughout all generations; every male among you shall be circumcised. And this shall be a token of the covenant between Me and you. And he that is eight days old shall be circumcised."

### THREE MEN VISIT ABRAHAM

AS ABRAHAM WAS sitting at the entrance of his tent [1] in the heat of the day, he looked up and saw three men standing near him. When he saw them, he ran

---

୶ [1] THE HOSPITABLE ABRAHAM: Abraham lived for many years in Beer-sheba, where he built a gracious dwelling. It stood in the midst of a beautiful garden which had gates facing in every direction, so that travelers might find their way inside with ease.

Abraham became known far and wide because his home was open, day and night, to any traveler or wandering beggar. If his guest was hungry, Abraham gave him food; if he needed clothing, Abraham gave him garments; and he provided him with food and money for his journey.

When thanked, Abraham had one reply, "Do not thank me. Give thanks to God, who provides food and drink to all His creatures." Then the visitor would acknowledge God, and bless Him. Thus, Abraham's home was not only a place of rest for the weary wanderer, but also of the teaching of the knowledge of God and His Law.

One stormy night, an old man stumbled across the threshold. Abraham made a fire to warm the wanderer. He washed his feet, gave him fresh garments, and served him food.

"Now I will thank my god who led me to your dwelling," the old man said. From his bosom he took a small wooden idol, and before it he knelt in prayer.

Abraham spoke softly, "Old man, are you not ashamed to bow

וְהָיָה לְאוֹת בְּרִית בֵּינִי וּבֵינֵיכֶם. וּבֶן שְׁמֹנַת יָמִים יִמּוֹל לָכֶם כָּל זָכָר.

34

to meet them and bowed down to the ground, and said, "My lords, if I have found favor in your eyes, please do not pass by without stopping with your servant. Let a little water be brought and wash your feet, and recline under the tree while I fetch a bit of bread to refresh you. After that, you may go on your way." And they said, "Do as you have said."

Abraham hurried into the tent to Sarah and said, "Make ready quickly three measures of fine flour, knead it, and make cakes."

And Abraham ran to the herd and fetched a calf, tender and good, and gave it to the servant, who hastened to prepare it.

And he took curd and milk and the calf which had been prepared, and set it before them. And he waited on them under the tree as they ate.

---

before a piece of carved wood, an image made by the hand of man? Thank the true God who created the heaven and the earth."

The stranger interrupted him. "This is the god which I have worshiped all my days. I will not forsake him."

Angered, Abraham drove him from the house. The old man went out into the night.

Abraham lay upon his bed, but could not sleep. Then God's voice spoke: "Where is the old man whom you sheltered from the storm?"

"I drove the idolater from my house," Abraham answered, "for I could tolerate him no longer."

"I have tolerated him for full seventy years," said God, "and for full seventy years kept him and sustained him. But you could not endure him a single night!"

Shame-faced, Abraham went out into the darkness to bring back the old man. He apologized and promised the stranger that he could worship as he chose.

The next morning, God revealed Himself to Abraham, and said, "As you overcame your pride before the old man, so will I be long-suffering and forgiving to your descendants. Though they rebel and turn from Me so that I must punish them, it will be with compassion. Never will I abandon them. I will remember My covenant: they will be My people, and I will be their God."

יֻקַּח נָא מְעַט מַיִם וְרַחֲצוּ רַגְלֵיכֶם וְהִשָּׁעֲנוּ תַּחַת הָעֵץ וְאֶקְחָה פַת לֶחֶם וְסַעֲדוּ לִבְּכֶם, אַחַר תַּעֲבֹרוּ.

And they said to him, "Where is your wife Sarah?"

And he said, "Inside the tent."

Then one said, "I will return to you next year at this season; and Sarah, your wife, shall have a son."

Sarah was listening behind the tent door. Now Abraham and Sarah were very old. And Sarah laughed to herself, and said, "I am old, and my lord is old also. Can I bear a child at this age?"

Then the Lord said to Abraham, "Why did Sarah laugh, saying: Can I really bear a child, when I am so old? Is anything impossible for the Lord? At the set time I will return to you, and Sarah shall have a son."

Then the men rose, and turned toward Sodom; and Abraham went with them to see them off.

And the Lord said, "Shall I hide from Abraham what I am about to do? I have singled him out that he may instruct his children and his family after him, to keep the way of the Lord, to do righteousness and justice."

## ABRAHAM PRAYS FOR SODOM

THE LORD SAID, "The outcry of Sodom and Gomorrah is great, and their sins are very grave. I will go down, [2] and see whether they have done altogether according to the outcry that has reached Me. [3] And if not, I will know."

But Abraham stood before the Lord

[2] I WILL GO DOWN: Why did God Himself descend to see how Sodom and Gomorrah sinned? Did He not see from above?

From this example is derived the Jewish law that no judge may determine innocence or guilt without facing the accused.

[3] THE OUTCRY THAT HAS REACHED ME: Those who lived in Sodom and Gomorrah were the richest of all men. Their land blossomed as the Garden of Eden. Its stones were sapphire, and its dust gold. The trees were heavy with fruit, and crops sprang untended from the soil.

As their wealth grew, so did their greed. "We do not wish strangers among us," they said. "They come here to take something from us." Any traveler who strayed into their cities was made to regret that he had come.

If by chance a poor man wandered their way, they welcomed him with false smiles, and gave him marked coins. When he tried to buy

הֲיִפָּלֵא מֵיְיָ דָּבָר? לַמּוֹעֵד אָשׁוּב אֵלֶיךָ כָּעֵת חַיָּה וּלְשָׂרָה בֵן.

and said, "Wilt Thou destroy the righteous along with the guilty? Suppose there are fifty righteous men in the city; wilt Thou still destroy and not spare the place for the sake of the fifty righteous men who are in it? Far be it from Thee to do such a thing, to make the righteous perish with the wicked, so that good and bad fare alike. Shall not the Judge of all the earth act justly?"

And the Lord said, "If I find fifty righteous men within the city, I will forgive the entire place for their sake."

Abraham answered and said, "Now that I have dared to speak to the Lord, I who am but dust and ashes, [4] suppose there are five short of the fifty righteous men; wilt Thou destroy the whole city for lack of five?"

And He replied, "I will not destroy it if I will find forty-five there."

Abraham spoke to Him still again,

---

food, no one would accept the marked coins, and the stranger starved though his purse was full. When he had perished, each man took back his marked coins.

They did not look after widows and orphans, though they hungered. They devised evil each against his fellow, seized gold by oppression, and in their laws favored the rich over the poor. Despite their greed, iniquity and shedding of innocent blood, God did not smite them—for He is gracious and long-suffering—until a certain cry reached His ears.

It came about through the friendship of two young girls. The father of one was robbed of all he possessed by a gang of clever thieves. They had asked him to guard fifty gold coins which they had secretly dipped in an aromatic oil. Soon after, they broke into his house and stole all his money as well as their own gold, which they located easily by its scent. What is more, they brought him to trial and demanded the money they had entrusted to him. Because he could not pay it, he was sold into slavery. His family was left penniless.

One day his daughter met her friend at the well. "Why are you so pale?" the second girl asked.

"I am faint for food," she replied. "It is two days since I have eaten."

"Wait here until I come back," her companion said. When she

הַאַף תִּסְפֶּה צַדִּיק עִם רָשָׁע?

and said, "Perhaps forty will be found there?"

And He said, "I will not do it for the sake of forty."

Then Abraham said, <u>"Oh, let not the Lord be angry if I should say: perhaps thirty will be found there."</u>

And the Lord said, "I will not do it if I find thirty."

And Abraham said, "Now that I have dared to speak to the Lord, suppose twenty are found there?"

And He said, "I will not destroy it for the sake of twenty."

---

returned, she murmured, "Let us exchange pitchers." Her pitcher was full of flour.

For some days the friend smuggled food to the hungry girl, until the men of Sodom sought to know how the poor family survived. When they learned the answer, the kind-hearted girl was arrested and condemned to death. Her body was smeared with honey and she was bound between two beehives. The girl screamed in agony as the bees stung her to death.

It was then that the Lord said, "The outcry of Sodom and Gomorrah is great. I will go down."

[4] I HAVE DARED TO SPEAK: How dared Abraham question God? His act may seem bold, but it typifies the relationship of the Jew to God. Abraham was only the first who acted in the Jewish tradition that injustice must be protested, even to God Himself.

It was in this spirit that, in a time of great oppression, Rabbi Levi Yitzhak of Berditchev stood before the open *Aron Kodesh* and contended with God:

"Oh, Master of the world,
I, Levi Yitzhak, son of Sarah of Berditchev,
Come in judgment against You
In behalf of Your people, Israel.
What do You want of Your people?
Why do You afflict us?
I shall not stir from here,
Until there be an end to this.
Magnified and sanctified be His great Name!"

אַל־נָא יִחַר לַאדֹנָי וַאֲדַבֵּרָה: אוּלַי יִמָּצְאוּן שָׁם שְׁלֹשִׁים.

Then Abraham said, "Oh, let not the Lord be angry if I should speak once more: perhaps ten shall be found there."

And the Lord said, "I will not destroy it for the sake of ten."

The Lord went His way when He had finished speaking to Abraham, and Abraham returned to his place.

### THE DESTRUCTION OF SODOM AND GOMORRAH

THE TWO ANGELS came to Sodom at evening, and Lot was sitting at the gate of Sodom. When Lot saw them, he rose and greeted them; and he bowed to the ground, and he said, "If you please, my lords, come into your servant's house and stay the night, and wash your feet. Then you may rise early and go on your way."

They said, "No, we will pass the night in the street."

But Lot urged them strongly, so that they went to his house. He prepared a feast for them, and he baked unleavened bread, and they ate.

But before they lay down, the men of Sodom, young and old, surrounded the house. And they shouted to Lot, "Where are the men who came to you tonight? Bring them out to us, and we will know what to do to them."

Lot went to the door and said, "I pray you, my friends, do not be wicked. Do nothing to these men, as they have come under the shelter of my roof."

But they said, "Get out of the way!" and added, "This fellow came to us as a stranger, and now he acts the judge. We will deal with you worse than with them."

They pressed hard against Lot, and tried to reach the door and break it. But the angels reached out their hands and pulled Lot into the house, and shut the door. And they struck the men that were at the door with blindness so that they searched in vain for the entrance.

And the angels said to Lot, "Is there anyone else here belonging to you—sons-in-law, sons, daughters, or anyone at all that belongs to you in the city? Take them out of the place, for we are about to destroy it, because the outcry is so great before the Lord that He has sent us to destroy it."

And Lot went out and spoke to his sons-in-law. "Leave this place at once, for the Lord will destroy the city." But his sons-in-law thought he was jesting.

When dawn appeared, the angels hastened Lot, saying, "Hurry, take your wife and your two daughters that are here; otherwise you will be swept away in the iniquity of the city."

But Lot hesitated, and the angels

הָאֶחָד בָּא לָגוּר וַיִּשְׁפֹּט שָׁפוֹט – עַתָּה נָרַע לְךָ מֵהֶם.

seized his hand, and the hand of his wife, and the hands of his two daughters, because the Lord had pity on them. They brought him out, and set him outside the city, and one said, "Escape for your life! Do not look behind you, nor stop anywhere in the Plain. Fly to the hills, lest you be swept away!"

And Lot said to them, "Oh, no, if your servant has found favor in your eyes, and in your mercy you have saved my life, I cannot escape to the mountains. The disaster may overtake me, and I will die. Here is a town nearby, and it is a little one; oh, let me escape there, and save my life."

And He said to him, "See, I grant you this also; I will not destroy the town of which you have spoken. Hurry, and fly there, for I can do nothing till you have come there."

As the sun rose over the earth, Lot came to Zoar, which was the name of the town. Then the Lord rained sulphur and fire from heaven on Sodom and Gomorrah. And He destroyed these cities, and all the Plain, with all its inhabitants and everything that grew. But Lot's wife looked back, and she became a pillar of salt.

In the morning, Abraham went to the place where he had stood before the Lord. And he looked out toward Sodom and Gomorrah, and toward all the region of the Plain, and saw the smoke from the land rising like the smoke of a furnace.

### THE BIRTH OF ISAAC

THE LORD KEPT His promise to Sarah as He had said. At the set time she bore a son to Abraham in his old age. And Abraham gave the name of Isaac to his son whom Sarah had borne to him.

And Abraham circumcised Isaac when he was eight days old, as God had commanded. Abraham was one hundred years old when his son Isaac was born to him.

And Sarah said, "God has brought me laughter; everyone who hears will laugh with me."

The child grew and was weaned. And Abraham made a great feast on the day Isaac was weaned.

וַיִּקְרָא אַבְרָהָם אֶת שֵׁם בְּנוֹ הַנּוֹלַד לוֹ, אֲשֶׁר יָלְדָה לוֹ שָׂרָה, יִצְחָק.

# 5. GENESIS [22–23]

THE BINDING OF ISAAC—AKÉDAH

IT CAME TO PASS that God put Abraham to test, and said to him, "Abraham." And he answered, "Here I am."

And He said, "Take your son, [1] your only son, Isaac, whom you love, and go to the land of Moriah; and offer him there as a burnt-offering upon one of the hills which I will tell you of." [2]

Abraham rose early in the morning, and saddled his donkey, [3] and took

---

[1] TAKE YOUR SON! The Hebrew reads *kaḥ-na*, which means "please take your son." Why did God say "please" to a mortal? Because He recognized how difficult His command was, said the Rabbis, but knew its lesson was important to mankind.

After Isaac had been released and the ram sacrificed, the puzzled father questioned the Lord. "Well You know, O Lord, that I would not withhold from You either my son or my soul. Why, therefore, did You find need to test me so?"

קַח־נָא אֶת בִּנְךָ, אֶת יְחִידְךָ, אֲשֶׁר אָהַבְתָּ, אֶת יִצְחָק, וְלֶךְ־לְךָ אֶל אֶרֶץ הַמּוֹרִיָה וְהַעֲלֵהוּ שָׁם לְעוֹלָה.

two of his servants with him, and his son Isaac. And he cut wood for the burnt-offering, and set out for the place of which God had told him.

On the third day Abraham raised his eyes and saw the place in the distance. Then Abraham said to his servants, "Stay here with the donkey while I and the boy will go there, and we will worship and return to you."

---

"That the world might know why I chose you from all others," was the reply, "when they witnessed your loyalty and trust in Me.

"And also because there are those who offer their first-born to their gods. I, the God of Righteousness, do not wish such offerings. You suffered an agony of fear that the world might know that human sacrifice is an abomination to Me."

[2] ONE OF THE HILLS: Why was a certain hill chosen over any other? Legend says that on opposite sides of this mount there lived two brothers. One was married and had sons and daughters, the other was unwed.

One moonlit night, after the harvest had been gathered, the brothers sat each in his own house. "My brother is alone," the married man was thinking. "There is no one to care for him when he grows old. He should have a larger share of the harvest. I shall take him a sack of wheat to store up for the time of his need."

At the same time the other brother was saying to himself, "My brother has many mouths to feed. It is not right that I share equally with him in the harvest. I shall bring him an extra sack in secret, so that his family will not want."

Both brothers rose and left their homes. Each filled a sack from his portion of the wheat. They climbed the hill from opposite sides, each bent under a heavy sack. At the summit of the hill they met in the moonlight. There they recognized each other, and took in the meaning of the gifts they bore. As they embraced, the Lord looked down and said, "This place is holy. Here shall My glory rest."

It was here that Abraham bound Isaac as a sacrifice, and here that the holy Temple was erected.

שְׁבוּ לָכֶם פֹּה עִם הַחֲמוֹר, וַאֲנִי וְהַנַּעַר נֵלְכָה עַד כֹּה וְנִשְׁתַּחֲוֶה וְנָשׁוּבָה אֲלֵיכֶם.

Abraham took the wood for the burnt-offering, and put it upon his son Isaac; and he took in his hand the fire and the knife; and the two of them went together. [4]

And Isaac said to his father Abraham, "My father."

And Abraham answered, "Here I am, my son."

And he said, "Here are the fire and the wood, but where is the lamb for a burnt-offering?"

And Abraham said, "God Himself will provide the lamb for a burnt-offering, my son."

So they went, both of them together. And they came to the place of which God had told him; and Abraham built the altar there, and laid the wood in order, and bound Isaac his son, and laid him on the altar, upon the wood. As Abraham put out his hand and took the knife to slay his son, the angel of the Lord called to him from heaven, "Abraham, Abraham!" [5]

And he replied, "Here I am."

And he said, "Do not lay your hand on the boy, neither do anything to him; for now I know that you revere God, for you did not withhold your son, your only son from Me."

Abraham looked up, and saw behind him a ram caught in the brushwood by its horns. And Abraham took the ram, and offered it up as a burnt-offering in place of his son.

---

[3] ABRAHAM SADDLED HIS DONKEY: Why did not Abraham summon his servants for so menial a task?

When God commands, reply our Sages, one does not call a servant. Abraham rose early and performed the service himself.

[4] THE TWO OF THEM WENT TOGETHER: The ancient legends tell us that Satan, who had instigated the entire matter of the sacrifice, tried to make the trial harder for Abraham by telling Isaac his fate. Neither Abraham nor Isaac heeded him, however. The reason? Not even the truth is accepted from the liar and the scorner.

[5] THE ANGEL OF THE LORD: It was the Lord who commanded that Abraham offer up his son, but an angel who told him to desist. Of this the Rabbis say: to destroy we need the authority of God Himself, but even the smallest angel can serve to show mercy.

אַל תִּשְׁלַח יָדְךָ אֶל הַנַּעַר וְאַל תַּעַשׂ לוֹ מְאוּמָה.

And the angel of the Lord called to Abraham a second time from heaven, and said, "The Lord says, because you have done this, and have not withheld your son, your only son, I will bless you, and will make your descendants as numerous as the stars of the heaven, and as the sand upon the seashore. And all the nations of the earth shall be blessed through your descendants, because you obeyed My command."

So Abraham returned to his servants, and together they went to Beer-sheba.

### THE DEATH OF SARAH

THE LIFE OF Sarah was one hundred and twenty-seven years. And Sarah died in Hebron, in the land of Canaan; and Abraham came to mourn for Sarah, and to weep for her.

Then Abraham rose from the side of his dead, and said to the children of Heth, "I am a stranger among you, but I live here. Sell me a burial-place for my dead."

And the children of Heth answered Abraham, "You are a mighty prince among us; in the best of our burial-places bury your dead."

Abraham rose and bowed to the people of the land, the Hittites, and he said to them, "If you consent that I bury my dead, entreat Ephron the son of Zohar on my behalf, that he may give me the Cave of Machpelah, which belongs to him. Let him sell it to me in your presence for the full price as a burial-ground."

Ephron the Hittite answered Abraham in the hearing of all, saying, "No, my lord, hear me. I give you the field, and I give you the cave that is in it. In the presence of my kinsmen I give it to you. Bury your dead."

And Abraham bowed before the people of the land. And he spoke to Ephron in their presence, saying, "Please hear me out! I will give you the price of the field. Take it from me, and I will bury my dead there."

And Ephron answered Abraham, "My lord, listen to me: a piece of land worth four hundred shekels of silver, what is that between me and you? Bury your dead."

Abraham accepted Ephron's offer; and Abraham weighed the silver, which he had named in the hearing of the children of Heth, four hundred shekels of silver, the current money among the merchants.

So the field of Ephron, which was in Machpelah, facing Mamre, and the cave which was in it, and all the trees that were in the field, passed into the possession of Abraham.

And Abraham buried Sarah his wife in the cave in the field of Machpelah, in Hebron, in the land of Canaan.

וְהִתְבָּרְכוּ בְזַרְעֲךָ כֹּל גּוֹיֵי הָאָרֶץ עֵקֶב אֲשֶׁר שָׁמַעְתָּ בְּקוֹלִי.

# 6. GENESIS [24–25]

ABRAHAM SENDS ELIEZER TO
ARAM-NAHARAIM

NOW ABRAHAM was old, well-advanced in years; and the Lord had blessed Abraham in all things. And Abraham said to the oldest servant of his house, who had charge over all that he had, "Swear by the Lord, the God of heaven and the God of the earth, that you will not let my son marry a daughter of the Canaanites, among whom I dwell; but you will go to my country and to my kindred, and take a wife for my son Isaac." [1]

And the servant said to him, "Suppose the woman will not be willing to follow me to this land, am I to take your son back to the land from which you came?"

---

[1] A DAUGHTER OF THE CANAANITES: Abraham commanded Eliezer not to allow Isaac to marry a Canaanite; however, Laban and his family were also idol-worshipers. What advantage was there in a wife from afar, who was also a pagan?

Some Rabbis explained that the Canaanite religion was worse than

וַיְיָ בֵּרַךְ אֶת אַבְרָהָם בַּכֹּל.

And Abraham said to him, "Beware that you do not take my son back there! The Lord, the God of heaven, who took me from my father's house and from the land of my birth, and who spoke to me and who swore to me, saying: 'To your descendants will I give this land;' He will send His angel before you, and you shall take a wife for my son from there. And if the woman is not willing to follow you, then you shall be free from this oath to me; but do not take my son back there."

And the servant swore to Abraham to do this thing. So the servant took ten of his master's camels and set out, bearing with him many of his master's valuables. And he went to Aram-naharaim, to the city of Nahor.

It was evening, the time that women come out to draw water, when he made the camels kneel outside the city by the well. And he said, "O Lord, the God of my master Abraham, give me success today and show kindness to my master Abraham. Here I stand by the well, and the daughters of the men of the city come out to draw water. Let the maiden to whom I say: Please, lower your pitcher for me to drink, answer: Drink, and I will give your camels drink also; let her be the one whom Thou hast appointed for Thy servant Isaac; and by this I shall know that Thou hast shown kindness to my master."

### ELIEZER MEETS REBEKAH

BEFORE HE HAD finished speaking, Rebekah came out with her pitcher upon her shoulder. [2] She was the daughter of Bethuel, the grandson of Nahor, Abraham's brother. And the girl was very beautiful; and she went down to the

---

the Haranite religion, because it included child sacrifice and other abominations.

Others believed that Abraham feared that a Canaanite girl, living near her friends and family, would hold on to pagan customs. A Haranite, however, finding Canaanite ways foreign, would not be lured by them nor lead Isaac astray.

[2] REBEKAH: Rebekah was born at the very moment that Sarah died. She grew to be a beautiful girl who found favor in everyone's eyes. Although her father was rich and gave her maids and servants, she helped in the home, even when very young. She went to the well

הוּא יִשְׁלַח מַלְאָכוֹ לְפָנֶיךָ וְלָקַחְתָּ אִשָּׁה לִבְנִי מִשָּׁם.

spring and filled her pitcher. As she came up, the servant ran to meet her and said, "Please let me drink a little water from your pitcher."

And she said, "Drink, sir;" and she quickly lowered the pitcher and let him drink. When he had drunk his fill she said, "I will draw for your camels also."

She hurriedly emptied her pitcher into the trough, and ran to the well to draw more water and drew for all his camels. And the man gazed steadily at her, and wondered in silence whether the Lord had made his journey successful or not.

When the camels had finished drinking, the man took a gold ring and two heavy golden bracelets, and he said, "Whose daughter are you, please tell me. Is there room in your father's house for us to lodge?"

And she said to him, "I am the daughter of Bethuel, the grandson of Nahor." And she added, "We have straw and fodder enough, and room to lodge in." [3]

And the man bowed his head, and kneeled before the Lord. And he said,

"Blessed be the Lord, the God of my master Abraham, who has not forsaken His kindness and truth to my master; the Lord has led me to the house of my master's brethren."

And the girl ran, and told her mother's household all that had happened.

REBEKAH LEAVES HER HOME

REBEKAH HAD a brother named Laban. When he saw the ring and the bracelets, and when he heard Rebekah's words, he went out to the man at the well.

And Laban said, "Come in, blessed of the Lord. Why do you stand outside when I have cleared the house and made room for the camels?"

Eliezer came into the house, and the camels were unharnessed and given straw and fodder, and water was brought to wash his feet and the feet of the men with him. Then food was set before him; but he said, "I will not eat until I have made known my errand."

And Laban said, "Speak on."

And the man said, "I am the servant

---

for water, in place of the servants, in order to meet the villagers and to see if any needed help.

Although Rebekah went out of her way to help the poor, there was little of kindness or charity among the other Haranites, her own family included. Therefore, when Eliezer told her how kind Isaac and his father were, she was pleased.

בָּרוּךְ יְיָ אֱלֹהֵי אֲדֹנִי אַבְרָהָם, אֲשֶׁר לֹא עָזַב חַסְדּוֹ וַאֲמִתּוֹ מֵעִם אֲדֹנִי.

of Abraham. The Lord has blessed my master greatly, and he has become very rich. He has given him flocks and herds, silver and gold, menservants and maidservants, camels and donkeys. And Sarah, my master's wife, bore a son to my master when she was old; and he is leaving him everything he has. And my master made me swear, saying: You shall not take a wife for my son of the daughters of the Canaanites, in whose land I dwell. But you shall go to my father's home, and take a wife for my son from my kindred. And I said to my master: Perhaps the woman will not follow me! And he said to me: The Lord, in whose path I walk, will send His angel with you and prosper your way; and you shall take a wife for my son of my kindred, and of my father's house. And now, if you will deal kindly and honorably with my master, tell me, and if not, tell me; that I may turn one way or another."

Then Laban and Bethuel answered, "This is the Lord's doing; we dare not say anything. Here is Rebekah. Take her and go, and let her become the wife of your master's son, as the Lord has spoken."

When Abraham's servant heard their words, he bowed down to the earth before the Lord. Then he brought out jewels of silver, and jewels of gold, and clothing, and gave them to Rebekah. He also gave precious gifts to her brother and to her mother.

Then he and the men with him ate

---

&ε [3] THE GRACIOUS REBEKAH: At the well, Eliezer saw a comely maiden approaching with a jug on her shoulder. She stopped beside a crying child, whose foot had been cut on a sharp stone. She washed the wound and bound it with her kerchief. "Do not worry," she comforted him. "It soon will heal."

A half-blind woman had come to the well to draw water. Rebekah helped her carry the full pitcher to her home. When she returned, Eliezer asked, "Will you give me a little water?"

"Drink, sir," she said, lowering her pitcher. Then she drew water for his camels. The other girls mocked her because she served a stranger, but she ignored their jeers.

Eliezer felt this was a suitable wife for Isaac, for she was kind as well as beautiful. "Whose daughter are you?" he inquired. When she told him, Eliezer blessed God who had not forsaken Abraham.

הִנֵּה רִבְקָה לְפָנֶיךָ קַח וָלֵךְ, וּתְהִי אִשָּׁה לְבֶן־אֲדֹנֶיךָ.

and drank, and stayed the night. When they arose in the morning, he said, "Send me away to my master."

But Rebekah's brother and mother said, "Let the maiden stay with us a few days, at least ten; after that she shall go."

But he said, "Do not delay me, since God has prospered my way. Let me go that I may return to my master."

And they said, "We will call the maiden, and ask her wishes." [4] And they called Rebekah and said to her, "Will you go with this man?"

And she said, "I will go."

So they sent Rebekah off with her nurse, and Abraham's servant and his men. And they blessed Rebekah, saying to her, "May you become the mother of thousands of ten thousands, and may

your descendants possess the gates of their enemies."

And the servant took Rebekah and her maids, and went his way.

REBEKAH BECOMES THE WIFE
OF ISAAC

ONE EVENING, Isaac went out to meditate in the field; and he lifted up his eyes, and there he saw camels coming.

And Rebekah looked up, and when she saw Isaac she dismounted from the camel. And she said to the servant, "Who is this man walking in the field toward us?"

And the servant answered, "It is my master." So she took her veil, and covered herself.

---

◆ [4] WE WILL CALL THE MAIDEN AND ASK HER WISHES: This line indicates, say our Rabbis, that a woman cannot be given in marriage by her father or older brother against her wishes. She must be asked and give her assent.

◆ [5] ISAAC WAS COMFORTED: Isaac had loved his mother dearly, our Sages said, for she had been a worthy and gracious woman, good to the poor, her door ever open to the needy. She baked fresh loaves for the Sabbath, kindled the Sabbath lights, and kept the festivals. When she died, there was sorrow among all the people.

Rebekah took Sarah's place. Once more the poor were welcomed; the lights twinkled in blessing every Sabbath and holiday; and joy returned to the home of Abraham and Isaac. So Isaac was comforted for his mother.

אֲחוֹתֵנוּ, אַתְּ הֲיִי לְאַלְפֵי רְבָבָה, וְיִירַשׁ זַרְעֵךְ אֵת שַׁעַר שֹׂנְאָיו.

Then the servant told Isaac all the things that he had done. And Isaac brought Rebekah to his mother's tent, and took her as his wife; and he loved her. Thus Isaac was comforted for his mother. [5]

### THE DEATH OF ABRAHAM

AND ABRAHAM lived a hundred and seventy-five years; and he died at a ripe old age. And his sons, Isaac and Ishmael, buried him in the Cave of Machpelah, in the field of Ephron, the field which Abraham had purchased from the children of Heth. There Abraham was buried with his wife Sarah.

And after the death of Abraham, God blessed his son Isaac.

וַיְהִי אַחֲרֵי מוֹת אַבְרָהָם וַיְבָרֶךְ אֱלֹהִים אֶת יִצְחָק בְּנוֹ.

# 7. GENESIS [25–28]

### ESAU AND JACOB ARE BORN

ISAAC WAS FORTY years old when he married Rebekah. And Isaac prayed to God on behalf of his wife, because she was barren. The Lord heard his prayers, and Rebekah became pregnant. And the children struggled within her; [1] and she said, "If it is to be like this, why do I live?"

So she inquired of the Lord. And the Lord said to her,

"Two nations are in your body,
And two peoples shall be separated from you;

---

[1] THE STRUGGLING OF JACOB AND ESAU: Though twins, Esau and Jacob were entirely different from one another. Esau was selfish and cruel; Jacob was virtuous. Even before they were born, they began their eternal quarreling.

Each brother wished to be born first, so as to win the birthright. When Esau threatened to kill their mother, Jacob let him go first, but held on to his heel.

שְׁנֵי גוֹיִם בְּבִטְנֵךְ וּשְׁנֵי לְאֻמִּים מִמֵּעַיִךְ יִפָּרֵדוּ.

And the one people shall be
stronger than the other;
And the elder shall serve the
younger."

When the time of delivery came, there
were indeed twins within her. And the
first-born was ruddy, and hairy all over;
so they called him Esau [the hairy one].
Then his brother was born, with his
hand holding on to Esau's heels; and so
his name was called Jacob [one who
holds by the heel]. And Isaac was sixty
years old when they were born.

The boys grew up; and Esau became
a skillful hunter, a man of the field; but
Jacob was a quiet man, [2] dwelling in
tents. [3]

Now Isaac loved Esau, because he
was fond of game; [4] and Rebekah
loved Jacob.

---

⤐ [2] JACOB WAS A QUIET MAN: "Why did Isaac favor Esau?" the
Rabbis asked. "Could he not see that Jacob was the faithful son?"

It was hard to judge Esau and Jacob when they were young. All
trees look alike when they are shoots; when they mature, one may
be green and fruitful, the other dry and covered with thorns. Both
brothers went to school in their childhood, and their ways did not
part until their thirteenth year. Then Jacob continued to study in the
*Bét ha-Midrash* of Shem and Eber, but Esau became a hunter and
a worshiper of idols.

⤐ [3] THE HUNTER VERSUS THE DWELLER IN TENTS: Esau was a tireless
hunter who enjoyed the excitement of tracking and killing animals;
Jacob liked to study the wisdom taught in the academies.

Through the centuries ever since, the descendants of Jacob have
abhorred war, and have rejoiced in study and in doing of good deeds.
Their models have been heroes of the spirit: prophets and scholars.
The descendants of Esau, however, have been warriors; their delight
has been in warfare, and their peacetime spent in bloody sports.

⤐ [4] FOND OF GAME: The Hebrew words *tzayid b'fiv* are usually translated to mean "fond of game." That is, Isaac favored his son Esau
because of the kind of food he brought him. But these words can
also be translated "skillful with his mouth." Esau was a deceiver,
adept at flattery; he fooled Isaac.

וַיִּגְדְּלוּ הַנְּעָרִים, וַיְהִי עֵשָׂו אִישׁ יוֹדֵעַ צַיִד אִישׁ שָׂדֶה, וְיַעֲקֹב אִישׁ תָּם יוֹשֵׁב
אֹהָלִים.

### ESAU SELLS HIS BIRTHRIGHT

ONE TIME, WHEN Jacob was making pottage, Esau came in from the field, and he was famished. And Esau said to Jacob, "Let me swallow some of this red pottage, for I am famished." [5]

But Jacob said, "Sell me first your birthright."

And Esau said, "I am at the point of dying, so what use is this birthright to me?"

Then Jacob said, "Swear to me first."

And Esau gave him his oath, and he sold his birthright to Jacob. Then Jacob gave Esau bread and stewed lentils; and he ate and drank, and rose and went his way. Thus Esau despised his birthright. [6]

### ISAAC AND THE WELLS

THERE WAS A famine in the land, besides the first famine that was in the days of Abraham. And Isaac went to Abimelech, king of the Philistines, in Gerar.

And the Lord appeared to him and said, "Do not go down to Egypt; stay in this land for a while, and I will be with you, and will bless you. To you and to your children I will give all these lands, to fulfill the oath which I swore to Abra-

---

&#8269;   [5] LET ME SWALLOW SOME OF THIS RED POTTAGE: Esau asked Jacob, "Why are you preparing lentils?"

"Our grandfather Abraham has passed away, and I am preparing lentils for our father's mourner's meal," Jacob replied. "You know that lentils and eggs are the mourner's meal, for they are round as a wheel. Life too is like a wheel: for every death there is a birth; life ends, and life begins."

Esau's voice was harsh. "The old man died, like anyone else. Abraham, the friend of God, is gone too!" He looked at the pot of food. "Come, give me some of your lentil pottage! I am famished!"

"I did not prepare it for you," Jacob replied.

"I'll give you my birthright for the pottage," his brother offered. Jacob was shocked. "Your birthright!"

"Of what use is my birthright?" said the other. "I am a hunter, always close to death. Whatever I can get today, I take."

So Esau sold his birthright to Jacob for a bowl of lentils.

הַלְעִיטֵנִי נָא מִן הָאָדֹם הָאָדֹם הַזֶּה.

ham. And I will multiply your descendants as the stars of heaven, so that all the nations of the earth will bless one another by them, because Abraham listened to My voice and observed My commandments, My statutes, and My laws."

And Isaac dwelled in Gerar. And Isaac sowed a crop in that land, and obtained that year a hundredfold; and the Lord blessed him. And the man became great, and grew more and more until he was very great. He had flocks of sheep, and herds of cattle, and a great household; and the Philistines envied him.

And all the wells which his father's servants had dug in the time of Abraham his father, the Philistines had stopped up and filled them with earth.

And Abimelech said to Isaac, "Go from us, for you have grown too powerful for us."

Isaac left there, and settled in the valley of Gerar. He reopened the wells of water which had been dug in the days of Abraham his father, but which the Philistines had stopped up after Abraham's death. And he gave them the same names his father had called them. But when Isaac's servants dug in the valley and found there a well of living water, the herdmen of Gerar disputed over it, saying, "The water is ours."

So Isaac's servants dug in another place, and the herdmen of Gerar disputed over that also. So he moved from there, and dug another well; and there was no dispute over this. And he called it Rehoboth; and he said, "For now the Lord has made room for us."

And he went up from there to Beersheba. And the Lord appeared to him the same night, and said, "I am the God of Abraham, your father. Do not fear, for I am with you, and will bless you, and multiply your children for the sake of My servant Abraham."

And Isaac built an altar there, and

---

≈§ [6] ESAU DESPISED HIS BIRTHRIGHT: How do we know that Esau despised his birthright? Because he brought his friends to Jacob's tent and said to them, "Look at the fool! I ate his lentils, drank his wine, and do you know what I gave him for these good things? My birthright!"

They all laughed at Jacob and jeered at him.

Later, however, Esau complained that Jacob had deceived him and had taken the birthright away by cunning.

אָנֹכִי אֱלֹהֵי אַבְרָהָם אָבִיךָ. אַל תִּירָא כִּי אִתְּךָ אָנֹכִי.

called upon the name of the Lord, and pitched his tent there.

Then Abimelech came to him from Gerar, with his friends. And Isaac said to them, "Why have you come to me, seeing that you hate me, and drove me away from you?"

And they said, "We saw plainly that the Lord was with you, and we said: Let there be an oath between us and you. Let us make a covenant with you, that you will do us no harm, as we have not touched you, but have sent you away in peace. You are indeed the blessed of the Lord."

And he made a feast for them, and they ate and drank. When they arose in the morning, they swore to one another; and they departed from him in peace. And it came to pass that same day that Isaac's servant came and told him about the well which they had dug, and said to him, "We have found water."

So Isaac called the place Shibah [fortunate]. Therefore the name of the city is Beer-sheba to this day.

## JACOB GETS HIS FATHER'S BLESSING

WHEN ISAAC HAD become old and his eyes were too dim to see, he called Esau, his elder son, and said to him, "My son."

And Esau replied, "Here I am."

Then Isaac said, "See, I am old, and know not the day of my death. Therefore, please take your quiver and your bow, and go out to the field, and get some game for me. Then make me a tasty dish, such as I love, and bring it to me to eat, that my soul may bless you before I die."

So Esau went to the field to hunt for

---

[7] MY BROTHER'S BLESSING: When Rebekah told Jacob to prepare the meat that he might receive Isaac's blessing, he protested, "I cannot take my brother's blessing."

But Rebekah insisted, "Esau holds the worship of God in contempt. Why, then, should he receive God's blessing?" Still Jacob refused to go.

Then Rebekah said, "If there is a sin in this, let it be on my soul. It is Esau's mother who says he does not deserve the blessing, for he spurns God and takes foreign wives. I command you to take his place!"

Only then, and reluctantly, did Jacob prepare to go in to Isaac.

עַל־כֵּן שֵׁם הָעִיר בְּאֵר שֶׁבַע עַד הַיּוֹם הַזֶּה.

game to bring to Isaac. Rebekah was listening when Isaac spoke to his son Esau. And she said to Jacob, "I heard your father say to your brother Esau: Bring me some game and make me a tasty dish, that I may bless you before the Lord before I die. Now, my son, listen to that which I command you. Go to the flock and get me two choice kids; and I will make them into a savory dish for your father, such as he loves. Then you will bring it to your father to eat, so that he may bless you before he dies."

And Jacob said to his mother, "But my brother Esau is a hairy man, while I am smooth-skinned. Perhaps my father will touch me, and I shall seem to him a deceiver; and I shall bring a curse on myself, not a blessing." [7]

But his mother said, "Let any curse for you, my son, fall on me; only obey me, and go fetch them for me."

Jacob went and fetched, and brought them to his mother; and his mother made a tasty dish, such as his father loved. And Rebekah took the finest clothes of Esau, her elder son, which she had in the house, and put them on Jacob, her younger son. And she put the skins of the kids upon his hands and upon the smoothness of his neck. She put into the hands of her son Jacob the savory food and the bread which she had prepared. Then he went to his father and said, "My father."

And he said, "Here I am; who are you, my son?"

Jacob said to his father, "I am Esau, your first-born; I have done as you bade me. Sit up, I beg you, and eat of my game, that you may give me your blessing."

And Isaac said to his son, "How is it that you have found it so quickly, my son?"

And he said, "Because the Lord, your God, gave me good fortune."

Isaac then said to Jacob, "Come near, my son, that I may feel you, to see whether you are really my son Esau, or not." [8]

And Jacob drew close to his father,

---

ৼ [8] COME NEAR THAT I MAY FEEL YOU: Why did Isaac doubt Jacob when he brought him food in Esau's place? Because Jacob answered that the Lord had helped him in the hunt. Even though he had been careful to say, "The Lord, your God," Isaac was suspicious, for it was not Esau's way to mention the Lord. Therefore he asked to feel him.

וַתֹּאמֶר לוֹ אִמּוֹ: עָלַי קִלְלָתְךָ בְּנִי, אַךְ שְׁמַע בְּקוֹלִי וְלֵךְ קַח־לִי.

who felt him and said, "The voice is the voice of Jacob, but the hands are the hands of Esau." He did not recognize him, because his hands were hairy.

And Isaac said, "Serve me, and I will eat of my son's game that I may give you my blessing."

So Jacob brought it to him, and he ate; and he brought him wine, and he drank. Then his father Isaac said to him, "Come close now, and kiss me, my son."

And he came near, and kissed him. And when Isaac smelled his clothing, he blessed him, saying, "The smell of my son is like the smell of a field which the Lord has blessed.

"May God give you of the dew of heaven
And of the fat of the earth,
And abundance of grain and wine.
Let peoples serve you,
And nations bow down to you.
Be master over your brothers,
And let your mother's sons bow
 down to you.
Cursed be everyone who curses you,
And blessed be everyone who
 blesses you."

No sooner had Isaac finished blessing Jacob, and Jacob scarcely had left the presence of his father, than his brother Esau came in from his hunt. He, too, made tasty food and brought it to his father. And he said, "Let my father arise, and eat some of his son's game, that you may give me your blessing."

And Isaac his father said, "Who are you?"

And he answered, "I am Esau, your first-born."

And Isaac trembled violently, and said, "Who was it then who took some game, and brought it to me? I ate heartily of it before you came, and blessed him. Indeed, he shall be blessed!"

When Esau heard his father's words, he burst into loud and bitter cries, and said to his father, "Bless me also, O my father."

But Isaac said, "Your brother came with guile, and has taken your blessing."

And Esau said, "He pushed me aside twice: he took away my birthright, and now he has taken away my blessing. [9] Have you not reserved a blessing for me?"

---

[9] HE TOOK AWAY MY BIRTHRIGHT: Both brothers desired the birthright, but for different reasons. Esau was concerned about the double share of inheritance that went with it. Jacob wished it because the priestly service was the right of the first-born.

הַקּוֹל קוֹל יַעֲקֹב, וְהַיָּדַיִם יְדֵי עֵשָׂו.

And Isaac answered and said, "I have made him master over you, and all his brothers I have made his servants; and I have provided him with grain and wine to sustain him; and what then shall I do for you, my son?"

And Esau said to his father, "Have you only one blessing, my father? Bless me also, O my father." And Esau wept aloud.

Then Isaac his father said to him,
"The fat places of the earth
   shall be your dwelling,
   And the dew of heaven from
   above.
And by your sword you shall live,
And you shall serve your brother;
But when you shall break loose,
You shall shake his yoke from off
   your neck."

And Esau hated Jacob because of the blessing which his father had given him. And Esau said to himself, "The days of the mourning for my father are near. Then I will slay my brother Jacob."

When the words of Esau, her elder son, were told to Rebekah, she sent for her younger son, Jacob, and said to him, "Your brother Esau consoles himself by planning to kill you. Now, my son, listen well: flee to my brother Laban, at Haran; and stay with him until your brother's anger subsides, and he forgets what you have done to him. Then I will send to fetch you. Why should I be bereaved of you both in one day?"

And Rebekah said to Isaac, "I am weary of my life, because of the Hittite women. If Jacob marries a Hittite woman, what good will life be to me?"

So Isaac called Jacob and blessed him, and charged him, "You shall not take a wife of the daughters of Canaan. Arise, go to Paddan-aram, to the house of Bethuel, your mother's father, and take a wife from the daughters of Laban, your mother's brother. May God Almighty bless you and make you fruitful and multiply you, that you may become a congregation of peoples."

And Isaac sent Jacob away, and he went to Paddan-aram.

וְשָׁלַחְתִּי וּלְקַחְתִּיךָ מִשָּׁם; לָמָה אֶשְׁכַּל גַּם שְׁנֵיכֶם יוֹם אֶחָד?

# 8. GENESIS [28–35]

JACOB'S DREAM

JACOB LEFT BEER-SHEBA and went toward Haran. [1] He came to the place, [2] and stayed there all night, for the sun had set; and he took of the stones of the place to put under his head, and lay down to sleep.

And he dreamed, and he saw a ladder set up on the earth, its top reached to heaven; and the angels of God ascended and descended on it. [3] Then the Lord

---

[1] JACOB LEFT BEER-SHEBA: Why does the Bible repeat that Jacob left Beer-sheba? It is emphasizing that when a righteous man leaves a community, his absence is felt. A righteous man is the splendor, beauty and glory of a town; when he leaves, these depart with him.

[2] HE CAME TO THE PLACE: Why is it written that Jacob came to "the" place? the Rabbis asked.

On his journey he came to a resting place for travelers, set up by

וַיַּחֲלֹם: וְהִנֵּה סֻלָּם מֻצָּב אַרְצָה וְרֹאשׁוֹ מַגִּיעַ הַשָּׁמַיְמָה, וְהִנֵּה מַלְאֲכֵי אֱלֹהִים עוֹלִים וְיוֹרְדִים בּוֹ.

stood over him, and said, "I am the Lord, the God of Abraham your father, and the God of Isaac. The land on which you are lying I will give to you and to your descendants. And your descendants shall be as the dust of the earth, [4] and shall spread out to the west, and to the east, and to the north, and to the south. In you and in your descendants shall all the peoples of the earth be blessed. And I will be with you, and will guard you wherever you go, and will bring you back into this land; for I will not leave you, until I have done what I have promised to you."

Jacob awoke from his sleep, and he said, "Surely the Lord is in this place, and I did not know it."

And he was filled with fear, and said, "How awesome is this place! This is none other than the House of God, and this is the gate of heaven."

---

thoughtful people because there was no inn. The spot was fenced in, as a protection against wild beasts; there were stones for tables and for stools. Here Jacob rested, and slept without fear; and here he had his wonderful dream of the ladder and the angels. When he awoke, he said, "I know now that God is found not only in sanctuaries, but wherever people do good for their fellow man."

◦§ [3] ANGELS ASCENDING AND DESCENDING: The Rabbis pointed out that the angels in Jacob's dream seemed to originate on earth, since they go up before they come down. It is as though man's deeds give rise to the angels.

Why did the angels ascend by ladders? The Rabbis pointed out that even angels must ascend to heaven one step at a time.

◦§ [4] THE DUST OF THE EARTH: Though it may seem strange, this is a lofty blessing, our Sages said. As the earth, though trampled and buffeted, still produces rich harvests, so the Children of Israel, though oppressed and downtrodden, still survive their oppressors. The Jews have outlived the great empires of Egypt, Assyria, Babylonia and Rome. They have produced wonderful creations of mind and spirit. As long as heaven and earth exist, the Jews shall be the world's conscience, bringing God's light to mankind.

מַה נּוֹרָא הַמָּקוֹם הַזֶּה; אֵין זֶה כִּי אִם בֵּית אֱלֹהִים וְזֶה שַׁעַר הַשָּׁמָיִם.

Jacob rose early in the morning, and took the stone that he had put under his head [5] and set it up as a pillar, and poured oil upon its top. And he called that place Beth-el, the House of God.

And Jacob made this vow, "If God will be with me, and will watch over me on this journey which I am taking, and will give me bread to eat and clothing to wear so that I return safely to my father's house, then the Lord shall be my God. And this stone, which I have set up as a pillar, shall be God's house; and of all that Thou shalt give me, I will surely give a tenth to Thee." [6]

JACOB MEETS RACHEL

THEN JACOB LIFTED up his feet [7] and went to the land of the East. He looked about and saw a well in the field, and three flocks of sheep lying nearby, for the flocks were watered from this well. The stone over the well was very large. Only after all the flocks were gathered there would the stone be rolled off the mouth of the well, and the sheep watered; then the stone was put back upon the mouth of the well.

Jacob said to them, "My friends, where are you from?"

They replied, "We are from Haran."

And he asked, "Do you know Laban, the son of Nahor?"

And they said, "We know him."

And he asked of them, "Is it well with him?"

And they answered, "He is well; and see, there is Rachel his daughter coming with the sheep."

And Jacob said, "Why, the sun is still high, and it is not yet time for the cattle to be gathered together. Go, water the sheep, and pasture them."

---

[5] TOOK THE STONE: Jacob used stones as a pillow, we read, but when he arose after his dream, he took "the" stone. How did the many stones become one? The Rabbis answered that the very stones were jealous of one another, and fought to be the one on which the righteous man rested his head. Rather than let them disturb the tired youth's sleep, God made them into one.

Another explanation is also offered. God had promised Jacob that he would father twelve sons, and that each would become an important tribe. Jacob prayed that the twelve tribes be ever as one, united as brothers and in serving the Lord. In token of God's answer to this prayer, the twelve stones beneath Jacob's head became one.

וְשַׁבְתִּי בְשָׁלוֹם אֶל בֵּית אָבִי – וְהָיָה יְיָ לִי לֵאלֹהִים.

And they answered, "We cannot until all the flocks are gathered together, and they [the shepherds] roll the stone off the mouth of the well; and then we will water the sheep."

While he was still talking to them, Rachel came with her father's sheep. And when Jacob saw Rachel, he went near, and rolled the stone off the mouth of the well, and watered the flock of Laban, his mother's brother. Then Jacob kissed Rachel, and wept. And he told her that he was Rebekah's son; and she ran and told her father.

And it came to pass when Laban heard about Jacob that he ran to meet him and embraced him and brought him to his house. And Jacob told Laban his whole story. And Laban said to him, "Surely you are my bone and my flesh." And Jacob stayed with him for a month.

And Laban said to Jacob, "Because you are my kinsman, should you work for me for nothing? Tell me, what shall your wages be?"

## LABAN DECEIVES JACOB

NOW LABAN HAD two daughters: the name of the elder was Leah, and the name of the younger was Rachel. Leah had weak eyes, but Rachel was beautiful of form and lovely. And Jacob loved Rachel; so he said to Laban, "I will serve you seven years for Rachel, your younger daughter."

And Laban said, "It is better that I give her to you than to another man. Stay with me."

Jacob served seven years for Rachel; and they seemed but a few days, because of his love for her. Then Jacob said, "Give me my betrothed, for my days are fulfilled, and let me marry her."

So Laban gathered all the people of the place, and made a feast. And in the evening, he took his daughter Leah, and brought her to Jacob; and Laban gave Zilpah, his maidservant, to his daughter Leah as a maid.

And in the morning, Jacob discovered

---

෪ [6] A TENTH TO THEE: Jacob was the first man to give a tenth of what he earned to God in a worthy cause. From this example we learn that we must give a tenth of our earnings to charity.

෪ [7] JACOB LIFTED UP HIS FEET: What is meant by the phrase, "Jacob lifted up his feet"? It indicates that Jacob did not merely walk: he strode. His heart filled with the promise of his dream; he saw new meaning to life. He lifted his feet and strode toward Haran.

וְעֵינֵי לֵאָה רַכּוֹת, וְרָחֵל הָיְתָה יְפַת תֹּאַר וִיפַת מַרְאֶה.

that it was Leah; and he said to Laban, "What is this you have done to me? Did I not serve you for Rachel? Why, then, have you deceived me?"

And Laban said, "It is not customary in our country to give the younger in marriage before the elder. Finish the week's festivities for this one, and we will give you the other also, in return for another seven years of service with me."

And Jacob did finish the week; and then Laban gave him his daughter Rachel as wife. And he also gave Bilhah, his maidservant, to Rachel to be her maid.

Jacob loved Rachel more than Leah, and he served Laban seven years more.

### JACOB'S CHILDREN

WHEN GOD SAW that Leah was unloved, He gave her children; but Rachel was childless. Leah became pregnant, and bore a son, and she called his name Reuben; and she said, "Now my husband will love me."

And she became pregnant again, and bore a son; and said, "Because God saw that I am unloved, He has therefore given me this son also." And she called his name Simeon.

And she bore another son; and said, "Now will my husband be attached to me, because I have borne him three sons." Therefore his name was called Levi.

And she gave birth to a fourth son; and she called his name Judah. And she stopped bearing children.

When Rachel saw that she bore no children to Jacob, she envied her sister, and she said to Jacob, "I want to have children, or else I will die." And Jacob became angry with Rachel, and he said, "Can I take the place of God, who has withheld children from you?"

And she said, "Here is my maid Bilhah. Marry her, that I may raise up children."

And Jacob took Bilhah. And she became pregnant, and bore Jacob a son. And Rachel said, "God has judged me, and has also heard my voice, and has given me a son." Therefore she called his name Dan.

And Bilhah, Rachel's maid, became pregnant again, and bore a second son. And Rachel called his name Naphtali.

Then Leah gave her maid Zilpah to Jacob as wife. And Zilpah bore Jacob a son; and Leah called his name Gad. And Zilpah bore Jacob a second son; and Leah called his name Asher.

And God heard Leah, and she became pregnant again; and she bore Jacob a fifth son, and she called his name Issachar. And she became pregnant again, and bore a sixth son to Jacob; and she called his name Zebulun. And afterward

דָּנַנִּי אֱלֹהִים וְגַם שָׁמַע בְּקוֹלִי וַיִּתֶּן־לִי בֵּן, עַל כֵּן קָרְאָה שְׁמוֹ דָּן.

she bore a daughter, and she called her name Dinah.

And God remembered Rachel, and she became pregnant and bore a son; and she called his name Joseph, saying, "May the Lord add another son for me."

### JACOB FLEES FROM LABAN

JACOB HEARD THE things that Laban's sons were saying: "Jacob has taken away all that our father had; and from that which was our father's he has gotten all his wealth."

And he also saw that Laban's manner to him was not as it had been before. And the Lord said to Jacob, "Return to the land of your fathers, and to your place of birth; and I will be with you."

So Jacob called Rachel and Leah to the field and said to them, "I see that your father's manner toward me is not as it was before. You know how hard I worked for your father, but he has cheated me and changed my wages ten times; but God did not allow him to do me any harm. If your father said, 'The speckled animals are to be your wages,' then all the sheep had speckled lambs; and if he said, 'The striped animals are to be your wages,' all the sheep had striped lambs. And I had a dream, and in it the angel of God said to me, 'Jacob!' And I said, 'Here I am.' And he said, 'I am the God of Beth-el where you

anointed a pillar and where you made a vow to Me. Now, come, leave this land and return to the land of your birth.' "

Rachel and Leah answered and said to him, "Have we any share or inheritance in our father's house? He has treated us as strangers, for he has sold us and has also kept for himself our price. For all the riches which God has taken away from our father really belong to us and to our children. Now then, do whatever God has told you."

Then Jacob arose and set his sons and his wives upon the camels; and he carried away all his cattle and all his property, and set out to go to Isaac his father, to the land of Canaan.

### LABAN PURSUES JACOB

ON THE THIRD DAY it was told Laban that Jacob had fled. And Laban took his kinsmen and pursued Jacob a way of seven days; and he overtook him in the mountain of Gilead.

In the night God appeared to Laban, the Aramean, in a dream, and said, "Beware of attempting anything with Jacob."

And Laban caught up with Jacob, and said, "Why did you flee in secret, and carry away my daughters, and rob me? If you had told me you longed for your father's home, I would have sent you off with festive music."

הִשָּׁמֶר לְךָ פֶּן תְּדַבֵּר עִם יַעֲקֹב מִטּוֹב עַד רָע.

Jacob answered, "Because I was afraid that you would take your daughters from me by force. Now search my camp and take whatever is yours." And Laban searched all the tents but found nothing which belonged to him.

Then Jacob said to Laban, "What is my offense and what is my sin that you have hotly pursued me? I served you fourteen years for your two daughters and six years for your sheep; and you have changed my wages ten times."

And Laban answered, "What can I do about my daughters or the children that they have borne? Come then, let us make a covenant."

And Jacob and his men gathered stones and made a heap. And Laban said, "Let this heap be witness that I will not pass over it to you, and that you shall not pass over it to me for harm."

And Laban rose early in the morning, and kissed his daughters and his grandchildren, and left for home. And Jacob continued his journey.

JACOB SENDS MESSENGERS TO ESAU

JACOB SENT MESSENGERS before him to Esau his brother to the land of Seir, the field of Edom. And he commanded them, "Thus shall you say to my lord Esau, 'Thus says your servant Jacob: I have sojourned with Laban and stayed until now. And I have oxen and donkeys and flocks, and male and female servants; and I have sent to tell my lord in the hope that I may find favor in your sight.'"

And the messengers returned to Jacob, saying, "We came to your brother Esau, and he is on his way to meet you, and four hundred men are with him."

Then Jacob was greatly afraid and distressed. And he divided the people who were with him, and the flocks and the herds and the camels, into two camps. And he said, "If Esau comes on one camp and attacks it, then the camp which is left may escape."

Then Jacob said, "O God of my father Abraham, and God of my father Isaac, O Lord, who said to me: 'Return to your country and to your place of birth and I will do you good;' I am not worthy of all the kindness that Thou hast shown Thy servant; for with nothing but my staff I crossed this Jordan, and now I have become two camps. Deliver me, I pray Thee, from the hand of my brother, from the hand of Esau; for I fear that he will come and smite me, as well as the mothers and the children."

And he selected from what he had with him a gift for Esau, his brother: two hundred and twenty goats, two hundred and twenty sheep, and thirty camels, and cattle and donkeys.

כִּי בְמַקְלִי עָבַרְתִּי אֶת הַיַּרְדֵּן הַזֶּה, וְעַתָּה הָיִיתִי לִשְׁנֵי מַחֲנוֹת.

## JACOB WRESTLES WITH AN ANGEL

THE GIFT WENT before him, and he himself spent that night in the camp.

And that night he arose, and took his two wives and his two maidservants and his eleven children, and crossed the ford of the Jabbok. He also sent everything that belonged to him across the stream.

And Jacob was left alone. Then a man wrestled with him until daybreak. And when he saw that he could not prevail against him, he touched the hollow of his thigh, so that Jacob's thigh was strained as he wrestled with him. Then he said, "Let me go, for the day is breaking."

But he replied, "I will not let you go unless you bless me."

And he said to him, "What is your name?"

And he replied, "Jacob."

Then he said, "Your name shall no longer be called Jacob, but Israel [Contender with God]; [8] because you have struggled with God and with man and have prevailed." [9] And Jacob asked him, "Tell me, I pray, your name."

And he answered, "Why ask my name?" And he blessed him there.

And Jacob called the name of the place Peniel [Face of God], for Jacob said, "I have seen God face to face, and yet my life has been spared."

And the sun rose upon him, and he limped upon his thigh.

## JACOB MEETS ESAU

AND JACOB LIFTED his eyes and looked, and behold, Esau came with four hundred men.

---

⪧ [8] PEOPLE OF ISRAEL: Why are the Jewish people referred to as the "Children of Israel," and never as the "Children of Abraham," or the "Children of Isaac"? Were not all three patriarchs?

The Rabbis pointed out that Abraham was the father of two peoples, the Ishmaelites and the Israelites. Isaac was the ancestor of two peoples, the Edomites and the Israelites. All of Jacob's children, however, and their children's children, were Israelites.

⪧ [9] STRUGGLED WITH GOD: Despite his victory over the angel, Jacob limped off the field. From this we understand that he who struggles with God may survive but he is touched in a vital spot.

לֹא יַעֲקֹב יֵאָמֵר עוֹד שִׁמְךָ כִּי אִם יִשְׂרָאֵל, כִּי שָׂרִיתָ עִם אֱלֹהִים וְעִם אֲנָשִׁים וַתּוּכָל.

And Jacob bowed himself to the ground seven times, until he came near to his brother. And Esau ran to meet him, and embraced him and kissed him, and they wept.

And Esau lifted his eyes and saw the women and the children, and he said, "Who are these with you?" And Jacob said, "The children whom God has graciously given to your servant."

And Esau said, "What do you mean by all this camp I met?" And Jacob said, "To find favor in the sight of my lord." And Esau said, "I have enough, my brother. Let that which you have be yours." But Jacob urged him and he took it.

So Esau returned that day on his way to Seir.

### BENJAMIN IS BORN

AND THEY JOURNEYED from Beth-el; and Rachel was in childbirth, and she had hard labor. When her labor was at its hardest her midwife said to her, "Fear not, for you have another son!"

But as she was breathing her last—for she died—she named her son Ben-oni [the "son of my sorrow"]; but his father called him Benjamin [the "son of the right" hand].

And Rachel died, and was buried on the road to Ephrath, which is now Bethlehem. And Jacob set up a monument upon her grave, the same monument that is on Rachel's grave to this day.

### THE DEATH OF ISAAC

AND JACOB CAME to his father Isaac at Mamre—that is Hebron—where Abraham and Isaac had sojourned. Now the days of Isaac were a hundred and eighty years.

And Isaac died and was gathered to his people, old and full of days. And his sons, Esau and Jacob, buried him.

וַיְהִי בְּצֵאת נַפְשָׁהּ כִּי מֵתָה וַתִּקְרָא שְׁמוֹ בֶּן־אוֹנִי, וְאָבִיו קָרָא לוֹ בִנְיָמִין.

# 9. GENESIS [37–41]

JOSEPH'S DREAM

THESE ARE THE generations of Jacob. Joseph was seventeen years old. [1] He was still a boy and was tending the flock with his brothers. And Joseph brought bad reports of them to their father.

Now Israel loved Joseph more than all his other children, because he was the son of his old age; and he made him a coat of many colors. [2] And when his

---

[1] JOSEPH WAS SEVENTEEN YEARS OLD: Why do the generations of Jacob begin with Joseph, although Jacob had eleven other sons?

Joseph was the cause of all that later happened to Jacob and to the Jewish people. Because he was sold as a slave and brought to Egypt, the descendants of Jacob became a nation, worthy of being freed and of receiving the Torah.

[2] A COAT OF MANY COLORS: This story teaches that a father should not favor one child over another, Rabbi Eleazar pointed out. Joseph's

וַיִּשְׂרָאֵל אָהַב אֶת יוֹסֵף מִכָּל בָּנָיו כִּי בֶן־זְקוּנִים הוּא לוֹ, וְעָשָׂה לוֹ כְּתֹנֶת פַּסִּים.

brothers saw that their father loved him more than all his brothers, they hated him, and could not speak peaceably to him.

And Joseph dreamed a dream and he told it to his brothers: "Hear this dream which I dreamed: We were binding sheaves in the field, and my sheaf arose and stood upright, and your sheaves gathered and bowed to my sheaf."

And his brothers said to him, "Would you rule over us?" And they hated him all the more for his dreams and for his words.

Then he had another dream and told it to his brothers, and said, "I have dreamed another dream: I saw the sun and the moon and eleven stars bow down to me."

When he told it to his father and to his brothers, his father rebuked him and said to him, "What is this dream that you have dreamed? Am I and your mother and your brothers come to bow before you?"

While his brothers were jealous of him, his father kept this matter in mind.

### THE BROTHERS SELL JOSEPH

HIS BROTHERS WENT to pasture their father's flocks at Shechem. And Israel said to Joseph, "Your brothers are pasturing at Shechem. Go now, see whether it is well with your brothers and with the flocks, and bring me back word."

So Joseph went out from the valley of Hebron, and he came to Shechem. A man found him wandering in the field and asked him, "What do you seek?"

And he said, "I seek my brothers. Tell me please where they are pasturing."

The man said, "They have moved from here; for I heard them say: Let us go to Dothan."

So Joseph went after his brothers, and found them in Dothan. And they saw him in the distance, and before he came near them they plotted to kill him. They said to one another, "Here comes the dreamer. Let us kill him and throw him into one of the pits, and we will say a wild beast devoured him. Then we shall see what will become of his dreams."

But Reuben heard them and tried to save Joseph from their hand, and said, "Do not shed blood. Throw him into this pit in the wilderness, but do not lay hand upon him," so that he might save him from their hand and restore him to his father.

---

coat did not weigh more than two *selas,* and it could be held in the palm of the hand; but this trifle caused the exile of the Children of Israel into Egypt.

אַל תִּשְׁפְּכוּ דָם. הַשְׁלִיכוּ אֹתוֹ אֶל הַבּוֹר הַזֶּה אֲשֶׁר בַּמִּדְבָּר וְיָד אַל תִּשְׁ

When Joseph came to his brothers, they stripped him of his coat of many colors, and they took him and threw him into the pit. The pit was empty; there was no water in it.

Then they sat down to eat bread; [3] and they looked up and saw a caravan of Ishmaelites coming from Gilead, their camels laden with spices and balm, on their way to Egypt. And Judah said to his brothers, "What do we gain if we kill our brother and conceal his murder? Come, let us sell him to the Ishmaelites and not lay hand on him; for he is our brother." And his brothers agreed.

They pulled Joseph out of the pit and sold him for twenty shekels of silver to the Ishmaelites, who brought him to Egypt. [4]

The brothers took Joseph's coat, and killed a he-goat, and dipped the coat in the blood; [5] and they brought it to

---

[3] JOSEPH IN THE PIT: After the brothers had thrown Joseph into the pit, they sat down to eat. Joseph cried to them to free him, but they moved away so as not to hear. When they were about to bless God for their meal, they paused in realization. "How can we thank God while we are putting our brother to death?" They immediately pulled Joseph out of the pit, but now they feared he would report their misdeeds to their father. When a caravan of Midianites passed by, Judah suggested that they sell the boy, rather than shed his blood.

[4] WHO SOLD JOSEPH? Some of our Rabbis believed that the brothers did not sell Joseph, but meant only to frighten him. While they were eating, however, passing Midianites carried Joseph away and sold him to the Ishmaelites. This explains why Joseph said years later, "For indeed I was stolen away out of the land of the Hebrews."

Our Rabbis declare further that when Joseph told his brothers, "You sold me here," he meant, "Because you threw me into the pit, I was sold here. You were as direct a cause as if you yourselves had sold me."

[5] A LIE PRODUCES A LIE: After the brothers had sold Joseph, Reuben returned, planning to release him. To his horror, he found the pit

מַה בֶּצַע כִּי נַהֲרֹג אֶת אָחִינוּ וְכִסִּינוּ אֶת דָּמוֹ? לְכוּ וְנִמְכְּרֶנּוּ לַיִּשְׁמְעֵאלִים וְיָדֵנוּ
אַל תְּהִי בוֹ כִּי אָחִינוּ בְשָׂרֵנוּ הוּא.

their father. They said, "We have found this. See whether it is your son's coat or not." And he recognized it, and said, "It is my son's coat; a wild beast has devoured Joseph."

And Jacob rent his garments, and mourned for his son many days. And all his sons and all his daughters tried to comfort him, but he refused to be comforted; and he said, "I will go down to the grave to my son mourning."

JOSEPH IN EGYPT

JOSEPH WAS BROUGHT down to Egypt; and Potiphar, an officer of Pharaoh, bought him from the Ishmaelites.

And Joseph lived in the house of his master, the Egyptian, and the Lord was with Joseph and made all that he did prosper under his hand. When his mas-

ter saw that the Lord was with him, [6] and that the Lord made everything that he did prosper, Joseph found favor in his sight, and he made him overseer of his house.

Now Joseph was handsome and good-looking, and his master's wife cast her eyes upon Joseph; and she said, "Love me!" [7] Joseph refused, and said to her, "My master trusts me. You are his wife. How can I commit this great wickedness and sin against God?"

She spoke to him day after day, but he did not listen to her. One day, when he went into the house to do his work and none of the men of the house was at home, she caught him by his coat, saying, "Stay with me."

Joseph left his coat in her hand and fled, and went outside. When she saw that he had fled, she called to the men

empty. When he learned what the others had done, Reuben was beside himself with anguish. "How could you have done this?" he asked. "I had thought but to frighten him, not to sell him! What shall we tell our father?"

When the brothers realized that they would have to face their father with the terrible news, they set out after the Midianites. "We will buy him back, or take him by force," they said. But they searched for days, and could not find the traders.

"We must tell our father that a wild beast devoured Joseph," they said. "Woe to him who reveals the truth! We must live with this lie all our days."

וַיְמָאֵן לְהִתְנַחֵם וַיֹּאמֶר: כִּי אֵרֵד אֶל בְּנִי אָבֵל שְׁאוֹלָה.

of her house, and said, "See, my master has brought in a Hebrew to insult us; he came in to make love to me and I cried out loudly, so that he left his garment with me and fled outdoors."

And she kept his coat by her until Joseph's master came home. Then she told him the same story: "The Hebrew slave, whom you have brought to us, came in to insult me. But when I screamed for help he fled, leaving his garment with me."

Joseph's master became wrathful. And he took Joseph and put him in prison, where the king's prisoners were kept.

But the Lord was with Joseph and

---

ᴥ  [6] THE LORD WAS WITH HIM: Potiphar observed that Joseph prayed three times a day. "What are you doing?" the Egyptian asked. "Are you trying to cast a spell on me?"

"No," answered Joseph, "I am praying to God."

"To God?" asked Potiphar. "Who is your God? Show him to me."

Replied Joseph, "Would my master please look up at the sun while I count to a hundred?"

Potiphar gazed at the sun for a few moments, then closed his eyes and turned away. "No man can look at the sun for any length of time," he said.

"If you cannot look at the sun, which is only one of His many works, how can you look at God Himself—at the Creator of heaven and earth, of the sun and the planets, and of all that is in the world!"

ᴥ  [7] THE SELF-SATISFIED YOUNG MAN: When Potiphar saw that God was with Joseph, he put him in charge of his entire household. Joseph was in command both in the field and in the house. Soon he was enjoying his power and his comfort. He began to curl his hair and to dress elegantly after the Egyptian fashion. He forgot about his grieving father.

God observed, and said, "Your father mourns you in sackcloth and ashes, while you preen in your finery. I will send a tigress after you." Then did Zuleika, Potiphar's wife, begin to cast her eyes on the handsome young slave.

אָבִיךָ מִתְאַבֵּל עָלֶיךָ בְּשַׂק וָאֵפֶר, וְאַתָּה אוֹכֵל וְשׁוֹתֶה וּמְסַלְסֵל בִּשְׂעָרֶךָ ·

showed kindness to him and gave him favor with the chief jailer. The jailer put Joseph in charge of all the prisoners. The jailer did not attend to anything because the Lord was with Joseph and whatever he did, the Lord made it prosper.

### THE CUPBEARER AND BAKER OF PHARAOH

IT CAME TO PASS that the cupbearer of the king of Egypt and his baker offended their lord the king. And Pharaoh was enraged at his two officers, and he put them in the prison where Joseph was confined. And the captain of the guard assigned Joseph to them, and they were in custody some time.

And they dreamed a dream, both of them, the cupbearer and the baker, on the same night. When Joseph came to them in the morning he saw that they were worried. And he asked the two imprisoned officers, "Why do you look so sad today?"

And they said to him, "We have dreamed a dream, and there is no one that can interpret it." And Joseph said to them, "Do not interpretations belong to God? Tell it to me, I pray you."

The cupbearer told his dream to Joseph, and said, "In my dream I saw a vine before me, and on the vine were three branches; and as soon as it budded, its blossoms shot forth and immediately its clusters ripened into grapes. And Pharaoh's cup was in my hand, and I took the grapes and pressed them into Pharaoh's cup, and I gave the cup into Pharaoh's hand."

And Joseph said to him, "This is the interpretation: the three branches are three days. In three days Pharaoh will restore you to your position; and you shall place Pharaoh's cup in his hand as you did when you were his cupbearer.

"But keep me in mind when it shall be well with you, and show kindness to me, I pray you, and mention me to Pharaoh, and bring me out of this house. For I was stolen away out of the land of the Hebrews; and here also I have done nothing that I should be put into the dungeon."

When the chief baker saw that the interpretation was good he said to Joseph, "I too had a dream. I saw three wicker baskets on my head, and in the top basket there was every kind of baked goods for Pharaoh, and birds were eating them out of the basket which was on my head."

And Joseph answered and said, "This is the interpretation: the three baskets are three days. Within three days Pharaoh shall hang you on a tree, and the birds shall eat your flesh."

כִּי גֻנֹּב גֻּנַּבְתִּי מֵאֶרֶץ הָעִבְרִים וְגַם פֹּה לֹא עָשִׂיתִי מְאוּמָה כִּי שָׂמוּ אֹתִי בַּבּוֹר.

And on the third day, which was Pharaoh's birthday, he made a feast for all his servants. And he restored the cupbearer to his office, so that he put the cup into Pharaoh's hand. But he hanged the chief baker, as Joseph had interpreted to them. [8]

The cupbearer, however, did not keep Joseph in mind, but forgot him.

### PHARAOH'S DREAM

AND IT CAME to pass two years later that Pharaoh dreamed that he stood by the Nile. And there came up out of the river seven beautiful, fat cows, and they fed in the reed-grass. And then seven other cows came up after them out of the river, ugly and lean, and stood by the other cows upon the bank of the Nile. And the ugly and lean cows ate up the seven beautiful and fat cows. So Pharaoh awoke.

And he slept and dreamed a second time: seven fine, good ears of grain came up on one stalk. And after them sprouted seven other ears, thin and blasted by the east wind. And the thin ears swallowed up the fine, full ears. Then Pharaoh awoke, and behold, it was a dream.

In the morning his spirit was troubled; so he sent for all the magicians of Egypt and all its wise men and he told them his dreams, but no one could interpret them.

Then the cupbearer said to Pharaoh, "My sins I now recall. Pharaoh was angry with his servants, and he put me and the chief baker in the prison of the captain of the guard. We had a dream on the same night, I and he. And there was a young Hebrew, a slave of the captain, and we told him our dreams and he interpreted them. And exactly as he interpreted them to us, so they came to pass: I was restored to my post, and the baker was hanged."

---

⤳ [8] CUPBEARER YES, BAKER NO! Why was the cupbearer forgiven, but the baker hanged? Both had seemed lax in their duties. The cupbearer had handed Pharaoh a goblet of wine with a fly in it. The baker had delivered bread with splinters of wood in it.

Pharaoh's counselors reasoned: "The cupbearer could have poured the wine carefully into a clean cup, but the fly flew in as he had handed it to his master. The baker was negligent, for if he had sifted the flour carefully, he would have removed the splinters." Therefore, the baker was hanged while the cupbearer resumed his duties.

וַיְהִי כַּאֲשֶׁר פָּתַר לָנוּ כֵּן הָיָה: אוֹתִי הֵשִׁיב עַל כַּנִּי וְאוֹתוֹ תָלָה.

Then Pharaoh sent for Joseph, and they brought him hurriedly out of the dungeon. And he shaved himself and changed his clothing, and he came to Pharaoh. And Pharaoh said to Joseph, "I have dreamed a dream, and there is no one that can interpret it. Now I have heard it said that when you hear a dream you can interpret it."

And Joseph answered Pharaoh, saying, "It is not I; God will give Pharaoh an answer of peace."

And Pharaoh told his dreams to Joseph. [9]

And Joseph said to Pharaoh, "The dream of Pharaoh is one; God has revealed to Pharaoh what He is about to do. There are coming seven years of great plenty throughout all the land of Egypt. And there shall be after them seven years of famine, and all the plenty shall be forgotten; famine will devastate the land. The dream was twice shown to Pharaoh, because the thing is decreed by God, and God will shortly bring it to pass. Therefore let Pharaoh seek out a man discerning and wise, and set him over the land of Egypt. Let Pharaoh do this, and let him appoint overseers over the land. And let them gather all the food of these good years to come, and lay up grain under the hand of Pharaoh, and keep the food in cities. It shall serve as a store against the seven years of famine which shall be in the land of Egypt, that the land may not perish because of the famine."

## JOSEPH IS MADE GOVERNOR OF EGYPT

THE PLAN PLEASED Pharaoh and all his servants. So Pharaoh said to his servants, "Can we find a man with the spirit of

---

◦§ [9] AND PHARAOH TOLD HIS DREAMS: Pharaoh described his dream twice: once to his magicians and once to Joseph. The second telling has many more details.

Nachmanides held that Pharaoh did not realize the importance of these details (such as, the lean cows not getting fatter after eating the fat cows) until he recounted it to Joseph.

Similarly, a great painting or magnificent symphony may mean nothing to an uninformed person. In the company of a man of spirit and understanding, even before he has been given an explanation, he begins to get hints of what is important.

בִּלְעָדָי, אֱלֹהִים יַעֲנֶה אֶת שְׁלוֹם פַּרְעֹה.

God in him like this one?" And Pharaoh said to Joseph, "Since God has shown you all this, there is none so discerning and wise as you. You shall be in charge over my house, and according to your word all my people shall be ruled; only in respect to the throne itself will I be greater than you. I have appointed you over all the land of Egypt." [10]

And Pharaoh took off his signet ring and put it upon Joseph's hand, and arrayed him in garments of fine linen, and put a gold chain about his neck. And he made him ride in the second chariot, and they cried before him, "Kneel!"

And Pharaoh gave him a wife, Asenath, the daughter of Poti-phera, priest of On. And Joseph was thirty years old when he stood before Pharaoh.

Then Joseph went throughout all the land of Egypt. And he gathered up all the food of the seven good years which were in the land of Egypt, and stored the food in the cities. And Joseph stored up grain as the sand of the sea, until they gave up counting it.

---

[10] VICTORY TO PHARAOH: Why did Pharaoh appoint as viceroy a Hebrew youth, fresh from prison, a slave who had displeased his master? Surely the great Pharaoh had officers of nobler lineage and greater experience?

The worried Pharaoh had asked his soothsayers and magicians to explain his dreams. Their interpretations were many and fantastic. One declared that Pharaoh would have seven daughters who would marry seven brothers; the daughters would all die, and the brothers would rebel against Pharaoh. Another proclaimed that the king would have seven wives, each of whom would die young, leaving a child who would rebel against him.

What most angered Pharaoh was that each magician claimed that he alone could prevent disaster. Pharaoh recognized that their interpretations were ruses to gain power for themselves.

By contrast, Joseph's interpretation was reasonable, and his plan to avert years of famine was clear. He did not offer himself as the man to administer the plan, but suggested that Pharaoh choose a wise man to direct it. Joseph's wisdom and his modesty appealed to Pharaoh, who made him second in the realm.

אַחֲרֵי הוֹדִיעַ אֱלֹהִים אוֹתְךָ אֶת כָּל זֹאת, אֵין נָבוֹן וְחָכָם כָּמוֹךָ. אַתָּה תִּהְיֶה עַל בֵּיתִי וְעַל פִּיךָ יִשַּׁק כָּל עַמִּי.

To Joseph were born two sons before the years of famine came. And Joseph named the first-born Manasseh, which means "making to forget": for "God has made me forget all my hardship, and all my father's house." The second he called Ephraim, which means "to be fruitful": for "God has made me fruitful in the land of my misfortune."

And the seven years of plenty that were in the land of Egypt came to an end. And the seven years of famine began, as Joseph had said. And there was famine in all lands; but in all the land of Egypt there was bread.

Moreover, all the world came to Egypt to Joseph to buy grain, because the famine was severe over all the earth.

וְכָל הָאָרֶץ בָּאוּ מִצְרַיְמָה לִשְׁבֹּר אֶל יוֹסֵף, כִּי חָזַק הָרָעָב בְּכָל הָאָרֶץ.

# 10. GENESIS [42–45]

JOSEPH'S BROTHERS COME TO EGYPT

NOW JACOB SAW that there was grain in Egypt, and he said to his sons, "Why do you look at one another? I have heard that there is grain in Egypt. [1] Go down and buy food for us, that we may live and not die."

And Joseph's ten brothers went down to buy grain in Egypt. [2] But Jacob did

---

[1] GRAIN IN EGYPT: Although Joseph was selling the stored grain at a good price and turning the money over to the king's treasury, Pharaoh had visions of empty granaries and of starvation in his own palace. He ordered Joseph not to sell grain, so that he and the royal household would have plenty, even though the rest of Egypt starved.

Joseph showed him the many store-cities he had built, holding grain enough for all the people for seven long years. In consequence, Joseph was permitted to sell rations to those in need, and the people loved him, and blessed him.

רְדוּ שָׁמָּה וְשִׁבְרוּ לָנוּ מִשָּׁם וְנִחְיֶה וְלֹא נָמוּת.

not send Benjamin, Joseph's brother, with his brothers lest harm befall him. And the sons of Israel came among others to buy grain, for the famine was in the land of Canaan.

Joseph was the governor over the land, and it was he who sold the grain to the people. [3] And Joseph's brothers came and bowed down to him with their faces to the earth. [4] When Joseph saw his brothers he recognized them, but acted as though he were a stranger to them, and spoke harshly to them, "Where do you come from?"

And they said, "From the land of Canaan, to buy food."

And Joseph remembered the dreams which he had dreamed about them, and he said to them, "You are spies. You came to see the nakedness of the land."

And they said to him, "No, my lord, your servants came to buy food. We are

---

[2] JOSEPH'S TEN BROTHERS: Why does Scripture refer to "Joseph's ten brothers" instead of to "Jacob's ten sons"? The Rabbis read the phrase as indication that the brothers were filled with remorse, and that they set out to search for Joseph in Egypt. They intended to offer ransom for him, and, if refused, to take him by force, at the risk of their lives.

[3] JOSEPH WAS GOVERNOR: After he was made governor, why did not Joseph send word to his aged father, who still grieved for him?

Joseph did send messengers to Jacob, we are told, but they could not find him, for Jacob and his family were nomads who wandered from place to place with their herds.

[4] JOSEPH'S BROTHERS CAME: Why did Jacob send ten sons to Egypt? Surely a smaller number, accompanied by servants, would have been sufficient.

The cause was Joseph who, unable to locate his father and brothers, decided to let them find him. He sent word over all the trade routes that servants of foreigners were forbidden to buy grain in Egypt during the famine. Only free men might come, each with one donkey. Therefore, when Jacob needed food for his family, he found it necessary to send ten sons to carry back food enough.

וַיַּרְא יוֹסֵף אֶת אֶחָיו וַיַּכִּרֵם וַיִּתְנַכֵּר אֲלֵיהֶם וַיְדַבֵּר אִתָּם קָשׁוֹת.

all one man's sons. We are honest men, not spies."

And Joseph said to them, "No, you came but to see the nakedness of the land."

And they said, "Your servants are twelve brothers, the sons of one man in the land of Canaan; and the youngest is today with our father, and one is no more."

But Joseph said to them, "It is as I said: you are spies! By this shall you be tested: [5] as Pharaoh lives, you shall not leave this place unless your youngest brother comes here. Send one of you and let him bring your brother, while the rest of you remain in custody, so that the truth of your word may be proved. Else,

as Pharaoh lives, surely you are spies." And he put them all together in prison for three days.

On the third day Joseph said to them, "Do this and you shall live, for I fear God. If you are honest men, let one of your brothers remain in prison; but the rest of you go, carry grain home for your starved households. But bring your youngest brother to me so that your words shall be verified, and you shall not die."

And they said to one another, "Truly, we are guilty about our brother in that we saw the distress of his soul when he pleaded with us for mercy, and we would not hear. Therefore this distress has come upon us."

---

ʕ§ [5] YOU SHALL BE TESTED! The text repeats that Joseph recognized his brothers when they came to Egypt. Why did he not reveal himself to them?

When they bent low before him, Joseph was reminded of his childhood dreams in which they bowed before him. He also remembered how he had begged in vain for mercy when he was thrown into the pit. Were they still so cruel, he asked himself? Had they harmed Benjamin, out of hatred for him? Was his father still alive? He awaited answers to these questions before revealing himself.

Moreover, Joseph had a sense of destiny, a belief that he was in Egypt as part of God's plan. Otherwise, the dedication of his ancestor, Abraham, would have been in vain. Would the Children of Israel persist as a spiritual force, or would they be no more than a tribe of quarrelsome brothers?

All this he would test and see.

אֲבָל אֲשֵׁמִים אֲנַחְנוּ עַל אָחִינוּ, אֲשֶׁר רָאִינוּ צָרַת נַפְשׁוֹ בְּהִתְחַנְנוֹ אֵלֵינוּ וְלֹא שָׁמָעְנוּ.

And Reuben said to them, "Did I not say to you: Do not sin against the boy? But you would not listen."

They did not know that Joseph understood them, for he had an interpreter between them. [6]

He turned away from them and wept; but he returned to them and spoke to them, and took Simeon and bound him before their eyes. Then Joseph gave orders to fill their sacks with grain, and to return each one's money into his sack, and to give them provisions for their journey; and this was done for them. And they loaded their donkeys with their grain and departed.

When they camped, one of them opened his sack to give his donkey fodder, and saw his money in the mouth of the sack. And he said to his brothers, "My money has been returned. See, it is here inside my sack."

And their hearts sank, and they turned trembling one to another, and said, "What is this that God has done to us?"

## THE BROTHERS RETURN TO CANAAN

THEY CAME TO Jacob their father in the land of Canaan, and they told him all that had befallen them.

And when they emptied their sacks, they found each man's money in his sack; and when they and their father saw their bundles of money, they were frightened.

And Jacob their father said, "You have bereaved me. Joseph is no more, and Simeon is no more, and now you would take Benjamin away."

Then Reuben said to his father, "You may slay my two sons if I do not bring him to you. [7] Put him in my charge, and I will bring him back to you."

And Jacob said, "My son shall not go down with you, for his brother is dead, and he only is left. If harm befalls him on the journey that you take, then you

---

✥ [6] THE INTERPRETER: According to the Midrash, the interpreter was Joseph's elder son, Manasseh. Although born and reared in Egypt, the youth had been taught the language and traditions of his ancestors. Despite the fact that they were the only Israelites in Egypt, Joseph's family maintained their identity.

✥ [7] SLAY MY TWO SONS: Though Reuben meant well, he was not the wisest of the brothers. When he suggested that Jacob kill Reuben's two sons if Benjamin did not return, Jacob might have retorted, "It is

לֹא יֵרֵד בְּנִי עִמָּכֶם, כִּי אָחִיו מֵת וְהוּא לְבַדּוֹ נִשְׁאָר.

will bring down my gray hairs with sorrow to the grave."

But the famine was very severe in the
land. And when they had eaten up the
grain they had brought from Egypt,
their father said to them, "Go again, and
buy us a little food."

And Judah said to him, "The man
warned us, saying: Do not see my face
unless your brother is with you. If you
will send our brother with us, we will
go down and buy you food; but if you
will not send him, we will not go down."

And Judah said to his father, "Send
the lad with me, and we will arise and
go, that we may live and not die, both
we and you and our little ones. [8] I will
be surety for him; hold me responsible.
If I do not bring him back to you and
set him before you, let me bear the
blame forever."

And Israel their father said to them,
"If it must be so, then do this: take some
of the best fruits of the land in your
vessels and carry down a gift to the man,
some balm, some honey, spices, pistachio
nuts and almonds. And take double the
money in your hands, because the money
that was returned in the mouth of your
sacks might have been an oversight.
Take your brother, too, and go and return to the man. And may God Almighty give you mercy before the man,
that he may release to you your other
brother and Benjamin. As for me, if I
am to be bereaved of my children, I
shall be bereaved."

## THE BROTHERS' SECOND VISIT TO EGYPT

THE MEN TOOK the gifts, and they took

---

a wild and foolish scheme! Joseph and Simeon are already lost to me.
If disaster befalls Benjamin, will I be happier for slaying my grandchildren as well?" But he replied only, "My son shall not go down
with you."

As the verse says, "Answer not a fool according to his folly" (Proverbs 26:4).

⇜ [8] SEND THE LAD WITH ME: The Midrash says that Judah's main ar-
gument was, "Father, we cannot foresee what may befall Benjamin.
However, we know that if we do not go to Egypt, you and I and all
our little ones will perish of hunger. Is it not better to risk one soul
than to abandon all?"

קְחוּ מִזִּמְרַת הָאָרֶץ בִּכְלֵיכֶם וְהוֹרִידוּ לָאִישׁ מִנְחָה: מְעַט צֳרִי וּמְעַט דְּבַשׁ, נְכֹאת
וָלֹט, בָּטְנִים וּשְׁקֵדִים.

double money in their hands, and Benjamin; and they rose up and went down to Egypt, and stood before Joseph.

When Joseph saw Benjamin with them, he said to the steward of his house, "Bring the men into the house and prepare meat, for the men shall eat with me at noon." And the man did as Joseph bade.

When Joseph came home, they brought him the gifts in their hands and bowed down to him to the ground. And he asked of their health, and said, "Is your father well? The old man of whom you spoke, is he still living?"

And they said, "Your servant, our father, is well. He is still alive." And they bowed their heads in obeisance.

And Joseph looked up and saw Benjamin his brother, his mother's son, and asked, "Is this your youngest brother of whom you spoke to me?" And he said to him, "May God be gracious unto you, my son."

And Joseph hastily sought a place to weep, for his heart yearned toward his brother; so he went to his chamber, and wept there. And he washed his face and came out, and he controlled himself, and said, "Set out bread."

They were seated in his presence according to their age; the first-born according to his birthright, and the youngest according to his youth; and the men looked at each other in astonishment.

Portions were taken to them from his table, but Benjamin's portion was five times as much as any of theirs. And they drank and were merry with him.

Then he commanded his house steward, saying, "Fill the men's sacks with food, as much as they can carry, and put each man's money in the mouth of his sack. And put my silver goblet in the mouth of the sack of the youngest." And he did as Joseph had told him.

When the morning dawned, the men were sent away, they and their donkeys. And when they were gone out of the city and were not yet far, Joseph said to his steward, "Quick! go after the men! And when you overtake them, say to them, 'Why have you repaid evil for good? It is the cup from which my lord drinks. You have done an evil thing.' "

So he overtook them, and he spoke these words to them. And they said to him, "Why does my lord speak such things? Far be it from your servants to do such a thing! Behold, the money which we found in our sacks we brought back to you from the land of Canaan; why then should we steal silver or gold from your lord's house? If it is found on one of your servants, he shall die, and the rest of us will become slaves to your lord."

And he said, "Although it should indeed be as you say, yet only the one in whose possession it is found shall be-

וַיְמַהֵר יוֹסֵף כִּי נִכְמְרוּ רַחֲמָיו אֶל אָחִיו וַיְבַקֵּשׁ לִבְכּוֹת.

come a slave; but the rest of you shall be blameless."

Then each one hastily lowered his sack to the ground and opened it. And he searched, beginning with the eldest and finishing with the youngest; and the goblet was found in Benjamin's sack. Then they rent their clothes, and every man reloaded his donkey, and they returned to the city.

Judah and his brothers came to Joseph's house, and they fell before him on the ground. And Joseph said to them, "What deed is this that you have done?"

And Judah said, "What can we say to my lord? What shall we speak? Or how shall we clear ourselves? God has discovered the iniquity of your servants. We are our lord's slaves, both we and he in whose hand the goblet was found."

But Joseph said, "Far be it from me that I should do so! Only the man in whose hand the goblet was found shall be my slave; but as for the rest of you, go in peace to your father."

### JOSEPH REVEALS HIMSELF

THEN JUDAH CAME near to him, and said, "Oh, my lord, [9] let your servant, I pray you, speak a word in the ears of my lord, and do not let your anger burn against your servant; for you are equal to Pharaoh himself. My lord asked his servants: Have you a father or a brother? And we said to my lord: We have a father, an old man, and a child of his old age, a little one; and his brother is dead, and he alone is left of his mother, and his father loves him. But you said to your servant:

---

&ᴈ [9] "BE, ADONI"—OH, MY LORD: When did Joseph decide to reveal himself? When Judah cried, "Oh, my lord!" Joseph understood that the Hebrew phrase could mean, "Me, my lord." Judah was saying, "Take me instead of Benjamin! If you need a soldier, I am the stronger. If you wish a servant to draw water, or to work in the fields, or to do any work whatever, I am better suited than the frail Benjamin."

This was precisely what Joseph had been waiting to hear. Until this moment, he had no knowledge that his brothers had changed; but now they did not try to save themselves at Benjamin's expense, even though it appeared that he had brought trouble upon them. Judah offered his freedom and, if need be, his very life for his brother.

Now Joseph made himself known to the brothers he knew to be worthy.

וַיִּגַּשׁ אֵלָיו יְהוּדָה וַיֹּאמֶר בִּי אֲדֹנִי, יְדַבֶּר־נָא עַבְדְּךָ דָבָר בְּאָזְנֵי אֲדֹנִי.

Bring him down to me that I may set eyes upon him. But we said to my lord: The lad cannot leave his father; for if he should leave his father would die. And you said: Unless your youngest brother comes down with you, you shall not see my face again. When we returned to our father, we told him the words of my lord.

"Our father said: Go again and buy us a little food. But we said: We cannot go unless our youngest brother be with us. Now if I come to your servant, my father, without the lad, in whose life his life is bound up, when he sees that the boy is not with us, he will die. And your servants will bring down the gray hairs of our father with sorrow to the grave.

"And your servant became surety for the lad to my father. Therefore, let your servant, I pray you, remain in the lad's place, a slave to my lord; but let the lad go back with his brothers. For how shall I go back to my father if the lad is not with me, and witness the sorrow that will come upon my father?"

Joseph could not control himself before his attendants, and he cried, "Let everyone go out from here!" And so there was no one else present with Joseph when he made himself known to his brothers.

And he wept aloud and he said to his brothers, "I am Joseph. Is my father yet alive?"

And his brothers could not answer him, so dismayed were they to see him. And Joseph said to his brothers, "Come near to me, I pray you."

And they came near and he said, "I am Joseph, your brother, whom you sold into Egypt. Now do not be distressed nor reproach yourselves that you sold me, for God sent me before you to preserve life. God sent me before you to insure you a remnant on earth and to save your lives in a great deliverance. It was not you who sent me here, but God.

"Hasten and go to my father, and say to him, 'Thus speaks your son, Joseph: God has made me lord of all Egypt; come down to me, without delay. You shall live in the land of Goshen, and be near me, you and your children and your children's children, and your flocks and your herds, and all that you have. And I will provide for you.' And you shall tell my father of all my glory in Egypt and of all that you have seen, and you shall hasten to bring my father here."

And he fell upon his brother Benjamin's neck and wept; and Benjamin wept upon his neck. And he kissed all his brothers and wept.

אֲנִי יוֹסֵף. הַעוֹד אָבִי חָי?

# 11. GENESIS [45–50]

### JACOB LEARNS THAT JOSEPH IS ALIVE

THE NEWS WAS heard in Pharaoh's house that Joseph's brothers had come, and Pharaoh and his servants were pleased. And Pharaoh said to Joseph, "Say to your brothers: Do this, load your beasts and go back to the land of Canaan; and take your father and your households and come to me; and I will give you the best of the land of Egypt and you shall eat the fat of the land. Now you are commanded to do this: Take wagons from the land of Egypt for your little ones and for your wives, and bring your father, and come. Do not worry about your belongings, for the best of all the land of Egypt is yours."

So Joseph gave them wagons as Pharaoh commanded, and supplied them with provisions for the journey. To each of them he gave changes of clothing, but to Benjamin he gave three hundred shekels of silver and five changes of clothing. And to his father he sent ten donkeys laden with the best things of Egypt, and ten laden with grain and bread and provisions for his father's journey.

And he said to them, "See that you do not quarrel on the way!"

So he sent his brothers away, and they

וּלְאָבִיו שָׁלַח כְּזֹאת עֲשָׂרָה חֲמֹרִים נֹשְׂאִים מִטּוּב מִצְרַיִם וְעֶשֶׂר אֲתֹנֹת נֹשְׂאֹת בָּר וָלֶחֶם וּמָזוֹן לְאָבִיו לַדָּרֶךְ.

went up from Egypt and came to the land of Canaan, to Jacob their father. And they told him, saying, "Joseph is yet alive, and he is ruler over all the land of Egypt." [1]

And his heart stood still, for he did not believe them. But when he saw the wagons which Joseph had sent to carry him, the spirit of Jacob their father revived.

"Enough," said Israel. "Joseph my son is still alive! I will go and see him before I die." [2]

### JACOB'S JOURNEY TO EGYPT

ISRAEL SET OUT on his journey with all that he had, and came to Beer-sheba, and offered sacrifices to the God of his father Isaac. And God spoke to Israel

---

[1] THE BROTHERS RETURN: When the brothers returned to Canaan, they reported to Jacob that Joseph was alive and ruler over all Egypt. They told of his importance and influence, his titles and honor, his servants and his wealth; but this was not of concern to Jacob.

"What of his good works," his father asked, "his charity and his good name?"

"There is none to equal him in all Egypt for good deeds and charity," they immediately said. "He gives generously to the needy, the widowed and the orphaned. He protects the weak and restores justice to the wronged. His kindnesses have made his name blessed."

Jacob rose, looked heavenward, and prayed, "Praised be the Lord who strengthened my son Joseph in his time of trouble, and caused him to live according to His Torah of lovingkindness."

[2] JACOB'S HAPPINESS: Jacob celebrated his happiness with a great banquet for his sons and their households. Canaanites, too, came to congratulate them on the good news. "When Joseph was lost to me many years ago," Jacob told them, "I mourned and would not be comforted. In my heart I said: God has embittered my life.

"Now I have learned not only that my son lives, but that he is governor over all of Egypt, and is known for his charity and good works. God is righteous and faithful: that which seems evil to us, He turns for good. May His great Name be blessed!"

רַב, עוֹד יוֹסֵף בְּנִי חָי; אֵלְכָה וְאֶרְאֶנּוּ בְּטֶרֶם אָמוּת.

in a vision by night, and said, "Jacob, Jacob!"

And he answered, "Here I am."

And He said to Israel, "I am God, the God of your father. Do not be afraid to go down into Egypt, for there I will make you a great nation. I will go down with you into Egypt; and I will also surely bring you up again; and Joseph will close your eyes."

Then Jacob rose up from Beer-sheba; and the sons of Israel carried Jacob their father and their little ones and their wives in the wagons which Pharaoh had sent to carry him. And they took their cattle and their goods which they had gotten in the land of Canaan, and came into Egypt, Jacob and all his children with him. All the souls belonging to Jacob that came into Egypt were sixty-six. And the sons of Joseph, who were born to him in Egypt, were two; all who came into Egypt were seventy. [3]

And he sent Judah ahead of him to Joseph, to show him the way to Goshen; and they came into the land of Goshen.

And Joseph ordered his chariot, and went up to meet Israel his father; and he presented himself to him and fell on his neck and wept a long time. <u>Then Israel said to Joseph, "Now I can die, since I have seen your face, that you are yet alive."</u>

### JACOB BEFORE PHARAOH

THEN JOSEPH WENT in and told Pharaoh, and said, "My father and my brothers, and their flocks and their herds and all that they possess, have come from the land of Canaan; and they are in the land of Goshen."

And from among his brothers he took five men and presented them to Pharaoh. And Pharaoh said to his brothers, "What is your occupation?"

---

⋙ [3] THE SEVENTY: Jacob was troubled when he learned that Joseph wished him to go down into Egypt, and there to reside. "Shall I leave the land of my ancestors, the Holy Land, where the *Shechinah,* the Divine Presence, is in every valley and field, to go to an unclean land, where men worship idols and do not fear God?"

Then God spoke, "I will go with you to Egypt."

It is written: "All who came into Egypt were seventy." Yet at the border of Egypt, when the males of Jacob's family were counted, they were found to number only sixty-nine, including Joseph and his two sons. The seventieth was the Almighty.

וַיֹּאמֶר יִשְׂרָאֵל אֶל יוֹסֵף: אָמוּתָה הַפַּעַם אַחֲרֵי רְאוֹתִי אֶת פָּנֶיךָ כִּי עוֹדְךָ חָי.

And they said to Pharaoh, "Your servants are shepherds, as were also our fathers. And we have come to sojourn in the land, for there is no pasture for your servants' flocks, since the famine is severe in the land of Canaan. Therefore, we pray you, let your servants dwell in the land of Goshen."

And Pharaoh spoke to Joseph, saying, "Now that your father and your brothers have come to you, let them live in the best part of the land; let them dwell in the land of Goshen. And if you know any able men among them, put them in charge of my cattle."

Joseph brought in Jacob his father, and presented him to Pharaoh. And Jacob blessed Pharaoh.

And Pharaoh said to Jacob, "How old are you?" And Jacob said to Pharaoh, "The days of the years of my sojournings are a hundred and thirty years. Few and hard were the years of my life, and they have not reached the years of my fathers in their sojournings." And Jacob blessed Pharaoh, and left Pharaoh's presence.

Then Joseph settled his father and his brothers, and gave them a possession in the land of Egypt, in the best part of the land, as Pharaoh had commanded. And Joseph provided for his father, his brothers and all his father's household.

And Israel dwelt in the land of Egypt in the province of Goshen; and they were fruitful and became very numerous.

### THE DEATH OF JACOB

JACOB LIVED IN the land of Egypt seventeen years. And when the time drew near for Israel to die, he called his son Joseph, and said to him, "If I have found favor in your eyes, I pray you, show kindness and faithfulness to me, and do not bury me in Egypt. When I lie down with my fathers, carry me out of Egypt and bury me in their burial-place. When I was coming from Paddan, Rachel died, to my sorrow, in the land of Canaan, some distance from Ephrath; and I buried her there on the road to Ephrath—now Beth-lehem."

And Joseph said, "I will do as you have said."

And Jacob said, "Swear to me."

And Joseph gave him his oath. And Israel settled back on the head of his bed.

Now Israel's eyes were so dim with age that he could not see. And Joseph brought his two sons to his father, and when Israel saw them, he said, "Who are these?" [4]

And Joseph said to his father, "They

---

⋰§   [4] WHO ARE THESE? Joseph brought his sons to his father that he might bless them. When they entered, Jacob saw two boys dressed as

וְעָשִׂיתָ עִמָּדִי חֶסֶד וֶאֱמֶת: אַל־נָא תִקְבְּרֵנִי בְּמִצְרָיִם.

are my sons, whom God has given me here."

And Israel said, "Bring them to me that I may bless them."

Then Joseph brought them near to him, and he kissed them and embraced them. And Israel said to Joseph, "I did not expect to see your face, but God has let me see your children also."

And Israel stretched out his right hand, and laid it upon the head of Ephraim, who was the younger, and his left hand upon Manasseh's head, crossing his hands, for Manasseh was the first-born. When Joseph saw that his father was laying his right hand upon the head of Ephraim it displeased him, and he raised his father's hand to remove it from Ephraim's head to Manasseh's head. And Joseph said to his father,

"Not so, my father, for this is the first-born. Put your right hand upon his head."

But his father refused, and said, "I know it, my son, I know it. He also shall become a people, and he also shall be great; however his younger brother shall be greater than he, and his descendants shall become a multitude of nations."

And Jacob blessed Joseph's children, and said, "The God before whom my fathers Abraham and Isaac did walk, the God who has been my shepherd all my life long unto this day, the angel who has redeemed me from all evil, bless the lads; and in them let my name be recalled and the name of my fathers Abraham and Isaac. And let them grow into a multitude in the midst of the earth."

---

Egyptians and speaking together in the Egyptian tongue. "Who are these?" Jacob asked. "They are not ours and should not receive my blessing."

"Father, they are my sons," Joseph answered. "They appear strange in your eyes because they were born and reared in Egypt, but they are true descendants of Abraham, worthy of your blessing."

This did not satisfy his father. "You did not marry one of our kin. Were you wed according to the laws and customs of our people?" Jacob asked.

In reply, Joseph brought his wife, Asenath, to Jacob, and showed him their marriage contract, the k'tubah. "Father, this is my wife, whom I married according to our laws and traditions, with a marriage contract and proper ceremony. Bless my sons, I beg you, if only for the sake of this pious woman."

הַמַּלְאָךְ הַגּוֹאֵל אוֹתִי מִכָּל רָע, יְבָרֵךְ אֶת הַנְּעָרִים, וְיִקָּרֵא בָהֶם שְׁמִי וְשֵׁם אֲבוֹתַי,
אַבְרָהָם וְיִצְחָק.

And Jacob called in all his sons and blessed them. [5] And he charged them, saying, "I am to be gathered to my people. Bury me with my fathers in the cave that is in the field of Ephron, in the cave that is in the field of Machpelah, in the land of Canaan, which Abraham bought from Ephron, the Hittite, for a burial-place. [6] There Abraham and his wife Sarah were buried; and there Isaac and his wife Rebekah were buried; and there I buried Leah."

When Jacob finished charging his sons, he drew his feet up into the bed and expired, and was gathered to his people.

And Joseph fell upon his father's face and wept upon him, and kissed him. And Joseph commanded his servants, the physicians, to embalm his father. And the physicians embalmed Israel.

And when the days of weeping for him were past, Joseph went up to bury his father in the land of Canaan. And with him went up all the officials of Pharaoh, the elders of his house, and all the elders of Egypt, and all the house of Joseph and his brothers, and his father's household.

## THE DEATH OF JOSEPH

AND JOSEPH RETURNED into Egypt after he had buried his father, he and his brothers, and all who went up with him to bury his father.

When Joseph's brothers saw that their father was dead, they said, "It may be that Joseph will hate us, and will pay us back all the evil which we did him." And they sent a message to him, saying: "Your father commanded before he died, saying, 'This you shall say to Joseph: Forgive now the wickedness and the sin of your brothers for the evil they did to you.'"

And Joseph wept when they spoke to him. Then his brothers fell down before him; and they said, "Here, we are your bondmen."

And Joseph said to them, "Do not be afraid, for am I in the place of God? You

---

༄ [5] JACOB SUMMONED HIS SONS: When Jacob's end was near, he called his sons together. They assembled about his bed for his blessing. Before he would bless them, the aged patriarch was obliged to ask, "Have you, my sons, been tempted by the animal gods of Egypt to forsake the God of Israel?"

With one voice they replied, "Hear, O Israel [our father], the Lord is our God, the Lord is One!"

וַיֹּאמֶר אֲלֵיהֶם יוֹסֵף: אַל תִּירָאוּ, כִּי הֲתַחַת אֱלֹהִים אָנִי?

meant to do me harm, but God meant it for good, in order to save the lives of many people. Now therefore do not be afraid; I will provide for you, and for your little ones." And he comforted them, and spoke kindly to them.

Joseph dwelt in the land of Egypt, he and his father's household; and Joseph lived one hundred and ten years. And he lived to see his sons' children of the third generation.

And Joseph said to his brothers, "I am about to die; but God will surely remember you and bring you up out of this land unto the land which He promised to Abraham, to Isaac, and to Jacob."

And Joseph then took an oath from the sons of Israel: "When God will remember you, you shall carry up my bones with you from here."

So Joseph died when he was one hundred and ten years old. And they embalmed him, and he was put in a coffin in Egypt.

---

[6] BURY ME WITH MY FATHERS: Despite the fact that he did not grant the same favor to Rachel, Jacob requested that he be buried in the Cave of Machpelah. Why had he been so indifferent to the last resting place of Rachel, whom he had loved the most?

The Midrash tells us that it was God who commanded Jacob to bury Rachel on the road to Beth-lehem, along which the Jewish people would pass, centuries later, as they went into exile. Then would the matriarch Rachel have compassion on her people, as Jeremiah prophesied: "A voice is heard on high, the sound of weeping—Rachel weeping for her children" (31:15).

וְאַתֶּם חֲשַׁבְתֶּם עָלַי רָעָה – אֱלֹהִים חֲשָׁבָהּ לְטוֹבָה.

# 12. EXODUS [1–4]

## THE OPPRESSION OF THE ISRAELITES IN EGYPT

JOSEPH DIED, AND all his brothers, and all that generation. [1] And the Children of Israel multiplied and increased greatly and grew mighty, so that the land was filled with them.

Now there arose a new king over Egypt, who knew not Joseph. And he said to his people, "The people of the Children of Israel are too many and too

---

[1] AND ALL THAT GENERATION: Why did the Egyptians come to despise the Children of Israel?

The change came about when Jacob's sons died and their descendants began to ape the ways of the Egyptians. They thronged to the shrines of the animal gods of Egypt, forsook their own traditions, and became a people without a heritage. Then the Egyptians' goodwill turned to hate, and Pharaoh said, "Come, let us deal wisely with them!"

וַיָּקָם מֶלֶךְ חָדָשׁ עַל מִצְרָיִם אֲשֶׁר לֹא יָדַע אֶת יוֹסֵף.

mighty for us. Come, let us deal wisely with them, lest they become so numerous that if a war comes, they will join with our enemies and fight against us, and go out of the land."

Therefore they set over them taskmasters to afflict them with hard labor. And they built for Pharaoh store-cities, Pithom and Raamses. But the more they were oppressed, the more numerous they multiplied and the more they spread out. And the Egyptians made their lives bitter with hard labor, in mortar and in brick and in all kinds of work in the field. [2]

### PHARAOH COMMANDS TO KILL ALL NEWBORN BOYS

THEN THE KING of Egypt spoke to the Hebrew midwives, and he said, "When

---

[2] BITTER WITH HARD LABOR: The Egyptians deliberately tried to break the spirit of the Children of Israel by making them humiliate each other. Each Egyptian taskmaster had under his command ten Israelite foremen. Each foreman had to see that his group of ten slaves fulfilled the prescribed day's work, or he was cruelly whipped. As a result, the foremen drove their men and beat them, in order to complete their quota. This system was intended to divide the Hebrews and to make them hate each other.

Often the Egyptians forced the Israelite foremen to put too heavy a load on the young, or to compel a woman or an old man to carry the load of a young, strong man. They humiliated a man by making him do women's work.

When the day's work was done, the taskmasters would rout their slaves from their miserable beds and set them to chopping wood and bringing water from the river. The slaves' reward for their labors was ever a kick and a curse.

Yet the Egyptians did not break the spirit of the Hebrews. Our Rabbis say that the Israelites did not give up hope because of four things: they never changed their names; they never changed their language; they did not inform on one another; and they always married their own people.

These strong family ties gave them fortitude to bear hardship with dignity, and to hope that they would be redeemed.

וְכַאֲשֶׁר יְעַנּוּ אוֹתוֹ כֵּן יִרְבֶּה וְכֵן יִפְרֹץ.

you help the Hebrew women [3] give birth, if it is a boy you shall kill him; but if it is a girl, she shall live."

But the midwives feared God and did not do as the king of Egypt commanded them, but let the boys live. [4] And the king of Egypt called for the midwives and said to them, "Why have you done this thing, and let the boys live?"

And the midwives said to Pharaoh, "Because the Hebrew women are not like the Egyptian women; for they are vigorous. Before the midwives come to them, they have given birth."

And God dealt well with the midwives; and the people multiplied, and grew very mighty. And Pharaoh commanded all his people, saying, "Every son that is born you shall cast into the Nile, but every girl you shall let live."

### THE BIRTH OF MOSES

THERE WAS A man from the tribe of Levi who took a wife, a daughter of the tribe of Levi. And the woman bore a son; and when she saw how fair he was, she hid him for three months. And when she

---

᳹ [3] THE HEBREW WOMEN: The Israelites did not break down under slavery, but were equal to freedom. Through the efforts of their loyal wives, they kept their courage, though overworked and mistreated.

The Hebrew women did not desert their husbands. They followed the men and camped near the slave barracks. During the day they netted fish or gathered vegetables; as night fell they prepared a savory dish for their weary husbands. When the men came home, exhausted and spiritless, their wives helped them wash, served their food, and spoke kind and loving words. Their devotion kept up the strength and courage of the Israelites under the rigors of slavery.

᳹ [4] THE MIDWIVES: Our Rabbis pointed out that the phrase, "did not do as the king of Egypt commanded them," implies they "let the boys live." Why were both phrases used?

This was double praise, our Sages explained. Not only did the midwives refuse to obey the king's command to kill the male infants, they also cared for the mothers, and washed and fed the infants. Moreover, they went among the other Hebrew women and asked for food and drink for the poor mothers, and for clothes for their babies.

וַתִּירֶאןָ הַמְיַלְּדֹת אֶת הָאֱלֹהִים וְלֹא עָשׂוּ כַּאֲשֶׁר דִּבֶּר אֲלֵיהֶן מֶלֶךְ מִצְרָיִם, וַתְּחַיֶּיןָ אֶת הַיְלָדִים.

could no longer hide him, she took a basket of papyrus reeds and daubed it with bitumen and with pitch; and she put the child in it and placed it among the reeds by the river's edge. And his sister stood at a distance to learn what would happen to him.

The daughter of Pharaoh came down to bathe in the river; and her maids walked along the river-side. She saw the basket among the reeds and sent her maid to fetch it. When she opened it, she saw a child, a boy crying. And she had pity on him.

And she said, "This is one of the Hebrews' children."

Then his sister said to Pharaoh's daughter, "Shall I go and call a nurse of the Hebrew women, that she may nurse the child for you?"

And Pharaoh's daughter said to her, "Go!"

So the maiden went and called the child's mother. And Pharaoh's daughter said to her, "Take this child and nurse it for me, and I will give you your wages."

So the woman took the child and nursed it. When the child grew she brought it to Pharaoh's daughter, and he became her son. And she called his name Moses, for she said, "I drew him out of the water." [5]

MOSES SEES THE SUFFERING OF HIS BRETHREN

AND IT CAME to pass, when Moses had grown up, that he went out to his kinsmen and saw their labor. [6] And he saw an Egyptian smiting a Hebrew, one of his kinsmen. And he looked this way and that way, and when he saw that there was no one around, he smote the Egyptian and he hid him in the sand.

He went out the next day and saw that two Hebrews were fighting. He said to the wrongdoer, "Why do you strike your fellow?"

[5] WHY WAS HE NAMED MOSES? Bithiah, Pharaoh's daughter, was taken by the infant's beauty. Her maidservants urged her to throw the baby back into the river. "It is the law that the Hebrew boys be drowned," they reminded her.

Bithiah did not heed them. "I shall raise him as my own," she said. "He shall be called Moshe, for I drew him from the water."

Though Moses had been given seven names by his family, to this day we know him only by the name of Moses.

וַתִּקְרָא שְׁמוֹ מֹשֶׁה וַתֹּאמֶר: כִּי מִן הַמַּיִם מְשִׁיתִהוּ.

And he said, "Who made you ruler and judge over us? Do you mean to kill me, as you killed the Egyptian?"

Then Moses was afraid and said, "Surely, the thing is known."

When Pharaoh heard of the matter, he sought to kill Moses. But Moses fled from Pharaoh.

### MOSES SETTLES IN MIDIAN

MOSES CAME TO the land of Midian, and he sat down by a well. Now the priest of Midian had seven daughters; and they came and drew water, and filled the troughs to water their father's flock. The shepherds came and drove them away; but Moses arose and helped them, and watered their flock.

When they came to their father, he said, "How is it that you have come so soon today?"

And they said, "An Egyptian delivered us from the shepherds. He even drew water for us and watered the flock."

And he said to his daughters, "Where is he? Why did you leave the man? Call him, that he may eat bread!"

And Moses was content to dwell with the man; and he gave Moses his daughter Zipporah as wife. And she bore a son, whom he called Gershom; because, he said, "I have been a stranger in a strange land."

### THE BURNING BUSH

A LONG TIME later the king of Egypt died. The Children of Israel groaned because of the bondage, and their cry came

---

ﻭ [6] HE WENT OUT TO HIS KINSMEN: Moses was reared in the palace as foster son of Pharaoh's favorite daughter. He grew handsome and tall, and was dressed in the finest of robes. Pharaoh himself gave him a proud horse to ride.

One day, when he was twenty, he rode out to Pithom and Raamses, where the Hebrews were building store-cities for Pharaoh. There he saw their enslavement, the harsh treatment they received, the ready whips that drove them to their labors. Dismounting, Moses went to their aid, bending his back beneath the huge stones they were struggling to put into place. When he walked among them, helping and encouraging them, his eyes were filled with tears. Then it was that he recognized these were his brethren, and that he must lead them.

וַתֵּלֶד בֵּן וַיִּקְרָא אֶת שְׁמוֹ גֵּרְשֹׁם, כִּי אָמַר: גֵּר הָיִיתִי בְּאֶרֶץ נָכְרִיָּה.

up to God. And God heard their groaning, and God remembered His covenant
with Abraham, with Isaac, and with Jacob. And God took notice of their plight.

Now Moses was tending the flock of
Jethro, his father-in-law, [7] the priest
of Midian; and he led the flock into the
wilderness and came to the mountain of
God, to Horeb. And he looked and he
saw a thorn bush, and behold the bush
was burning with fire, and the bush was
not consumed. [8]

Then Moses said, "Let me turn and
see this great sight; why is the bush not
consumed?"

And when the Lord saw that he
turned aside to see, God called to him out
of the midst of the bush, and said,
"Moses, Moses!"

And he answered, "Here I am."

And He said, "Do not come nearer;
take your shoes off your feet, for the
the place on which you stand is holy
ground." Moreover, He said, "I am the
God of your father, the God of Abraham,
the God of Isaac, and the God of Jacob."

---

[7] WHY WAS MOSES CHOSEN? God does not raise a man to greatness
until He has tested him in small things. The Almighty observed the
way Moses tended Jethro's flocks, leading them into the wilderness
to keep them from grazing, even by accident, on other men's fields.

Once a young kid ran away. Moses pursued it until it stopped at
a water hole to drink. "I did not know that you ran away because of
thirst," Moses said. "You must be weary from running so far!" He put
the kid on his shoulders and carried it back to the flock.

"You have shown kindness and compassion to the sheep," God said.
"You shall therefore shepherd My flock, My beloved Children of
Israel."

[8] WHY FROM THE THORN BUSH? Gazing at the thorn bush, Moses
thought, "My people are like this lowly bush: small and unimportant.
Will they ever be freed from slavery?"

As he spoke, flames began to envelop the bush, and Moses exclaimed with a trembling heart, "O God, now the bush is in flames!
Does this mean that my people will be destroyed by the Egyptians?"

The bush burned, but was not consumed; and a voice within him
said, "Your people are like this burning bush. It burns and it is not

וַיִּקְרָא אֵלָיו אֱלֹהִים מִתּוֹךְ הַסְּנֶה וַיֹּאמֶר: מֹשֶׁה, מֹשֶׁה! וַיֹּאמֶר: הִנֵּנִי.

And Moses hid his face, for he was afraid to look at God.

And the Lord said, "I have indeed seen the affliction of My people that are in Egypt, and have heard their cry under the oppressors; and I know their suffering. And I have come down to deliver them from the hand of the Egyptians and to bring them up out of that land to a spacious and a good land, to a land flowing with milk and honey, to the country of the Canaanites. Come now, therefore, and I will send you to Pharaoh, that you may bring forth My people, the Children of Israel, out of Egypt."

And Moses said, "Who am I, that I should go to Pharaoh and that I should bring the Children of Israel out of Egypt?"

And He said, "I will be with you."

And Moses said to God, "Behold, when I come to the Children of Israel and shall say to them: The God of your fathers has sent me to you; and they shall say to me: What is His name? what shall I say to them?"

And God said to Moses, "Thus shall you say to the Children of Israel: *Eh'yeh Asher Eh'yeh*, I Am Who I Am—*Eh'yeh* has sent me to you. This is My name forever, and this is My memorial to all generations.

"Go and gather the elders of Israel together, and say to them: The Lord, the God of Abraham, of Isaac and of Jacob, has appeared to me, and said: I have indeed remembered you, and seen that which is done to you in Egypt. And I will bring you up out of the affliction of Egypt to the land of the Canaanite, to a land flowing with milk and honey."

And Moses said, "But perhaps they will not believe me nor listen to me, for they will say: The Lord has not appeared to you."

And the Lord said to him, "What is that in your hand?"

And he replied, "A rod."

The Lord said, "Cast it on the ground." And Moses cast it on the ground and it became a serpent; and Moses recoiled from it. [9]

---

consumed. The Israelites suffer, but they will never be destroyed."

Our Rabbis also explain: God spoke from the lowly thorn bush to teach that no place, no matter how small and humble, is without God's presence and care.

⋙ [9] MOSES RECOILED FROM IT: A Roman matron boasted to Rabbi Yosé ben Halafta, "From your own Bible I can prove that my idols

וָאֵרֵד לְהַצִּילוֹ מִיַּד מִצְרַיִם וּלְהַעֲלוֹתוֹ מִן הָאָרֶץ הַהִיא אֶל אֶרֶץ טוֹבָה וּרְחָבָה,
אֶל אֶרֶץ זָבַת חָלָב וּדְבָשׁ.

And the Lord said to Moses, "Stretch out your hand and take it by the tail." And he stretched out his hand and seized it, and it became a rod in his hand.

But Moses said to the Lord, "O Lord, I am not a man of words; for I am slow of speech and of a slow tongue."

And the Lord said to him, "Who has given man a mouth? Who makes a man dumb or deaf, or seeing or blind? Is it not I, the Lord? Therefore, go now, and I will be with your mouth, and teach you what to speak."

And Moses said, "O Lord, I pray Thee, send anyone but me."

Then the Lord became angry at Moses, and He said, "There is your brother Aaron, the Levite. I know that he can speak well. And he is coming to meet you; and when he sees you, he will be overjoyed. You shall speak to him and put words in his mouth; and he shall be your spokesman to the people. He shall be to you a mouth, and you shall be in God's stead to him. And you shall take in your hand this rod with which to perform the signs."

### MOSES RETURNS TO EGYPT

THEN MOSES WENT and returned to Jethro, his father-in-law, and said to him, "Let me go, I beg of you, and I will return to my brethren in Egypt and see whether they are still alive." [10]

---

are greater than your God. When the God of Israel appeared in a thorn bush, Moses merely covered his face; but when the rod turned into a serpent, he fled. This proves that the serpent, who is my god, is more powerful than your God!"

Rabbi Yosé rejoined, "Can you not see that there was no place Moses could flee from the true God, even should he so wish, for no place on earth is hidden from Him? But he had only to retreat a few paces to be beyond the reach of the fangs of your serpent-god."

[10] KINDNESS SHOULD NOT BE FORGOTTEN: Before Moses accepted the mission of redeeming Israel, he said to God, "First I must return to Midian to ask my father-in-law's permission to leave. I cannot go without his consent, for he befriended me when I was a stranger in Midian; he gave me a roof over my head, and food, and his daughter as a wife."

בִּי אֲדֹנָי, לֹא אִישׁ דְּבָרִים אָנֹכִי ... כִּי כְבַד פֶּה וּכְבַד לָשׁוֹן אָנֹכִי.

And Jethro said to Moses, "Go in peace." So Moses took his wife and his sons, and set them upon a donkey, and he returned to the land of Egypt. And Moses took the rod of God in his hand.

And the Lord said to Aaron, "Go into the wilderness to meet Moses." And he went and met him and kissed him. And Moses told Aaron all the words of the Lord with which He had sent him, and all the signs with which He had instructed him.

---

And God said, "Yes, even before you fulfill My command, ask Jethro's leave. No man should be ungrateful."

Jethro consented for Moses to leave Midian, but not that he take his wife and children with him. "Why take your family into trouble?" he asked.

Moses replied, "When people see that I have brought my wife and sons with me, they will believe that deliverance is near, for I would not bring my family into slavery."

At the border of Egypt, however, Moses met Aaron, who asked, "Who are they that travel with you?"

Moses answered, "My wife and children." Aaron said quickly, "The Egyptians will seize them and enslave them, for they are the family of a Hebrew. They are not used to slavery as our people have become, and will perish before the day of deliverance. Send them back!"

Moses did as his brother counseled.

וַיֹּאמֶר יִתְרוֹ לְמֹשֶׁה: לֵךְ לְשָׁלוֹם.

# 13. EXODUS [4-12]

MOSES AND AARON BEFORE PHARAOH

MOSES AND AARON went and gathered together all the elders of the Children of Israel. And Aaron spoke all the words which the Lord had spoken to Moses, and did the signs in the sight of the people. And the people believed; and when they heard that the Lord had remembered them, they bowed their heads and worshiped.

Then Moses and Aaron [1] came to

[1] ONLY MOSES AND AARON: The Israelite elders did not have courage enough to go with Moses and Aaron before Pharaoh. Even though Moses said he would speak in the name of the Lord, the elders furtively slipped away, one by one, as they approached the royal palace. Moses and Aaron appeared alone before the king.

The elders failed in their responsibility as leaders. Therefore when God gave the Ten Commandments to the Children of Israel, only Moses was allowed to ascend Mount Sinai; the timorous elders were not worthy of this privilege.

וַיַּאֲמֵן הָעָם, וַיִּשְׁמְעוּ כִּי פָקַד יְיָ אֶת בְּנֵי יִשְׂרָאֵל וְכִי רָאָה אֶת עָנְיָם, וַיִּקְדּוּ וַיִּשְׁתַּחֲווּ.

Pharaoh, and said, "Thus says the Lord, the God of Israel: Let My people go, that they may hold a feast unto Me in the wilderness."

And Pharaoh said, "Who is the Lord [2] that I should listen to His voice to let Israel go? I do not know the Lord, and I will not let Israel go."

And they said, "The God of the Hebrews revealed Himself to us. Pray, let us go three days' journey into the wilderness and sacrifice to the Lord our God."

And the king of Egypt said to them, "Moses and Aaron, why do you interrupt the people at their tasks? Go back to your burdens!" And the same day Pharaoh commanded the taskmasters of the people and their overseers, saying, "You shall no

---

&#8269; [2] WHO IS THE LORD? Thousands of soldiers guarded Pharaoh's magnificent palace, and fierce lions and leopards were chained at its doors. Only those who had been summoned by Pharaoh were permitted to enter the court.

However, Moses and Aaron strode in as though they owned the palace, and the brightness of their faces was such that the soldiers did not dare come near them. When the beasts reared up to strike, Moses lifted his rod and they fell back.

Pharaoh was amazed to see the brothers standing before him. Aaron delivered the message that God wished them to go into the wilderness to worship.

"What is your God's name?" the king answered calmly. "Where does He live? How great is His strength? How many countries bow to Him? How many wars has He won?"

Moses and Aaron declared that God rules over the entire earth, that the stars and planets are His creation, as well as all the creatures of the world.

Pharaoh replied angrily, "I am a god, and I created myself. I cause the Nile to irrigate my land."

He sent for the chronicles of Egypt, wherein were listed the gods of all the nations: Amon, Ra, Isis, Osiris, and the gods of Moab, Zidon, and many more. The name of the Lord, God of Israel, did not appear.

"You are seeking the living God in the graves of the dead," Aaron replied.

אָמְרוּ לוֹ: אֱלֹהֵינוּ כֹּחוֹ וּגְבוּרָתוֹ מָלֵא עוֹלָם.

longer give the people straw to make bricks as before. Let them go and gather straw for themselves. But the amount of bricks which they have made until now, you shall not diminish at all. For they are lazy; that is why they are crying, 'Let us go and sacrifice to our God.' Let heavier work be laid upon the men, that they may labor and not pay attention to lying words."

Then the taskmasters of the people and the overseers went out, and they spoke to the people, saying, "Thus says Pharaoh: I will not give you straw. Go yourselves, get straw wherever you can find it, but none of the work shall be diminished."

So the people scattered throughout all the land of Egypt to gather stubble for straw. And the taskmasters urged them, saying, "Fulfill your daily task as when there was straw!" And the overseers of the Children of Israel, whom Pharaoh's taskmasters had set over them, were beaten, for the taskmasters said, "Why have you not fulfilled your assignment of making bricks as before?" [3]

Then the overseers of the Children of Israel came and cried to Pharaoh, saying, "Why do you deal thus with your servants? There is no straw given to your servants, and yet we are told: 'Make bricks!' And your servants are beaten, though the fault is with your own people."

But Pharaoh said, "You are lazy, you

---

ᏹ [3] THE OVERSEERS WERE PUNISHED: "Why were the overseers beaten, rather than the Israelites who did not make their quota of bricks?" our Rabbis asked.

When Pharaoh commanded that the Hebrews were not to receive straw for bricks, they wandered over the land, gathering the straw they needed. The Egyptian farmers saw them in the fields and attacked them with whips and sticks, so that it was impossible to meet the daily quotas.

The Egyptian taskmasters asked the Israelite overseers to point out the slaves who had not fulfilled their tasks. The Israelite overseers refused to inform on them, and were flogged.

Then God said, "Because you refused to inform on your brethren, you are worthy to be elders of Israel." When Moses chose elders of Israel after they had gone out of Egypt, he picked from among the former overseers.

תֶּבֶן אֵין נִתָּן לַעֲבָדֶיךָ, וּלְבֵנִים אוֹמְרִים לָנוּ עֲשׂוּ.

are lazy; that is why you say: 'Let us go and sacrifice to the Lord.' Get to work now, for no straw will be given to you, yet you must deliver the quota of bricks!"

When they left Pharaoh, they met Moses and Aaron, who were standing outside. And the overseers said to them, "Let the Lord look upon you and judge you; because you have made us hateful in the eyes of Pharaoh and in the eyes of his servants. You have put a sword in their hands to slay us."

Then Moses returned to the Lord, and said, "Lord, why hast Thou dealt badly with these people? Why didst Thou send me? [4] Since I came to Pharaoh to speak in Thy name, he has dealt ill with this people; Thou hast not delivered Thy people at all."

And the Lord said to Moses, "You shall see what I will do to Pharaoh. For by a strong hand he shall let them go, and by a strong hand he shall drive them out of his land."

And God spoke to Moses and said to him, "I am the Lord; and I appeared to Abraham, to Isaac, and to Jacob. And I have established My covenant with them, to give them the land of Canaan, the land in which they sojourned. Moreover, I have heard the groaning of the Children of Israel, whom the Egyptians keep in bondage; and I have remembered My covenant. Therefore say to the Children of Israel: I am the Lord, and I will free you from the burdens of the Egyptians, and I will deliver you with an outstretched arm and with great judgments. And I will take you to Me for a people, and I will be your God; and you shall know that I am the Lord your God who brought you out from under the burdens

---

    [4] WHY DIDST THOU SEND ME? Moses was saddened, for he had not helped his people. Instead, Pharaoh had increased their burdens. "O Lord," Moses cried, "You sent me to rescue these people, but they suffer more than before! You sent me to save, and yet there is no redemption."

One of the angels heard Moses' plaint, and called, "Lord, punish him! He questions Your decrees!"

"He does not ask for himself, but for his people," God said. Then He turned. "Moses, you must learn to be patient, and to understand that nothing of worth comes quickly. The Hebrews will see My signs and learn My ways. Then will My purpose be revealed and will they become worthy of being redeemed."

וְגָאַלְתִּי אֶתְכֶם בִּזְרוֹעַ נְטוּיָה וּבִשְׁפָטִים גְּדוֹלִים, וְלָקַחְתִּי אֶתְכֶם לִי לְעָם וְהָיִיתִי לָכֶם לֵאלהִים.

of the Egyptians. And I will bring you into the land which I lifted My hand to give to Abraham, to Isaac, and to Jacob, and I will give it to you as a heritage; I am the Lord."

And Moses spoke so to the Children of Israel, but they would not listen to Moses because of their impatience, and because of cruel bondage.

### THE SIGNS

THEN THE LORD spoke to Moses, saying, "Go in, speak to Pharaoh, king of Egypt, that he may let the Children of Israel go out of his land." And Moses spoke before the Lord, saying, "Behold, the Children of Israel have not heeded me; how then shall Pharaoh heed me, since I am slow of speech?"

And the Lord said to Moses, "I have put you in God's stead to Pharaoh, and Aaron your brother will be your spokesman. You shall speak all that I command you, and Aaron your brother shall speak to Pharaoh, that he let the Children of Israel go out of his land. And I will harden Pharaoh's heart, and multiply My signs and wonders in the land of Egypt. But Pharaoh will not listen to you, and I will lay My hand upon Egypt and bring forth My people, the Children of Israel, out of the land of Egypt by mighty acts of judgment. Then the Egyptians shall know that I am the Lord, when I stretch forth My hand against Egypt, and bring out the Children of Israel from among them."

And Moses was eighty years old and Aaron eighty-three years old, when they spoke to Pharaoh.

And then the Lord said to Moses and to Aaron, "When Pharaoh shall speak to you, saying: 'Show us a wonder,' you shall say to Aaron: 'Take your rod, and cast it down before Pharaoh,' and it will become a serpent."

Moses and Aaron went to Pharaoh and they did as the Lord had commanded. And Aaron cast down his rod before Pharaoh and before his servants, and it became a serpent.

Then Pharaoh called the wise men and the magicians of Egypt; and they did the same thing with their secret arts. Each one cast down his rod, and they became serpents. But Aaron's rod swallowed up their rods.

However, Pharaoh's heart was hardened and he did not heed them, just as God had said.

### THE TEN PLAGUES—[5]
### THE FIRST PLAGUE

AND THE LORD said to Moses, "Pharaoh's heart is stubborn; he refuses to let the people go. Go to Pharaoh in the morning, as he goes out to the water, and take your stand on the banks of the river to meet

וַיֶּחֱזַק לֵב פַּרְעֹה וְלֹא שָׁמַע אֲלֵיהֶם, כַּאֲשֶׁר דִּבֶּר יְיָ.

him; and take in your hand the rod that was turned into a serpent.

"And you shall say to Pharaoh, 'The Lord, the God of the Hebrews, has sent me to you saying: Let My people go that they may serve Me in the wilderness; but till now you have not listened. Therefore, thus says the Lord: By this you shall know that I am the Lord—behold, I will strike with my rod that is in my hand upon the waters which are in the river, and they shall turn to blood.' "

And Moses and Aaron did so.

### THE SECOND PLAGUE

WHEN SEVEN DAYS passed after the Lord had struck the river, He spoke to Moses, "Go to Pharaoh and say to him: 'If you refuse to let my people go, I will plague all your borders with frogs.' "

And Aaron stretched out his hand, and the frogs came up and covered the land of Egypt. Then Pharaoh called for Moses and Aaron, and said, "Plead with the Lord to take away the frogs from me, and I will let the people go."

And Moses said, "Tomorrow the Lord will destroy the frogs." And the Lord did according to the word of Moses.

But when Pharaoh saw that there was relief, he hardened his heart and would not let the people go.

### THE THIRD PLAGUE

AND THE LORD said to Moses, "Tell Aaron to strike the dust of the earth, that it may become vermin throughout all the land of Egypt."

Aaron did so, and all the dust of the earth became vermin, over all the land of Egypt, upon man and upon beast.

But Pharaoh hardened his heart, and did not listen to them, as the Lord had spoken.

### THE FOURTH PLAGUE

AND THE LORD said to Moses, "Stand before Pharaoh and say to him: 'Let my people go; else if you will not let my people go, I will send swarms of gnats upon you. By tomorrow shall this sign be.' " And the Lord did so.

Then Pharaoh called for Moses and

---

⤚§ [5] THE TEN PLAGUES: The plagues were not brought upon Pharaoh and his people without warning. For fully twenty days before each plague, Moses warned the Egyptians of the affliction to come, in the hope that they would change their ways; but Pharaoh and his servants scoffed at the warnings.

יְיָ אֱלֹהֵי הָעִבְרִים שְׁלָחַנִי אֵלֶיךָ לֵאמֹר: שַׁלַּח אֶת עַמִּי וְיַעַבְדוּנִי בַּמִּדְבָּר.

for Aaron, and said, "Go, sacrifice to your God in this land."

And Moses said, "This would not be right. We will go three days' journey into the wilderness, and there we shall sacrifice to the Lord our God."

And Pharaoh said, "I will let you go that you may sacrifice to the Lord your God in the wilderness; only you shall not go very far away."

And the Lord removed the swarms of gnats from Pharaoh, from his courtiers, and from his people. But Pharaoh hardened his heart this time also, and he did not let the people go.

### THE FIFTH PLAGUE

THEN THE LORD said to Moses, "Now My hand will fall upon Pharaoh's cattle which are in the fields." And all the cattle of Egypt died.

But the heart of Pharaoh was stubborn, and he did not let the people go.

### THE SIXTH PLAGUE

THEN THE LORD said to Moses and to Aaron, "Take handfuls of soot of the furnace, and let Moses throw it heavenward. This will bring boils upon man and upon beast throughout all the land of Egypt."

And Moses did so. But the Lord hardened the heart of Pharaoh and he did not listen to them.

### THE SEVENTH PLAGUE

AND THE LORD said to Moses, "Pharaoh still oppresses My people. Tomorrow I will send a very heavy hail, such as has not been seen, in all the land of Egypt."

And the Lord sent thunder and hail, and fire flashing upon the earth.

And Pharaoh said to Moses and Aaron, "I have sinned; the Lord is righteous. Entreat the Lord, and let there be enough to these mighty thunderings and hail; and I will let you go, and you shall stay no longer."

And Moses prayed; and the thunder and hail ceased. But Pharaoh sinned again, and hardened his heart.

### THE EIGHTH PLAGUE

THEN MOSES AND AARON went to Pharaoh, and said to him, "If you refuse again to let the people go, tomorrow the Lord will bring locusts into your land."

Then Pharaoh said to Moses, "Go, serve the Lord your God. But who are they that shall go?"

And Moses replied, "We will go with our young and with our old, with our sons and with our daughters, with our flocks and with our herds."

וַיֹּאמֶר מֹשֶׁה: בִּנְעָרֵינוּ וּבִזְקֵנֵינוּ נֵלֵךְ, בְּבָנֵינוּ וּבִבְנוֹתֵינוּ, בְּצֹאנֵנוּ וּבִבְקָרֵנוּ נֵלֵךְ.

And Pharaoh said, "Not so! Only the men may go!" And they were driven out from Pharaoh's presence.

And when it was morning, God brought forth the locusts.

Then Pharaoh called for Moses and Aaron in haste, and he said, "I have sinned against the Lord your God. Forgive this once, and entreat your God that He may take away this death from me."

And the Lord caused a very strong west wind, which lifted the locusts and drove them into the sea. But when the locusts were gone, Pharaoh's heart was hardened and he did not let the Children of Israel go.

### THE NINTH PLAGUE

AND THE LORD said to Moses, "Lift your hand toward heaven that there may be darkness over the land of Egypt, a darkness that may be felt." And there was a thick darkness in all the land.

And Pharaoh called Moses, and said, "Go, serve the Lord. Only let your flocks and herds remain behind. Your little ones may go with you too."

But Moses said, "Our cattle also shall go with us; not a hoof shall be left behind."

The Lord hardened the heart of Pharaoh and he did not let them go.

Then Pharaoh said to him, "Begone from me! Beware never to see my face again, for on the day you see my face you shall die!"

And Moses said, "You have spoken well; I shall never see your face again."

### THE PASSOVER LAMB

AND MOSES CALLED all the elders of Israel and said to them, "Let each family draw a lamb out of the flock, and kill it as a Passover sacrifice. And you shall take a bunch of hyssop, and dip it in the blood that is in the basin, and smear it on the lintel and the two doorposts with the blood that is in the basin. And none of you shall go out of the door of his house until the morning.

"And when the Lord will pass through to smite the Egyptians, and when He sees the blood upon the lintel and on the two side-posts, the Lord will pass over the door and will not let the destroyer come into your houses to smite you. And this day shall be a memorial for you, and you shall keep it as a feast to the Lord.

"And you shall observe this thing as an ordinance to you and to your sons forever. And it shall come to pass, when you have come to the land which the Lord will give you, as He has promised, that you shall observe this service. And it shall come to pass, when your

וּפָסַח יְיָ עַל הַפֶּתַח וְלֹא יִתֵּן הַמַּשְׁחִית לָבוֹא אֶל בָּתֵּיכֶם לִנְגֹּף.

children shall say to you, 'What is the meaning of this service?' that you shall say, 'It is the Passover sacrifice to the Lord, for He passed over the houses of the Children of Israel in Egypt when He smote the Egyptians but spared our houses.'" And the people bowed their heads in reverence and worshiped.

And they went and did thus; they did just as the Lord had commanded Moses and Aaron.

### THE TENTH PLAGUE

AND IT CAME to pass at midnight that the Lord struck down all the first-born in the land of Egypt, from the first-born of Pharaoh that sat on the throne to the first-born of the captive that was in the dungeon; and all the first-born of the cattle.

And there was a great cry in Egypt, for there was not a house where there was not one dead.

Then Pharaoh rose up in the night, he and all his servants; and he called Moses and Aaron by night and said, "Arise, go out from among my people, you and the Children of Israel; and go, serve the Lord, as you have said. Take your flocks and your herds, as you have said, and be gone! And bless me also."

זֶבַח פֶּסַח הוּא לַיְיָ, אֲשֶׁר פָּסַח עַל בָּתֵּי בְּנֵי־יִשְׂרָאֵל בְּנָגְפּוֹ אֶת מִצְרַיִם וְאֶת בָּתֵּינוּ הִצִּיל.

# 14. EXODUS [12–15]

### THE COMMANDMENT OF MATZOT

THE EGYPTIANS URGED the people of Israel to go out of the land in haste, for they said, "We shall all be dead."

So the people took their dough before it was leavened, their kneading troughs wrapped up in their clothes on their shoulders. And the Children of Israel did as Moses told them; and they asked of the Egyptians [1] jewels of silver and jewels of gold and garments. And the Lord made the people find favor with the Egyptians, so that they gave them what they asked.

And the Children of Israel journeyed

---

[1] THEY ASKED OF THE EGYPTIANS: Years later, when Alexander the Great conquered the world, he let it be known that justice would prevail in his empire. And so the Egyptians came before him to demand justice. "The Hebrews stole from us!" they cried. "When they left our land, they borrowed much gold and silver which they have not returned. Justice, O king!"

The Hebrew elders replied, "O king, let them pay us the wages

וַיִּ נָתַן אֶת חֵן הָעָם בְּעֵינֵי מִצְרַיִם וַיַּשְׁאִלוּם וַיְנַצְּלוּ אֶת מִצְרָיִם.

from Rameses to Succoth, about six hundred thousand men on foot, besides children. And a mixed multitude [2] went up also with them; and much livestock, both flocks and herds.

And they baked unleavened cakes of the dough which they brought out of Egypt, for it was not leavened, because they were driven out of Egypt and could not tarry, nor prepare for themselves any provisions.

And Moses said to the people, "Remember this day, on which you came out of Egypt, out of the house of bondage; for by a strong hand the Lord brought you out from this place. And it shall be when the Lord shall bring you into the land of the Canaanite, which He swore to your fathers to give you, a land flowing with milk and honey, that you shall keep this service. *Matzot* shall be eaten seven days, and no leavened bread shall be seen among you in all your borders. And you shall tell your son in that day, saying: It is because of that which the Lord did for me when I came forth out of Egypt. You shall observe this ordinance in its season from year to year."

Now the time that the Children of Israel lived in Egypt was four hundred and thirty years. At the end of four hundred and thirty years, on the very day, all the host of the Lord went out from the land of Egypt.

And Moses took the bones of Joseph with him; for he had made the Children of Israel take an oath, saying, "God will surely remember you; then you shall carry up my bones away from here with you."

And the Children of Israel went up armed out of the land of Egypt.

### PHARAOH PURSUES

WHEN PHARAOH HAD let the people go, God did not lead them by way of the land of the Philistines, although that was the shortest way; for God said, "Lest

---

due for four hundred years of slavery, for the beatings, and for the drowned children, and we shall gladly return the silver and the gold."

The Egyptians silently left the court.

⁓ [2] A MIXED MULTITUDE: Who were the mixed multitude? They were Egyptians who had sympathized with Hebrew slaves, but had been unable to help them. When the Lord redeemed Israel, these Egyptians joined their band and went forth with them to serve the Lord.

מַצוֹת יֵאָכֵל אֵת שִׁבְעַת הַיָּמִים. וְלֹא יֵרָאֶה לְךָ חָמֵץ, וְלֹא יֵרָאֶה לְךָ שְׂאוֹר בְּכָל גְּבֻלֶךָ.

it happen that the people regret when they see war, and return to Egypt." [3] But God led the people around, by way of the wilderness by the Sea of Reeds. And they camped at Etham, on the edge of the wilderness. [4]

And the Lord went before them by day in a pillar of cloud, to lead the way, and by night in a pillar of fire, to give them light, so that they might travel by day and by night.

When the king of Egypt was told that the people had fled, the heart of Pharaoh and of his servants was changed toward the people, and they said, "What have we done, that we have let Israel go from serving us?"

And Pharaoh readied his chariots, and took six hundred chosen chariots, and all the chariots of Egypt, and captains over all of them. For the Lord hardened the heart of Pharaoh, king of Egypt, and he pursued the Children of Israel. [5]

And the Egyptians pursued them, all

---

⋙ [3] REGRET WHEN THEY SEE WAR: Why would the Hebrews be afraid of war? An ancient legend has it that the tribe of Manasseh had rebelled against their slavery long before Moses came to redeem his people. "The Lord promised the land of Canaan to Abraham and his descendants," they said. "Let us go up and claim our land."

They marched out of Egypt, driving Pharaoh's troops before them. When they reached the Promised Land, the Canaanites joined together and defeated them in battle. Only a few survivors managed to flee back to Egypt and slavery.

Because Moses did not want the newly-freed slaves to become fearful when they saw the relics of war, he took them the longer way.

⋙ [4] ON THE EDGE OF THE WILDERNESS: The Hebrews' trust in God was so complete that they marched into the wilderness without provisions. All they carried with them was the remainder of the *matzah* and the bitter herbs left from the night of Passover.

⋙ [5] HE PURSUED THE CHILDREN OF ISRAEL: Why did Pharaoh pursue the Hebrews despite his terrible experiences with them? Had he not had punishment enough?

Rabbi Levi compared him to a man who owned a piece of land

וַיְיָ הֹלֵךְ לִפְנֵיהֶם יוֹמָם בְּעַמּוּד עָנָן לַנְחוֹתָם הַדֶּרֶךְ, וְלַיְלָה בְּעַמּוּד אֵשׁ לְהָאִיר לָהֶם, לָלֶכֶת יוֹמָם וָלָיְלָה.

the horses and chariots of Pharaoh, and his horsemen and his army, and overtook them camping by the sea. And when Pharaoh drew near, the Children of Israel lifted up their eyes and saw the Egyptians, and they were dreadfully afraid.

And they said to Moses, "Is it because there are no graves in Egypt that you have taken us away to die in the wilderness? Why have you brought us out of Egypt? Is it not this that we told you in Egypt, when we said: Let us alone, that we may serve the Egyptians? For it would be better for us to serve the Egyptians than to die in the wilderness."

And Moses said to the people, "Fear not! Stand firm, and see how the Lord will save you today. For as surely as you now see the Egyptians, you shall never see them again. The Lord will fight for you, and you shall hold your peace."

MOSES DIVIDES THE SEA

THEN THE LORD said to Moses, "Why do you cry to Me? Speak to the Children of Israel, that they go forward. And lift up your rod, [6] and stretch out your hand over the sea and divide it; and the Children of Israel shall walk on dry ground into the midst of the sea. And I

---

covered with thorn bushes and stones. When he walked there, he barked his shins on the stones, and his skin was torn by the thorns. Annoyed, he sold the land cheaply.

The purchaser cleared the thorns, used the stones to erect a wall, and planted flowers and fruit. In a short while the plot was covered with greenery. The former owner passed and was startled to see vines, blossoms, and young fruit trees. He hastened to a court of law to reclaim the plot.

So it was with Pharaoh. As soon as the Israelites left Egypt, they began to act like free men. They stood straight, and sang as they strode along. When Pharaoh heard this, he took off in pursuit.

ᥫᦅ [6] LIFT UP YOUR ROD: When the army of Pharaoh overtook them at the sea, the Israelites were frantic. There were two opposing opinions among them as to what to do. One group, terrified, said, "Let us return to Egypt. Better slavery than death!" The other cried, "Let us try

וְאַתָּה הָרֵם אֶת מַטְּךָ וּנְטֵה אֶת יָדְךָ עַל הַיָּם וּבְקָעֵהוּ, וְיָבֹאוּ בְנֵי־יִשְׂרָאֵל בְּתוֹךְ הַיָּם בַּיַּבָּשָׁה.

will harden the hearts of the Egyptians, and they shall go in after them. And thus I will gain honor through Pharaoh, and all his army and his chariots and his horsemen. And the Egyptians shall know that I am the Lord.

The pillar of cloud which had gone before them now went behind them, and it came between the camp of Egypt and the camp of Israel. And there was the cloud and the darkness, so that the one did not come near the other all the night.

Then Moses stretched out his hand over the sea; and the Lord caused the sea to move back by a strong east wind all that night, and made the sea dry land, and the waters were divided.

Thus the Children of Israel went into the midst of the sea on dry ground; [7] and the waters were a wall on their right and on their left. [8]

And the Egyptians pursued, and went in after them into the midst of the sea, all Pharaoh's horses, his chariots, and his horsemen. And in the morning watch, the Lord looked forth upon the

---

to cross! Many will die, but some will reach the other shore." Nahshon, son of Amminadab, was the first to jump into the sea, and others of the tribe of Benjamin waded in after him. Soon the water reached their nostrils.

Moses stood before God and prayed, but God cut short his words, saying, "My children are in distress. The sea is before them, the enemy at their back. Lift up your rod, and stretch out your hand to divide the sea, that the Children of Israel may go on dry land."

ᦇ [7] INTO THE SEA ON DRY GROUND: If the Hebrews entered into the water, why is it written that they entered on dry ground? And conversely, if they entered on dry ground, why is it said that they entered the sea? The Rabbis explained that the sea did not divide until after they had demonstrated their faith by wading into it.

ᦇ [8] THE WALL IN THE SEA: To express their excitement and wonder at the crossing of the Sea of Reeds, the Rabbis of the Midrash wove many fanciful legends about it.

The walls of the sea, they said, were covered with fruit trees whose

וַיָּבֹאוּ בְנֵי־יִשְׂרָאֵל בְּתוֹךְ הַיָּם בַּיַּבָּשָׁה, וְהַמַּיִם לָהֶם חוֹמָה מִימִינָם וּמִשְּׂמֹאלָם.

host of the Egyptians through the pillar of fire and of cloud, and confused the army of the Egyptians. He locked their chariot wheels and made them drag heavily, so that the Egyptians said, "Let us flee from before the Israelites, for the Lord is fighting for them against the Egyptians."

And the Lord said to Moses, "Stretch out your hand over the sea, that the water may return upon the Egyptians, upon their chariots, and upon their horsemen."

And Moses stretched forth his hand over the sea, and the sea returned to its strength as morning broke; and the Egyptians fled against it. And the Lord overturned the Egyptians in the midst of the sea. The waters returned and covered the chariots and the horsemen; and of all the host of Pharaoh that went into the sea after the Israelites, not one remained. [9] But the Children of Israel walked upon dry land in the midst of the sea; and the waters were a wall for them on their right and on their left.

Thus the Lord saved Israel that day from the hand of the Egyptians; and

---

branches protected the Hebrews from the sun. The Israelite mothers could reach up and pluck an orange or pomegranate for their children.

Twelve paths were opened, they declared, one for each tribe. The walls of water were transparent as glass so that the tribes could see each other. Through the brackish water flowed a stream of clean, fresh water at which the Hebrews could quench their thirst.

~§ [9] NOT ONE REMAINED: Lessons come hard to some. Because Pharaoh had not let Israel go at once, his people had suffered plagues and lost their gold and silver. Nonetheless, he changed his mind again, and brought more trouble upon himself.

The Egyptians were like the servant who had served his master a spoiled fish. In anger, the man said, "Either you will eat the fish, or receive forty lashes, or pay forty silver pieces." The servant chose to eat the spoiled fish, but after eating half of it, cried out that he preferred the lash. After twenty strokes, however, he screamed that he would pay the fine. So he ate spoiled fish, and received twenty lashes, and paid the full fine besides.

וַיּוֹשַׁע יְיָ בַּיּוֹם הַהוּא אֶת יִשְׂרָאֵל מִיַּד מִצְרָיִם.

Israel saw the Egyptians dead upon the seashore. And the people feared the Lord; and they believed in the Lord and in His servant Moses.

### THE SONG OF MOSES

THEN SANG MOSES and the Children of Israel this song unto the Lord:

"I will sing unto the Lord,
For He has triumphed gloriously;
The horse and his rider
He has hurled into the sea.
The Lord is my strength and song,
For He has brought me salvation.
This is my God, and I will glorify
  Him,
My father's God, whom I shall
  extol.
The Lord is a man of war,
The Lord is His name.
Pharaoh's chariots and his host
He has cast into the sea;
And his chosen captains
Are sunk in the Sea of Reeds.
The deeps cover them;
They went down into the depths
  like a stone.
Thy right hand, O Lord, is glorious
  in power,
Thy right hand, O Lord, shatters
  the enemy!
And in the greatness of Thy
  triumph
Thou overthrowest Thine
  adversaries.
Thou sendest forth Thy wrath,
And it consumes them like straw.
At the blast of Thy nostrils the
  waters were piled up,
The floods stood upright as a wall;
The deeps were congealed in the
  heart of the sea.
The enemy said:
'I will pursue, I will overtake,
I will divide the spoil;
My desire shall be satisfied upon
  them;
I will draw my sword,
And my hand shall destroy them.'
Thou didst blow with Thy wind,
  and the sea covered them;
They sank like lead in the mighty
  waters.
Who is like Thee, O Lord, among
  the mighty? [10]

---

ᦉ [10] WHO IS LIKE THEE, O LORD? "Beware," cautioned the Rabbis, "of comparing God with mortal kings. A king's subjects run before him to clear the way, and spread carpets so that his feet do not touch the ground. They place pillows for him to lean on, and serve him sumptu-

אָשִׁירָה לַיָי כִּי גָאֹה גָּאָה, סוּס וְרוֹכְבוֹ רָמָה בַיָּם.

Who is like Thee, glorious in
   holiness,
Awe-inspiring, doing wonders?
The Lord shall reign for ever and
   ever."

### THE SONG OF MIRIAM

AND MIRIAM THE prophetess, the sister
of Aaron, took a tambourine in her hand;
and all the women followed her with
tambourines and with dances. And Miriam sang with them:
   "Sing to the Lord,
   For He has triumphed gloriously;
   The horse and its rider
   He has hurled into the sea."

---

ous meals. They light bright torches and adorn his palaces with tap-
estries and carpets.

"The King of Kings does the very opposite. He clothes the fields
with grass, so that man does not walk on the bare earth. He lights
the world with the sun and the moon, and prepares the widest variety
of foods. He adorns His palace, the world, with mountains and lakes.
The flowers bud for His subjects, and the birds sing for them. His
dominion is without end, and His reign is eternal."

מִי כָמֹכָה נֶאְדָּר בַּקֹּדֶשׁ, נוֹרָא תְהִלֹּת, עוֹשֵׂה פֶלֶא.

# 15 ♦ EXODUS [15–18]

JOURNEY TO SINAI—
THE PEOPLE HAVE NO WATER

AND MOSES LED Israel onward from the Sea of Reeds, and they went out into the wilderness of Shur; [1] and they journeyed for three days in the wilderness, and found no water. And when they reached Marah, they could not drink the water for it was bitter. And the people murmured against Moses, saying, "What shall we drink?"

And he cried to the Lord, and the Lord showed him a tree. And he cast it into the water, and the water became sweet.

There God gave them laws, and He said, "If you will diligently hearken to the voice of the Lord your God, and will do that which is right in His eyes, and

[1] THE WILDERNESS OF SHUR: The Children of Israel obeyed Moses and followed him without hesitation into the wilderness. This was proof of their faith in God, for the wilderness was a barren waste, crawling with snakes, lizards and scorpions.

וַיֹּאמֶר : אִם שָׁמוֹעַ תִּשְׁמַע לְקוֹל יְיָ אֱלֹהֶיךָ וְהַיָּשָׁר בְּעֵינָיו תַּעֲשֶׂה...

will obey His commandments and observe all His laws, I will not put any of the diseases upon you which I have put upon the Egyptians; for I am the Lord that heals you."

Then they came to Elim, where there were twelve springs of water and seventy palm trees. And they camped there by the water.

## THE PEOPLE HAVE NO FOOD

THEN THEY JOURNEYED from Elim, and the Children of Israel came to the wilderness of Sin, which is between Elim and Sinai, on the fifteenth day of the second month after their departure from Egypt.

And the whole congregation of the Children of Israel murmured against Moses and against Aaron in the wilderness, and said to them, "If only we had died by the hand of the Lord in the land of Egypt, where we sat by the fleshpots, where we ate our fill of bread; for you have brought us into this wilderness to kill all of us with hunger."

Then the Lord said to Moses, "I will send bread down to you from heaven like rain; and the people shall go out and gather all they need each day."

So Moses and Aaron said to the Children of Israel, "In the morning you shall see the glory of the Lord, for He has heard your murmuring; and what are we that you grumble against us? Your murmurings are not against us, but against the Lord."

In the morning there was a layer of dew around the camp. When the dew evaporated, there were upon the surface of the wilderness fine flakes, thin as frost on the ground. And when the Children of Israel saw it, they said to one another, "*Man hu?* What is this?"— for they did not know what it was.

And Moses said to them, "It is the bread which the Lord has given. Every man of you gather as much as he needs; an *omer* for each person, according to the number of souls in his tent."

## THE CHILDREN OF ISRAEL EAT
## MANNA FROM HEAVEN

THE CHILDREN OF ISRAEL did so, and some gathered much and some gathered little. But when they measured it with an *omer,* he who had gathered much had nothing over, and he who gathered little did not lack. Each gathered as much as he could use.

Then Moses said to them, "No one is to leave any of it till the morning." Nevertheless they did not listen to Moses, but some of them kept it until the morning, and it bred worms and rotted; and Moses was angry with them.

... וְהַאֲזַנְתָּ לְמִצְוֹתָיו וְשָׁמַרְתָּ כָּל חֻקָּיו – כָּל הַמַּחֲלָה אֲשֶׁר שַׂמְתִּי בְמִצְרַיִם לֹא אָשִׂים עָלֶיךָ כִּי אֲנִי יְיָ רֹפְאֶךָ.

So they gathered it every morning, [2] every man according to his needs; and as the sun grew hot, it melted.

On the sixth day they gathered twice as much bread, two *omers* for each; and all the leaders of the congregation came and told Moses. And he said to them, "That is what the Lord has spoken: Tomorrow is a day of rest, a holy Sabbath to the Lord. Bake what you need to bake, and cook what you need to cook; and whatever remains put aside to be kept until the morning."

And they laid it up till the morning, as Moses commanded; and it did not spoil, nor were there worms in it.

Then Moses said, "Eat this today, for today is a Sabbath to the Lord. Today you shall not find any in the field. Six days you shall gather it, but on the seventh day, which is the Sabbath, there shall be none."

However, some of the people went out to gather it on the seventh day, but they found none.

And the Lord said to Moses, "How long will you refuse to keep My commandments and My teachings? See, the Lord has given you the Sabbath; therefore on the sixth day He gives you bread for two days. Let no man go out of his place on the seventh day."

The House of Israel called it manna. [3] It was white, like coriander seeds;

---

◄§ [2] EVERY MORNING: Why did the bread from heaven (manna) fall every day?

In answer, Rabbi Simeon ben Yohai told of a king whose son was studying at an academy. Once a year the boy returned for money and supplies. The father complained because he saw his son so rarely. So he changed the practice and said, "Come every day for your provisions that I may see your face."

So, too, with Israel. In the daily search for manna, they turned their hearts to the Holy One, Blessed Be He, every morning.

◄§ [3] HOW DID THE MANNA TASTE? "My bread which I gave you, fine flour and oil and honey wherewith I fed you," wrote the prophet Ezekiel (16:19). The Rabbis say that this verse refers to the taste of the manna. To the young it tasted like bread; to the old, like honey; and to the infant, it was as milk.

בַּחוּרִים הָיוּ טוֹעֲמִים בּוֹ טַעַם לֶחֶם, זְקֵנִים טַעַם דְּבַשׁ, תִּינוֹקוֹת טַעַם חָלָב.

and its taste was like wafers made with honey.

Then Moses said, "This is what the Lord has commanded: Let an *omer* of it be kept throughout your generations, that they may see the bread with which I fed you in the wilderness when I brought you out of the land of Egypt."

And Moses said to Aaron, "Take a jar, and put an *omer* of manna in it, and store it up before the Lord, to be kept for future generations." And Aaron did as the Lord commanded Moses.

And the Children of Israel ate manna for forty years, until they came to the borders of the land of Canaan.

WATER FROM A ROCK

ALL THE CONGREGATION of the Children of Israel journeyed from the wilderness of Sin, and they camped at Rephidim; and there was no water for the people to drink. Therefore the people quarreled with Moses, and said, "Give us water to drink."

And Moses said to them, "Why do you find fault with me, and why do you put the Lord to test?"

But the people thirsted for water, and they complained to Moses, "Why have you brought us up out of Egypt to kill us and our children and our cattle with thirst?"

And Moses cried to the Lord, "What am I to do with this people? They are almost ready to stone me!" [4]

Then the Lord said to Moses, "Go before the people, and take with you some of the elders of Israel. Take in your hand

---

&#x297B; [4] READY TO STONE ME: Our Rabbis say that God was vexed with Moses for these words, and said, "You slander My people. Go before them, and see if they will stone you."

Moses went before the people of Israel and, behold, every man rose in his honor!

Then God said to Moses, "Be patient with My children, even as a shepherd is patient with his flock."

&#x297B; [5] STRIKE THE ROCK: When God told Moses to strike the rock, Moses pleaded, "But this rod has been used for evil; it became a snake, changed the Nile into blood. Now would you have it deal kindly?"

And God answered, "Let everyone see that a stick is but a stick. It is good or bad only as it is used."

וַיֹּאמֶר לָהֶם מֹשֶׁה: מַה תְּרִיבוּן עִמָּדִי, מַה תְּנַסּוּן אֶת יְיָ?

the rod with which you struck the river. Go to the rock in Horeb and I will stand there; and you shall strike the rock [5] and water will gush out of it that the people may drink."

And Moses did so before the eyes of the elders of Israel.

### AMALEK MAKES WAR ON THE ISRAELITES

THEN CAME AMALEK and attacked Israel in Rephidim. And Moses said to Joshua, "Choose us men, [6] and go out to fight with Amalek. I will take my stand tomorrow on the top of the hill with the rod of God in my hand."

So Joshua did as Moses told him, and fought with Amalek; and Moses, Aaron, and Hur went up to the top of the hill.

Whenever Moses held up his hand, [7] Israel prevailed; but when he let down his hand, Amalek prevailed.

But Moses' hands became tired; so they took a stone and put it under him, and he sat on it; and Aaron and Hur held up his hands. So his hands were steady until sundown.

And Joshua overwhelmed Amalek and his people with the sword.

### JETHRO COMES TO MOSES

NOW JETHRO, the priest of Midian, Moses' father-in-law, heard of all that God had done for Moses and for Israel, His people. And Jethro took Zipporah, Moses' wife, and her two sons, and came to Moses into the wilderness where he was encamped at the mountain of God.

---

[6] CHOOSE US MEN: Why did Moses use the word "us" in this line, rather than "me"? He was suggesting that Joshua choose men satisfactory to them both, for he treated Joshua as an equal. From this we learn, "Let the honor of your disciple be dear to you as your own honor, and the honor of your associate as the awe of your teacher, and the awe of your teacher as the awe for the Almighty" (Pirké Avot 4:15).

[7] WHEN MOSES HELD UP HIS HAND: Our Rabbis ask: Could Moses' hands bring victory when they were raised, defeat when lowered?

When the Israelites saw Moses raise his hand in prayer, they were inspired to renewed valor. When he dropped his hand, they lost faith and could not fight.

וְהָיָה כַּאֲשֶׁר יָרִים מֹשֶׁה יָדוֹ וְגָבַר יִשְׂרָאֵל, וְכַאֲשֶׁר יָנִיחַ יָדוֹ וְגָבַר עֲמָלֵק.

Moses went out to meet his father-in-law, and bowed down and kissed him. They asked of each other's welfare; [8] and they entered the tent.

And Moses told his father-in-law all that the Lord had done to Pharaoh and to the Egyptians for Israel's sake, all the hardship that had befallen them on the journey, and how the Lord delivered them.

And Jethro rejoiced in all the <u>goodness which the Lord had done for Israel.</u> And Jethro said, "Blessed be the Lord, who has delivered you from the hand of Pharaoh and from the hand of the Egyptians. Now I know that the Lord is greater than all the gods."

JETHRO'S ADVICE TO MOSES

IT HAPPENED on the next day that Moses sat to judge the people; and the people stood about Moses from the morning until the evening. When Moses' father-in-law saw all that he was doing for the people, he said, "Why do you judge the people all alone, and the people stand about you from morning until evening?"

And Moses said to his father-in-law, "Because the people come to me to inquire of God. And I judge between a man and his neighbor, and I make them know the statutes of God and His teachings."

And Moses' father-in-law said to him, "What you are doing is not good. You will surely wear yourself out, both you and the people that are with you; for the task is too heavy for you: [9] you cannot perform it alone. Listen to me, and let me advise you, that God may be with you. Select from the people able men,

---

◆ [8] THEY ASKED OF THEIR WELFARE: The Hebrew for "their welfare" is *l'shalom,* which means "to their peace." Our Rabbis say that before Moses told Jethro what God had done for Israel, he offered him the greeting of peace. Great is peace, for it precedes even the praise of God!

◆ [9] FOR THE TASK IS TOO HEAVY: Why was the judging too heavy for Moses, the man who had led his people out of slavery, and who had ascended Sinai? Because a judge has a grave responsibility: his decisions change the lives of those who come before him. The Talmud says he must judge as though a sword were suspended above him. If he is unjust, God Himself sits in judgment over him.

וַיִּחַדְּ יִתְרוֹ עַל כָּל הַטּוֹבָה אֲשֶׁר עָשָׂה יְיָ לְיִשְׂרָאֵל.

God-fearing men, honest men who hate bribery; and make them chiefs of thousands, chiefs of hundreds, chiefs of fifties, and chiefs of tens, and let them judge the people at all times. Every great matter they shall bring to you, but every small matter they shall judge themselves. So they shall make it easier for you, since they will share the burden with you. If you will do this, you shall be able to endure, and the people too shall go to their place in peace."

So Moses hearkened to the voice of his father-in-law, and did all that he had said.

And Moses let his father-in-law depart; and he went his way to his own land. [10]

---

[10] JETHRO RETURNS TO HIS OWN LAND: Why did Moses send his father-in-law home just before the revelation on Mount Sinai?

Because when Israel was in Egypt, slaving with clay and brick, Jethro lived in Midian in peace and quiet. He who suffers with the community shall know its joys, but he who does not share its suffering cannot rejoice with it.

וְהָיָה כָּל הַדָּבָר הַגָּדוֹל יָבִיאוּ אֵלֶיךָ, וְכָל הַדָּבָר הַקָּטֹן יִשְׁפְּטוּ הֵם.

# 16. EXODUS [19–31]

THE COVENANT:
REVELATION AT MOUNT SINAI

IN THE THIRD month after the Children of Israel had gone forth out of the land of Egypt, on that same day, they came to the wilderness of Sinai. And Israel camped there before the mountain.

And Moses went up to God, and the Lord called to him from the mountain, saying, "Thus shall you say to the House of Jacob and tell the Children of Israel: [1] You have seen what I did to the Egyptians, and how I bore you on eagles' wings and brought you to Myself. Now, therefore, if you will listen to My voice,

---

[1] THE HOUSE OF JACOB: Why does the text specify both the House of Jacob and the Children of Israel; are they not one? the Rabbis pondered.

They read "Children of Israel" to mean the whole people, but the "House of Jacob" as the women of Israel. The women are to be taught first because it is they who will first instruct the children in the ways of the Torah.

לָמָה לַנָּשִׁים תְּחִלָּה? כְּדֵי שֶׁיִּהְיוּ מַנְהִיגוֹת אֶת בְּנֵיהֶן לַתּוֹרָה.

and keep My Covenant, you shall be My own treasure from among all peoples; for all the earth is Mine. And you shall be to Me a kingdom of priests and a holy people."

Moses summoned the elders of the people and set before them all these words which the Lord commanded him. And all the people answered together, and said, "All that the Lord has spoken we will do." [2] And Moses reported the words of the people to the Lord.

And the Lord said to Moses, "I will come to you in a thick cloud, that the people may hear when I speak with you and may always believe you. Go to the people and sanctify them today and tomorrow, and let them wash their garments and be ready for the third day; for on the third day the Lord will come down on Mount Sinai in sight of all the people."

On the morning of the third day, there were thunders and lightnings and a dense cloud upon the mountain, and a very loud *Shofar* blast. And all the people in the camp trembled.

And Moses brought the people out of

---

ها [2] ALL THAT THE LORD HAS SPOKEN WE WILL DO: Before God gave the Torah to the Children of Israel, He approached the Edomites, the children of Esau, and said to them, "Will you accept My Torah?" "What is written in it?" they asked Him. "You shall not kill," God replied. "Our father Esau was blessed with these words: 'By the sword you shall live,'" replied the Edomites. "We cannot accept Your Torah."

Then God asked the children of Ishmael to accept His Torah. They asked, "What is written in it?" And He answered, "You shall not steal." "It was promised to our father Ishmael, that his hand would be against every man," they made reply. "How can we accept Your Torah?"

God offered the Torah to the Canaanites, who asked, "What is written in Your Torah?" He answered, "A just measure you shall use, a perfect scale . . ." The Canaanites replied, "How can we prosper by Your Torah?"

To each nation in turn He offered His Law, and none accepted.

Finally God turned to Israel: "Will you accept My Torah, wherein is written a guide to a righteous world?" And the Children of Israel answered, "All that the Lord has spoken we will do and we will obey."

וַיַּעֲנוּ כָל הָעָם יַחְדָּו וַיֹּאמְרוּ: כֹּל אֲשֶׁר דִּבֶּר יְיָ נַעֲשֶׂה.

the camp to meet God; [3] and they stood at the lower part of the mountain. Now Mount Sinai was covered with smoke, because the Lord descended upon it in fire; and the smoke rose like the smoke of a furnace, and the whole mountain quaked violently. And when the voice of the *Shofar* became louder and louder, Moses spoke, and God answered him aloud.

## THE TEN COMMANDMENTS

AND GOD SPOKE all these words, [4] saying,

1. "I am the Lord [5] your God, [6] who brought you out of the land of Egypt, out of the house of bondage.

2. "You shall have no other gods before Me. You shall not make for yourself a graven image, nor any manner of likeness

---

[3] WHO WILL BE YOUR SURETY? Even when the Children of Israel were gathered before Sinai, God hesitated, lest the Torah be not safe in their hands. Although the Hebrews desired the Torah, He foresaw that they might be unfaithful to its teachings. "O Children of Israel, what will be your surety for this most precious possession?" He asked. The Israelites replied, "All our gold and silver we give as pledge."

"The wealth of all the world does not measure to one line of the Torah," God answered.

Thereupon the Israelites declared, "Our fathers, Abraham, Isaac and Jacob, are our assurance to You."

"Your fathers are My debtors and cannot be your surety," was the answer.

Then the Israelites offered, "We give You our children in pledge."

"These I accept as surety," said the Lord.

And Israel responded, "We shall teach them diligently to our children, and to our children's children after them."

[4] GOD SPOKE ALL THESE WORDS: In Deuteronomy it is written: "Did ever a people hear the voice of God speaking out?" (4:33). Concerning this, the Rabbis say that if God had spoken in the full strength of His great voice, none could have withstood its power. God so spoke that each heard according to his ability: the young according to their capacity, the old to their understanding, and the children to theirs.

אָנֹכִי יְיָ אֱלֹהֶיךָ אֲשֶׁר הוֹצֵאתִיךָ מֵאֶרֶץ מִצְרַיִם מִבֵּית עֲבָדִים.

of anything that is in heaven above, or that is in the earth beneath, or that is in the water under the earth. You shall not bow down to them nor serve them; for I, the Lord your God, am a demanding God, visiting the iniquity of the fathers upon the children unto the third and fourth generation of them that hate Me; but showing lovingkindness unto the thousandth generation of them that love Me and keep My commandments.

3. "You shall not take the name of the Lord your God in vain; for the Lord will not hold him guiltless that takes His name in vain.

4. "Remember the Sabbath day to keep it holy. Six days shall you labor and do all your work, but the seventh day is a Sabbath to the Lord your God; in it you shall not do any manner of work, neither you, nor your son, nor your daughter, nor your manservant, nor your maidservant, nor your cattle, nor your stranger that is within your gates. For in six days the Lord made heaven and earth, the sea and all that is therein, and He rested on the seventh day; therefore the Lord blessed the Sabbath day and sanctified it.

5. "Honor your father and your mother, that your days may be long in the land which the Lord your God is giving you. [7]

6. "You shall not murder.

7. "You shall not commit adultery.

---

&❦ [5] I AM THE LORD: When God uttered these words, the whole world stood still: no bird sang, and that which flew in mid-air remained suspended without moving a wing. The waves in the ocean congealed. Not a creature uttered a sound. Never before had there been such silence in the world, and never will there be such a silence again. In this awesome stillness the world listened breathlessly to "I am the Lord your God."

&❦ [6] YOUR GOD: As the host of Israel stood before Sinai, the voice thundered, "I am the Lord your God!" "Your" is used in the singular, said our Sages, so that each man shall understand that though the voice spoke to everybody, yet it spoke to him alone.

&❦ [7] HAVE YOU PARENTS? When Moses ascended Mount Sinai he was taken to heaven, the Midrash tells us. The angels protested, "Is a mortal to receive the holy Torah? Leave the Torah with us, O Lord."

זָכוֹר אֶת יוֹם הַשַּׁבָּת לְקַדְּשׁוֹ. שֵׁשֶׁת יָמִים תַּעֲבֹד וְעָשִׂיתָ כָּל מְלַאכְתֶּךָ, וְיוֹם הַשְּׁבִיעִי שַׁבָּת לַיָי אֱלֹהֶיךָ.

8. "You shall not steal.

9. "You shall not bear false witness against your neighbor.

10. "You shall not covet your neighbor's house; you shall not covet your neighbor's wife, nor his manservant, nor his maidservant, nor his ox, nor his donkey, nor anything that is your neighbor's."

And all the people witnessed the thunder and lightning, and the blast of the *Shofar,* and the mountain smoking; [8] and when the people saw it, they trembled and stood afar off. And they said to Moses, "You speak with us and we will hear; but do not let God speak with us, lest we die."

And Moses said to the people, "Fear not, for God has come to prove you, and that reverence of Him may be with you, so that you will not sin."

And the people stood afar off; but Moses approached the thick darkness where God was.

And the Lord said to Moses, "Thus shall you say to the Children of Israel: You yourselves have seen that I have talked with you from heaven. Gods of silver or gods of gold, you shall not make for yourselves. An altar of earth shall you

---

God said to Moses, "Reply to them."

And Moses answered, "The Torah was meant for man. Were angels enslaved so that God had to redeem them? Do angels work, so that they require rest on the Sabbath? Do angels have parents to honor? Can they murder or steal? No, the Torah is meant for man."

[8] THE KINGS TAKE COUNSEL TOGETHER: Before the giving of the Ten Commandments, peals of thunder sounded throughout the earth. The heathen nations trembled, and their kings rushed to take counsel with Balaam, the heathen prophet, lest another flood drown the world. God had promised Noah that never again would He send such a flood. Balaam assured them. The thunder had sounded because God was giving the Hebrews His commandments.

The kings were not reassured. Israel had been freed from the yoke of Egypt, had witnessed the destruction of Pharaoh's army, and had smashed the Amalekites. Their new gift would further strengthen the former slaves.

Balaam calmed them with the words of Proverbs (3:17), "The ways of the Torah are pleasant and all her paths are peace."

וַיֹּאמְרוּ אֶל מֹשֶׁה: דַּבֵּר אַתָּה עִמָּנוּ וְנִשְׁמָעָה, וְאַל יְדַבֵּר עִמָּנוּ אֱלֹהִים פֶּן נָמוּת.

make unto Me, and shall sacrifice on it your offerings. In every place where I cause My name to be mentioned, I will come to you and bless you."

### THE ORDINANCES OF THE LORD

THESE ARE THE ordinances which you are to set before them:

#### Slaves

If you buy a Hebrew slave, he shall serve six years, and in the seventh he shall go free with no payment. If he came in alone, he shall go out alone; if he was married, his wife shall go out with him.

But if the slave shall say, "I love my master; I do not wish to be free," then his master shall bring him before God. And he shall bring him to the door or to the doorpost, and his master shall pierce his ear with an awl; and then he shall serve him forever.

#### Justice

You shall not utter a false report; do not join hands with the wicked to be a false witness.

You shall not follow a multitude to do evil; neither shall you bear witness in a suit to pervert justice by following a multitude. Nor shall you favor a poor man in a lawsuit because he is poor.

You shall not pervert the justice due to your poor in his case. Keep far from a false matter; and the innocent and the righteous you shall not slay, for I will not forgive the wicked.

You shall not oppress a stranger, for you know the heart of the stranger, because you were strangers in the land of Egypt.

If you chance upon your enemy's ox or his donkey going astray, you shall surely take it back to him.

If you see the donkey of your enemy lying under a burden, you shall not ignore him; you shall surely help him to free it.

#### Damages

If a man opens a pit, or if a man digs a pit and does not cover it, and an ox or a donkey falls into it, the owner of the pit shall be responsible; he shall pay money to the owner of the animal, and the dead beast shall be his.

If a man's ox hurts another's so that it dies, then they shall sell the live ox and divide its price; and the dead beast also they shall divide. But if it was known that the ox was likely to gore, and its owner has not kept it in, he must pay ox for ox, and the dead beast shall be his.

If a man steals an ox or a sheep, and kills it or sells it, he shall pay five oxen for an ox, and four sheep for a sheep. If what he stole is found alive in his possession, whether it be ox, or donkey, or sheep, he shall pay double.

If a man lets his beast loose, and it

לֹא תִהְיֶה אַחֲרֵי רַבִּים לְרָעוֹת, וְלֹא תַעֲנֶה עַל רִיב, לִנְטוֹת אַחֲרֵי רַבִּים, לְהַטּוֹת.

feeds in another man's field, he shall make restitution from the best of his own field and of his own vineyard.

### Widow and Orphan

You must not wrong any widow or fatherless child. If you wrong them in any way, and if they cry at all to Me, I will surely hear their cry.

### The Poor

If you lend money to any of My people, to the poor among you, you shall not act as a creditor to him; neither shall you charge him interest.

If you take your neighbor's garment in pledge, you shall return it to him by sundown, for that is his only covering. It is his garment for his skin; in what shall he sleep? When he will cry to Me, I will hear, for I am compassionate.

### Bodily Injury

If men quarrel and one strikes the other with a stone or with his fist, and he does not die but is laid up in bed, if he gets up again and walks around on his staff, the one who struck him shall be acquitted. However, he must pay him for the loss of his time, and have him fully restored to health.

Eye for eye, tooth for tooth, hand for hand, foot for foot. [9]

If a man strikes the eye of his manserv-

---

[9] EYE FOR EYE: The Torah does not seek revenge. In ancient times, men took vengeance for injuries. Unless the hurt was done by one of his own clan, vengeance was a matter of tribal loyalty.

The avengers sought not "measure for measure" from the culprit, as an eye for an eye, but his death.

In Genesis, Lamech boasts he is a great warrior. He killed a man whose fellow tribesman wounded him. He killed a child of another tribe because a member bruised him with a stone. He further boasts that while other tribes, such as the tribe of Cain, avenge injury sevenfold, he avenges seventy-sevenfold (4:23–24).

The Torah forbade wanton killing in revenge, and limited the punishment to fit the crime.

In the days of the Second Temple, the Rabbis worked out a law that is as modern and just as present damage laws. They read "an eye for an eye" to mean financial compensation. An injured person must receive payment for medical costs, loss of time, and permanent injury (see *Baba Kamma*, 83b).

הִיא שִׂמְלָתוֹ לְעוֹרוֹ, בַּמֶּה יִשְׁכָּב? וְהָיָה כִּי יִצְעַק אֵלַי וְשָׁמַעְתִּי, כִּי חַנּוּן אָנִי.

ant, or of his maidservant, and destroys it, he shall let him go free for his eye's sake. And if he knocks out his manservant's tooth, or his maidservant's tooth, he shall let him go free for his tooth's sake.

And if a man strikes his manservant or his maidservant with a rod, and he dies by his hand, he shall surely be punished.

If a man willfully plans to murder another, even from My altar you shall take him, that he may die.

And if he steals a man and sells him, or if he be found in his possession, he shall surely be put to death.

### The Sabbath

Six days you shall work, but on the seventh day you shall rest; that your ox and your donkey may have rest, and the son of your maidservant, and the stranger may be refreshed.

Faithfully you shall keep My Sabbaths, for it is a sign between Me and you throughout your generations, so that you may know that I am the Lord who sanctifies you.

The Children of Israel shall keep the Sabbath, to observe the Sabbath throughout their generations as a perpetual Covenant. It is a sign between Me and the Children of Israel forever, for in six days the Lord made heaven and earth, and on the seventh day He ceased from work and rested.

### THE CHILDREN OF ISRAEL ARE GIVEN LAWS

AND MOSES CAME and told the people all the words of the Lord and all the ordinances. And all the people answered with one voice, and said: "All the words which the Lord has spoken we will do."

And Moses wrote all the words of the Lord, and rose up early in the morning, and built an altar at the foot of the mountain, and put up twelve pillars, one for each of the twelve tribes of Israel.

And he took the book of the Covenant, [10] read it to the people, and they said: "All that the Lord has spoken we will do and we will obey."

---

ᑫᔕ [10] THE BOOK OF THE COVENANT: The Torah was given in the wilderness because it is the property of no nation or land. Whoever wishes may accept it or study it. The Torah belongs to everyone.

שֵׁשֶׁת יָמִים תַּעֲשֶׂה מַעֲשֶׂיךָ וּבַיּוֹם הַשְּׁבִיעִי תִּשְׁבֹּת, לְמַעַן יָנוּחַ שׁוֹרְךָ וַחֲמֹרֶךָ,
וְיִנָּפֵשׁ בֶּן אֲמָתְךָ וְהַגֵּר.

## 17. EXODUS [24–32]

### MOSES ON MOUNT SINAI

AND THE LORD said to Moses, "Come up to Me on the mountain, and be there; and I will give you the tablets of stone, and the Torah and the commandment which I have written, that you may teach them."

And Moses and Joshua his attendant rose up. And Moses said to the elders, "Wait here for us until we return to you. Aaron and Hur are with you; whoever has a dispute, let him bring it to them."

And Moses ascended the mountain, and the cloud covered the mountain.

And Moses entered into the midst of the cloud; and Moses was on the mountain forty days and forty nights.

### THE GOLDEN CALF

WHEN THE PEOPLE saw that Moses delayed in coming down from the mountain, they gathered around Aaron and said to him, "Come, make us a god [1] who shall go before us; for we do not know what has become of the man Moses, who brought us up out of the land of Egypt."

And Aaron said to them, "Take off the golden rings from the ears of your wives,

קוּם עֲשֵׂה לָנוּ אֱלֹהִים אֲשֶׁר יֵלְכוּ לְפָנֵינוּ. כִּי זֶה מֹשֶׁה הָאִישׁ אֲשֶׁר הֶעֱלָנוּ מֵאֶרֶץ מִצְרַיִם, לֹא יָדַעְנוּ מֶה הָיָה לוֹ.

of your sons and your daughters, and bring them to me."

Then all the people took off the golden rings which were in their ears, and brought them to Aaron. And he took them from their hands, and made a molten calf. And they said, "This is your god, O Israel, which brought you up out of the land of Egypt." [2]

And when Aaron saw this, he built an altar before it; and Aaron proclaimed, "Tomorrow shall be a feast to the Lord." So they rose up early the next day, and offered burnt-offerings, after which the

[1] MAKE US A GOD: Shocked at the people's request, Hur, Miriam's husband, cried, "You are a stubborn and thankless people! You have seen the glory of God, which He Himself revealed before you, yet you would worship an idol!"

The wrathful people stoned him to death, and then threatened Aaron, "Unless you make us a god, a visible god who shall go before us, we will kill you too." Aaron did not wish the Israelites to kill any more. He took it upon himself to make the idol, but he delayed, hoping that Moses would return before it was built. First he requested their wives' earrings, in the hope that the women would refuse to give up their adornments, but the men even brought the rings from their own ears. Finally Aaron began to fashion an idol.

When Moses still did not come, Aaron raised his eyes to heaven, and said, "Almighty God, I do this against my will, that You may not count the sin against the Children of Israel after they repent."

[2] THE GOLDEN CALF: Our Rabbis sought to explain how it was that only forty days after God revealed Himself on Mount Sinai, while Moses was preparing the tablets, the Israelites worshiped an idol.

Moses had promised he would return on the fortieth day, the Rabbis explained. The people counted from the day of his departure, whereas he did not include the days spent on the long, slow ascent. As Moses did not return when expected, they assumed he was dead. Like children, unable to comprehend an invisible God, they became frightened and called on a visible god for help.

תָּלָה אַהֲרֹן עֵינָיו לַשָּׁמַיִם וְאָמַר: אַתָּה יוֹדֵעַ שֶׁבְּעַל־כָּרְחִי אֲנִי עוֹשֶׂה.

people sat down to eat and to drink, and rose up to make merry.

And the Lord said to Moses, "Go down at once; [3] for your people, whom you brought up out of the land of Egypt, have become corrupt. They have turned aside quickly from the way which I commanded them." [4]

And Moses turned and went down from the mountain, with the two tablets of the testimony in his hand. The tablets were the work of God, and the writing

---

✌ [3] GO DOWN AT ONCE: God said to Moses, "Go down at once."

"What is my sin, Almighty?" asked Moses. And God said, "Your people whom you brought up out of the land of Egypt have become corrupt."

"Why are they now my people and not Yours?" queried Moses. "When You sent me to redeem them, You said, 'I have surely seen the affliction of My people'" (Exodus 3:7).

"I reject them as My people," God replied. "They have forgotten My word. In My place they worship the image of an ox."

And Moses said, trembling, "O Lord, what will You do to them?"

"I will destroy them, but of you I will make a great nation."

"You have made a vow to Abraham, Isaac and Jacob to multiply their children as the stars of heaven, and now You wish to destroy Israel and to make me a great nation? If a three-legged stool has no stability, how then shall the one-legged stool stand? If You will not forgive Your people their sin, Almighty, blot me out too, I pray You, from Your book of remembrance."

God answered, "They are not worthy to be My people. Though I gave them My Torah, they bowed to a calf of gold."

"Almighty God, why are You so wrathful? They made only an assistant to You. The calf will help You. You will make the sun and moon to shine, and the calf will light the stars. You will make the rain fall to the earth, and the calf will bring the dew."

God said to Moses, "Are you as misled as they? The calf they made with their hands has no power; it is a work of delusion." Said Moses, "Then why be concerned with it?"

"Is the fault not Yours?" he argued further. "You brought them

לֶךְ־רֵד, כִּי שִׁחֵת עַמְּךָ אֲשֶׁר הֶעֱלֵיתָ מֵאֶרֶץ מִצְרָיִם. סָרוּ מַהֵר מִן הַדֶּרֶךְ אֲשֶׁר צִוִּיתִים.

was the writing of God, engraved upon the tablets.

When Joshua heard the sound of the people as they shouted, he said to Moses, "There is a noise of war in the camp." And Moses said, "It is not the voice of the victor, neither is it the voice of the defeated. It is a noise of singing that I hear."

As soon as he came near the camp, he saw the calf and the dancing; and Moses' anger blazed, and he flung the tablets from his hands, and shattered them at the foot of the mountain. [5] And he took the calf which they had made and burned it, and ground it to powder and strewed it upon the water, and made the Children of Israel drink of it.

And Moses said to Aaron, "What did this people do to you that you have brought such a great sin upon them?" And Aaron said, "Let not the anger of my lord be so hot; you know that the people are set on evil. So they said to me:

---

into Egypt where men worship animal gods. In their bondage, the Children of Israel learned from their Egyptian masters. Remember from which land You set them free."

And God listened to the plea of Moses.

⋘ [4] MOSES' FACE DIMS: Moses' face was radiant with light when God finished teaching him the Torah. But when the Israelites made the golden calf, this light was dimmed. "You achieved your greatness through the people," said God. "When their greatness is dimmed, so is yours."

⋘ [5] WHY DID MOSES CAST DOWN THE TABLETS? As Moses descended the mountain, he heard jubilant cries from the camp below. At the sight of the calf, he was horrified. "How can I give these Tablets of the Covenant, which forbid idol-worship, to a people in the midst of their revels?"

As he said this to himself, the letters engraved upon the stone tablets vanished, and only the bare rock remained. Until then, the word of God had made the tablets light, and Moses had felt no weight; now he could not hold them; they fell from his hands, and were dashed to pieces on the boulders below.

וַיִּחַר אַף מֹשֶׁה וַיַּשְׁלֵךְ מִיָּדָיו אֶת הַלֻּחֹת וַיְשַׁבֵּר אוֹתָם תַּחַת הָהָר.

Make us a god which shall go before us, because we do not know what has become of the man Moses, who brought us up out of the land of Egypt. Then I said to them: Whoever has any gold, let him take it off. So they gave it to me and I cast it into the fire, and out came this calf."

Then Moses stood in the gate of the camp, and said, "Whoever is on the Lord's side, come to me!" And all the sons of Levi gathered to him.

On the next day Moses said to the people, "You have sinned a great sin; and now I will go up to the Lord, perhaps I shall win forgiveness for your sin."

And Moses returned to the Lord. The Lord said to Moses, "I have seen this people; it is a stiff-necked people. Now let My wrath blaze against them, that I may destroy them; [6] but of you I will make a great nation."

And Moses said, "Oh, this people has sinned a great sin, and have made themselves a god of gold. Yet now, if Thou wilt, forgive their sin—and if not, blot me out too, I pray Thee, from Thy book which Thou hast written."

But the Lord said to Moses, "He who has sinned against Me, him only will I blot out of My book."

And Moses beseeched God, "Lord, why dost Thy wrath blaze against Thy people, whom Thou hast brought forth out of the land of Egypt with great power and with a mighty hand? Why should the Egyptians say, 'With evil intent He brought them forth, to slay them in the mountains, and to wipe them from the face of the earth'? Turn from Thy fierce

---

[6] THAT I MAY DESTROY THEM: When God threatened to destroy Israel because of the golden calf, Moses asked, "Is Israel worse than Sodom? When Abraham pleaded, You offered to spare Sodom if there were in it ten righteous men. Yet in Israel there are eighty righteous men."

"Who are the righteous?" asked God.

"The seventy elders of Israel, and Aaron, Nadab, Abihu, Eleazar, Ithamar, Phinehas and Caleb."

"These are seventy-seven," said God.

"Do you not include Abraham, Isaac and Jacob, who join in pleading for their children?"

And God hearkened to Moses.

מִי לַיָי – אֵלָי!

wrath, and do not do this evil to Thy people. Remember Abraham, Isaac and Israel, Thy servants, to whom Thou didst swear by Thine own self: I will multiply your children as the stars of heaven, and all this land that I have spoken of I will give to your children, and they shall inherit it forever."

And the Lord set aside the punishment which He said He would do to His people. [7] And the Lord said to Moses, "Go, lead the people to the place of which I have spoken to you. My angel shall go before you. [8] Nevertheless, on the day I make an accounting, I will repay them for this sin."

---

    [7] THE LORD FORGAVE HIS PEOPLE: Moses was so angered by the golden calf that he moved his tent outside the camp and dwelt alone. The sorrowing people begged him to return, but he refused.

"Though we have repented our sins," they said, "God has left us. Now you abandon us too. We are as orphans."

Then Moses heard God's voice: "Return unto the camp."

And Moses said, "Return also unto Your people, O Lord, as I do now."

And God listened to Moses.

    [8] FORGIVENESS: The day on which God assured Moses that Israel was forgiven for the golden calf was Yom Kippur, the day set by Him for forgiveness.

וַיִּנָּחֶם יְיָ עַל הָרָעָה אֲשֶׁר דִּבֶּר לַעֲשׂוֹת לְעַמּוֹ.

# 18. EXODUS [33–40]

MOSES ASKS THAT GOD'S GLORY LEAD
THE HEBREWS

AND THE LORD spoke to Moses, "Go from here, you and the people that you have brought up out of the land of Egypt, to the land which I swore to Abraham, to Isaac, and to Jacob. And I will send an angel before you, to a land flowing with milk and honey; for I will not go up in your midst, for you are a stubborn people."

And when the people heard these dreadful words, they mourned, and no man put on his ornaments.

And Moses said to the Lord, "See, Thou sayest to me: Bring up this people; but Thou hast not let me know whom Thou wilt send with me. Therefore, I pray Thee, if I have found favor in Thy sight, show me now Thy ways, that I may know Thee; and consider that this nation is Thy people."

And He said, "My Presence shall go with you, and I will give you rest."

Then Moses said, "If Thy Presence goes not with me, do not take us from here. For how shall it be known that I have found favor in Thy sight, I and Thy people? How else are we distinguished from all people on the face of the earth?"

And the Lord said to Moses, "I will do this also, for you have found favor in My sight, and I know you by name."

וְנִפְלִינוּ אֲנִי וְעַמְּךָ מִכָּל הָעָם אֲשֶׁר עַל פְּנֵי הָאֲדָמָה.

And Moses said, "Show me, I pray Thee, Thy glory." [1]

And He replied, "I will make all My goodness pass before you, and will proclaim the name of the Lord before you; and I will be gracious to whom I will be gracious, and I will show mercy on whom I will show mercy."

And He said, "But you cannot see My face, for man shall not see Me and live."

### THE SECOND TABLETS

AND THE LORD said to Moses, "Hew two tablets of stone like the first; and I will write upon them the words that were on the first tablets, which you broke. Be ready in the morning, and ascend Mount Sinai, and present yourself to Me on the top of the mountain. No man shall come up with you, neither let any man be seen anywhere on the mountain."

Moses rose early in the morning, and he hewed two tablets of stone like the first, and went up to Mount Sinai as the Lord had commanded him, and took in his hands the two tablets of stone. And the Lord descended in a cloud and passed by before him, and proclaimed, "The Lord, the Lord, merciful and gracious God, long-suffering, and abundant in goodness and truth; keeping mercy unto the thousandth generation, forgiving iniquity and transgression and sin; but He will not clear the guilty."

---

~§ [1] SHOW ME THY GLORY: When Moses asked to see His glory, God showed him a huge arch, enclosing gates of light. "For whom are these gates?" asked Moses.

"For those who study My Torah," answered God. Another beautiful pair of gates then opened. "Whose are these?" asked Moses.

"These are the gates of comfort and salvation," said God. "They are for all who call upon Me in their need."

A third pair of gates, even more splendid, swung wide, and within them were heaps of crowns. On each crown were carved the words, "A Good Name." "For whom are these crowns?" asked Moses.

"For those who do charity and righteousness; who raise the orphaned; who feed the poor and clothe the tattered," answered God.

Finally, another heavenly set of gates appeared. "These are the gates of My Grace," God told Moses. "Those who strive to serve Me will enter here. Man can give Me nothing, nor can his service enrich Me; but when I see his heart and mind striving to serve Me, I will have compassion on him and he will become Mine."

יְיָ יְיָ, אֵל רַחוּם וְחַנּוּן, אֶרֶךְ אַפַּיִם וְרַב חֶסֶד וֶאֱמֶת. נוֹצֵר חֶסֶד לָאֲלָפִים, נוֹשֵׂא עָוֹן וָפֶשַׁע וְחַטָּאָה.

And Moses bowed his head to the ground and worshiped.

### MOSES' FACE BEAMS

MOSES WAS THERE with the Lord forty days and forty nights; he neither ate bread nor drank water. And he wrote upon the tablets the words of the Covenant, the Ten Commandments.

And it came to pass when Moses came down from Mount Sinai with the two tablets of the testimony, he did not know that his face was radiant.

When Aaron and all the Children of Israel saw Moses, and saw that the skin of his face was radiant, they were afraid to come near him. And Moses called to them; then Aaron and all the leaders of the congregation returned to him, and Moses spoke to them. And afterward all the Children of Israel came near, and he told them all that which he was commanded.

### THE MISHKAN—THE PORTABLE SANCTUARY

AND MOSES SPOKE to all the congregation, "The Lord has commanded: Take from among you gifts for the Lord. Let everyone whose heart is willing bring the Lord's offering: gold and silver and brass; and blue and purple and scarlet material, fine linen and goats' hair; and rams' skins dyed red and sealskins, and acacia wood; and oil for the light, and spices for the anointing oil and for the sweet incense. And let them make Me a sanctuary [2] that I may dwell among them. [3]

"And let every wise-hearted man among you come, and make all that the Lord has commanded: the Tabernacle, its tent, and its covering, its clasps and its boards, its pillars and its pedestals; the Ark with its poles, the Ark-cover, and the veil of the screen; the table, and its poles and all its vessels; and the showbread; the *menorah* also for the light, and its vessels and its lamps, and the oil for the light; and the altar of incense, and the altar of burnt-offering, and the laver with its base; and the plaited garments for ministering in the holy place."

And the Children of Israel brought voluntary offerings to God: every man

---

    [2] THE TABERNACLE OF TESTIMONY: When God forgave Israel, He said, "I will let My Presence dwell in their midst. They shall rear My Sanctuary as a testimony of My forgiveness."

The Tabernacle was not intended as a dwelling place for God, for the heavens cannot contain Him, and the earth is but His footstool.

וַיְהִי שָׁם עִם יְיָ אַרְבָּעִים יוֹם וְאַרְבָּעִים לַיְלָה, לֶחֶם לֹא אָכַל וּמַיִם לֹא שָׁתָה.

and every woman whose heart prompted him, for all the work which God had commanded to be made.

And Moses called Bezalel and Oholiab, and every wise-hearted man in whose heart the Lord had put wisdom in all manner of workmanship. And they took from Moses all the offering which the Children of Israel had brought for the construction of the Sanctuary.

And the people continued to bring freewill-offerings every morning. And all the skilled men that wrought all the work of the Sanctuary, said to Moses, "The people are bringing much more than is necessary for the work which the Lord commanded."

And Moses proclaimed throughout the camp, saying, "Let neither man nor woman bring anything more for the work of the Sanctuary." So the people were stopped from bringing any more.

And the skilled men made the Tabernacle with ten curtains. Bezalel made the Ark of acacia wood, and he overlaid it with pure gold. And he made the

---

"But," said God, "this Tabernacle shall be a token of My affection. When it is built, I shall dwell in their midst."

The Rabbis comment, "Note that God did not say He would dwell in the Tabernacle, but in their midst. When the people serve with a willing heart and erect in its beauty a Tabernacle to His Name, God is among them."

[3] GOD'S DWELLING PLACE: When God said, "Let them make Me a sanctuary," Moses was startled.

"These requests are beyond my understanding," he said. "You asked that each man give a ransom for his soul—half a shekel. Yet if a man were to give all he possesses for his soul, it would not be enough. Then You commanded the Children of Israel concerning the offerings made by fire! Who can bring sufficient offerings to You? The Lebanon with all its forests is not sufficient for a burnt-offering worthy of You. Now You request a dwelling place, a sanctuary. The heavens, and the heavens of the heavens, cannot contain You, much less a sanctuary we can build for You."

And God answered, "I do not need your offerings, your food, nor your sanctuary. They are for your sake, not for Mine."

וַיִּקְרָא מֹשֶׁה אֶל בְּצַלְאֵל וְאֶל אָהֳלִיאָב וְאֶל כָּל אִישׁ חֲכַם לֵב אֲשֶׁר נָתַן יְיָ חָכְמָה בְּלִבּוֹ.

144

EXODUS 37:17, 25-26, 29; 38:8; 40:33-34

*menorah* of pure gold. He made of acacia wood the altar of incense, and overlaid it with gold. [4] He made the holy anointing oil, and he made the laver and its base of brass. And he made a court round about the Tabernacle and the altar, and set up a screen at the gate of the court.

So Moses finished the work. [5] Then the cloud covered the Tent of Meeting, and the glory of the Lord filled the Tabernacle.

---

◦§ [4] THE CROWNS OF BEZALEL: When Bezalel made the Tabernacle according to God's plans, he carved crowns on the altar, on the table, and on the Ark. The crown of the altar was for the priesthood; and that on the table for the kings who would rule in Israel. But, asked our Sages, for whom was the crown of the Torah?

And they answered: Anyone who wishes to attain the crown of the Torah, let him come and take it!

◦§ [5] MOSES FINISHED THE WORK: A man who handles the community's money should publicly give a full accounting. Our teacher, Moses, set the example.

God said of Moses, "He is trusted in all My house." Yet people would remark, "Is it impossible that he who has charge of the Sanctuary should get rich?" Others winked and nodded their heads.

Therefore, when the work of the Sanctuary was complete, Moses gathered the whole congregation of Israel. "I collected from you many valuable materials," he told them. "Now that the work is done, I shall give you a full accounting."

The people sat with him, and together they began the tally. When they finished, they found the weight of seventeen hundred and seventy-five silver shekels missing.

Moses began to worry. "Woe is me! They will accuse me of stealing. Where is the weight of the missing shekels?"

He checked his figures and discovered that he had not counted the hooks on the pillars. Then he told the Israelites, "Weigh the hooks of the pillars."

The Israelites weighed the hooks, which were exactly the weight of the missing silver.

וַיְכַס הֶעָנָן אֶת אֹהֶל מוֹעֵד, וּכְבוֹד יְיָ מָלֵא אֶת הַמִּשְׁכָּן.

# 19. LEVITICUS [1–25]

### LAWS RELATING TO SACRIFICE

AND THE LORD [1] called [2] to Moses and spoke to him from the Tent of Meeting, saying, "Speak to the Children of Israel, and say to them: When [3] any man [4] of you brings an offering to the Lord of the herd or of the flock, it shall be a male without blemish. And when anyone brings a meal-offering, it shall be of fine flour."

And the Lord spoke to Moses, saying, "If anyone sins and commits a trespass against the Lord, [5] and deals falsely with his neighbor in a matter of a deposit, or of pledge, or has robbed his neighbor [6] or has found something that was lost and denies it, and swears to

---

[1] AND THE LORD: Why does Leviticus begin with "And"? The use of the conjunction shows the close connection between this book and Exodus, which recounts the establishment of the Jewish nation. Since a nation must develop a way of life and of worship, Leviticus deals mainly with sacrifice and priestly duties in the Sanctuary. The history in Exodus leads on to the worship and holiness in Leviticus.

וְאִם מִן הַצֹּאן קָרְבָּנוֹ מִן הַכְּשָׂבִים אוֹ מִן הָעִזִּים לְעוֹלָה, זָכָר תָּמִים יַקְרִיבֶנּוּ.

a lie; if he has sinned by doing any of all these, then when he is found guilty he shall restore what he took by robbery or by fraud, or what was deposited with him, or the lost article that he found, or anything about which he swore falsely. He shall restore it in full [7] and shall also add a fifth more to it, giving it to whom it belongs on the day he was found guilty. Then he shall bring a guilt-offering to the Lord, a perfect ram from his flock. And the priest shall make atonement for him before the Lord, and he shall be forgiven."

And the Lord spoke to Moses, saying, "If anyone of the House of Israel presents an offering, in order that it may be accepted it shall be a perfect animal, without blemish. Anything blind, or maimed, or mutilated, or scabbed, or diseased, you must not offer to the Lord.

"And you shall observe My commandments and do them, as I am the Lord. And you shall not profane My holy name. I will be hallowed among the Children of Israel: I am the Lord who hallows you, who brought you out of the land of Egypt to be your God; I am the Lord."

FESTIVALS

AND THE LORD spoke to Moses, saying, "Speak to the Children of Israel, and

---

⋙ [2] VAYIKRA: The Hebrew name for the Book of Leviticus is *Vayikra*. In every manuscript of the Torah it is spelled with a tiny *aleph*. Why?

In ancient writings there were no spaces between words. When the last letter of one word was the same as the first letter of the next, as in this case, one letter might serve for both. Later, when words were separated by spaces, the scribes wrote the *aleph* of *Vayikra* in smaller size, to show that it had not occurred in previous manuscripts.

This profound respect for each letter of the Scriptures is why the Bible has come down to us in its pure, sacred form.

⋙ [3] WHEN: Why is the word "When" used to introduce the laws of sacrifice? The phrase might have read, "You shall bring a sacrifice."

As the Prophets and Rabbis pointed out, God does not command these offerings. The Hebrews were accustomed to sacrifice, which was the religious custom of the ancient East. God would accept a sacrifice offered in the proper spirit; He did not demand it.

וְנִקְדַּשְׁתִּי בְּתוֹךְ בְּנֵי יִשְׂרָאֵל, אֲנִי יְיָ מְקַדִּשְׁכֶם.

say to them: The appointed festivals of
the Lord, which you shall proclaim to be
holy assemblies, these are My fixed
seasons."

SABBATH [8]

"SIX DAYS SHALL work be done, but
the seventh day is a Sabbath of complete

---

[4] WHEN ANY MAN: "Any man," this verse says, not "an Israelite" or
"Hebrew." This indicates that anyone may bring an offering to the
Lord. His faith, not his birth, is important to God.

The Hebrew word for "offering" is *korban*, which means "that
which is brought near" to God. Whatever may bring man closer to
God, be it sacrifice, prayer or charity, is a *korban*.

[5] AGAINST THE LORD: Rabbi Akiba held that these three simple
words were of utmost significance. A man who denies his oath or
swears falsely denies God, who is witness, and also denies His
teachings.

[6] ROBBERY, FRAUD: The Rabbis maintained that robbery includes
any injustice or trickery, whether or not it conforms to the letter of
the law. For example, if a farmer reserved the corners of his fields
for a poor relative, this was considered robbery, for it robbed other
poor people of their share.

[7] THE FIRST STEP: The first step in repentance for a wrong against
a fellow man is restitution of what has been stolen or defrauded.

Without this first step, there is no true repentance. Neither prayer
nor the Day of Atonement atones for the sin until the wronged man
has been repaid and his forgiveness sought. Only then may the re-
pentant sinner ask for God's forgiveness.

[8] AN EXTRA SOUL: The Sabbath is not merely a day of rest. Rabbi
Simeon ben Lakish declared that every Jew receives an extra soul
on that day. The delight of the Sabbath is so great that man's soul
expands to enjoy its holiness.

מוֹעֲדֵי יְיָ אֲשֶׁר תִּקְרְאוּ אוֹתָם מִקְרָאֵי קֹדֶשׁ, אֵלֶּה הֵם מוֹעֲדָי.

rest, a holy assembly; you shall not do any manner of work. [9] It is a Sabbath to the Lord [10] in all your dwellings." [11]


PESAḤ

"IN THE FIRST month, on the fourteenth day of the month at dusk, is the Lord's Passover. And on the fifteenth day of the same month is the Festival of Unleavened Bread to the Lord; seven days you shall eat *matzot*. [12] On the first day and on the seventh day you shall have a holy assembly; you shall do no manner of servile work."

---

[9] THE TASTE OF THE SABBATH: Emperor Antoninus dined with Rabbi Joshua ben Ḥananiah, and was served a hot meal. The next Sabbath, the Rabbi served him a cold meal. "The cold meal was even better than the hot," the Emperor observed. "How is that possible?"

"We have a spice called Sabbath," replied the Rabbi, "which gives this food its savor."

"Give me some of this spice," requested the Emperor.

The Rabbi smiled. "For him who keeps the Sabbath, the spice works; for him who does not keep it, it does not work."

[10] THE SABBATH IS FOR MAN: Hillel was poor when he came from Babylonia to the academy of Shemaiah and Avtalion. When he lacked even the meager funds for his tuition, he climbed to the roof and listened to the discussion through the grate.

Although it was winter, and the snow began to fall, he remained in his place to listen. He was still lying there when the class came to an end.

When the two rabbis returned for prayer the next morning, Shemaiah said to Avtalion, "Brother, it is always light at this hour, but today the room is dark." Looking up, they saw a figure outlined on the grate. They rushed to the roof and found Hillel lying there, covered with snow. They lifted him from the grate and carried him inside.

Although it was the Sabbath, they lit a fire to warm him. "We break the Sabbath this time to save his life," they said, "so that he may observe many hundreds of Sabbaths."

אָמְרוּ: רָאוּי זֶה לְחַלֵּל עָלָיו אֶת הַשַּׁבָּת.

SHAVUOT

ROSH HASHANAH AND YOM KIPPUR

"WHEN YOU HAVE come into the land which I give to you, and shall reap its harvest, then you shall bring the sheaf of the first-fruits of your harvest to the priest. And he shall wave the sheaf before the Lord that it may be accepted for you.

"And you shall count from the day after the day of rest, from the day that you brought the sheaf of the waving, seven full weeks, counting fifty days to the day after the seventh week. [13] And you shall proclaim a holy assembly; you shall do no manner of servile work. It is a statute forever in all your dwellings throughout your generations."

AND THE LORD spoke to Moses, saying, "Speak to the Children of Israel, and say: In the seventh month, on the first day of the month, shall be a solemn rest to you, a memorial proclaimed with the blast of the *Shofar,* a holy assembly. You shall do no manner of servile work.

"However, on the tenth day of this seventh month is the Day of Atonement; there shall then be a holy assembly, and you shall afflict your souls. [14] And you shall do no manner of work on that day, for it is the Day of Atonement, to make atonement for you before the Lord your God. [15] It is a statute forever throughout your generations in all your

---

   [11] A SABBATH FOR THE BEAST: Animals, too, are creatures of God and are entitled to a day of rest.

    The Rabbis decreed, therefore, that on the Sabbath an ox is not to be locked in its stall all day, for this is not rest, but imprisonment. The ox must be allowed to pasture in the field.

   [12] MATZOT—THE BREAD OF AFFLICTION: *Matzah* is known as *leḥem oni,* the bread of the poor. Even he who is rich and happy should eat *matzah* on Pesaḥ, to remind himself that there are those who are poor and unhappy, as were our ancestors who were enslaved in Egypt.

   [13] COUNTING SEVEN TIMES SEVEN: "Why do we count the days between Pesaḥ and Shavuot?" asked the Rabbis. "The giving of the Torah at Sinai was the whole purpose of the deliverance from Egypt," explained Maimonides. "We count the days from Pesaḥ as one counts the days until his best friend comes to visit."

וְכָל מְלָאכָה לֹא תַעֲשׂוּ בְּעֶצֶם הַיּוֹם הַזֶּה, כִּי יוֹם כִּפּוּרִים הוּא לְכַפֵּר עֲלֵיכֶם לִפְנֵי יְיָ אֱלֹהֵיכֶם.

dwellings. It shall be to you a sabbath
of complete rest, and you shall afflict
your souls. On the evening of the ninth
day, from evening to evening, you shall
keep your sabbath."

SUKKOT

AND THE LORD spoke to Moses, saying,
"Speak to the Children of Israel, and
say: On the fifteenth day of this seventh
month is the Festival of Booths for seven
days to the Lord. On the first day shall
be a holy assembly; you shall do no
manner of servile work.

"However, on the fifteenth day of the

seventh month, when you have gathered
in the produce of the land, you shall observe the feast of the Lord for seven
days. On the first day shall be a sabbath,
and on the eighth day shall be a sabbath.

"And on the first day you shall take
the fruit of the beautiful citron tree,
branches of the palm tree, and boughs
of the broad-leaved tree, and willows of
the brook, and you shall rejoice before
the Lord your God for seven days.

"You shall dwell in booths seven
days; [16] all the native-born in Israel
shall dwell in booths, that your generations may know that I made the Children of Israel to dwell in booths when I

---

[14] YOU SHALL AFFLICT YOUR SOULS: Our Rabbis say: "Afflict your
souls" does not mean that you are to mistreat your body. We fast so
that our attention may be directed on atonement. It is our souls we
afflict as we consider our deeds in the year past.

[15] THE HEART ALSO MUST SMITE: Rabbi Israel Meir, the sage
known as the Ḥafetz Ḥayyim, commented on the tradition of beating
one's breast when the sins are enumerated on Yom Kippur: "God
does not forgive the sins of one who smites his heart, but He pardons
those whose hearts smite them."

[16] DWELL IN BOOTHS: Why do we dwell in booths at the harvest
season? Naḥmanides, the Spanish commentator of medieval days, explained that the booths call to mind that our ancestors wandered in
the wilderness. At harvest time we must not say in our pride, "This
I achieved with my own strength." Just as it is God who redeemed
our ancestors, so it is He who brings the harvest.

וּלְקַחְתֶּם לָכֶם בַּיּוֹם הָרִאשׁוֹן פְּרִי עֵץ הָדָר, כַּפֹּת תְּמָרִים וַעֲנַף עֵץ עָבוֹת
וְעַרְבֵי נָחַל.

brought them out of the land of Egypt; I am the Lord your God."

### THE SABBATICAL YEAR

AND THE LORD spoke to Moses on Mount Sinai, saying, "When you come into the land which I give you, then the land shall keep a sabbath unto the Lord. [17] Six years you shall sow your field and six years you shall prune your vineyard and gather in its produce. But in the seventh year shall be a sabbath of complete rest for the land; you shall neither sow your field nor prune your vineyard. You shall not reap that which grows of itself of your harvest, and you shall not gather the grapes of your undressed vine; it shall be a year of rest for the land.

"And the produce of the land at rest shall be food for all: for you and for your manservant and for your maidservant, and for the stranger who lives with you; for your cattle and for the beasts in your land."

### THE YEAR OF JUBILEE

"AND YOU SHALL count seven sabbaths of years, seven times seven years, forty-nine years. Then on the tenth day of the seventh month, on the Day of Atonement, you shall make proclamation with the blast of the *Shofar* throughout your land. [18] And you shall hallow the fif-

---

ᵛᵍ [17] THE EARTH RESTS: There were emperors who respected the Jewish Sabbatical year, and did not require the Jews to pay tribute, since they reaped no harvest. Both Alexander the Great and Julius Caesar recognized that it was a religious duty of the Jews to let the ground lie fallow. Roman emperors who hated Judaism demanded the tribute money, however.

The Rabbis ruled that the people must work the soil throughout the Sabbatical year, so that the Romans would have no excuse to sell them into slavery.

ᵛᵍ [18] JUBILEE AND ATONEMENT: The year begins on Rosh Hashanah; the jubilee year with Yom Kippur. Both occasions celebrate human freedom: the Day of Atonement frees man from the slavery of sin, the jubilee from the slavery of poverty.

The blowing of the *Shofar* proclaimed both great freedoms.

וּבַשָּׁנָה הַשְּׁבִיעִית שַׁבַּת שַׁבָּתוֹן יִהְיֶה לָאָרֶץ. שָׂדְךָ לֹא תִזְרָע וְכַרְמְךָ לֹא תִזְמֹר.

tieth year, and proclaim liberty through-out the land to all the inhabitants thereof. It shall be a jubilee to you; and you shall return every man to his prop-erty and to his family.

"A jubilee shall that fiftieth year be to you; you shall not sow, neither reap that which grows by itself in it, nor gather the grapes of the undressed vines. For it is a jubilee; it shall be holy to you.

"And if you sell anything to your neighbor, or buy from your neighbor, you shall not wrong one another. Ac-cording to the number of years after the jubilee you shall buy from your neighbor, and according to the number of years of the crops he shall sell to you. If the years are many the price shall in-crease, and if the years are few the price shall diminish; for it is the number of crops that he sells to you. You shall not cheat one another; but you shall fear your God, for I am the Lord your God.

"And the land shall not be sold in perpetuity; for the land is Mine, and you are strangers and settlers with Me.

"If your brother becomes poor, and sells some of his property, then shall his nearest kinsman come and redeem what his brother has sold. And if a man has no one to redeem it, and he does well and has enough means to redeem it, let him count the years of its sale, and re-store the gain to the man to whom he sold it and return to his property.

"But if he does not have sufficient means to get it back for himself, then the land he sold shall remain with the buyer until the year of jubilee, and in the jubi-lee he shall return to his property.

"If your brother becomes poor and his means fail, then you shall help him; as a resident alien and a settler he shall live with you. Take no interest from him; but fear your God, that your brother may live with you.

"If your brother becomes poor, and sells himself to you, you shall not make him serve as a slave. [19] He shall be to you as a hired servant and as a settler; he shall serve with you until the year of jubilee. Then he shall be released from your service, he and his children with him, and shall return to his own family and to the property of his fathers. For the Children of Israel are My serv-ants whom I brought forth out of the land of Egypt; they shall not be sold as bondmen. You shall not rule over him harshly; but you shall fear your God."

---

[19] NOT SERVE AS A SLAVE: The Jews did not build their civilization on slavery. They remembered that they had been slaves in Egypt.

כִּי עֲבָדַי הֵם אֲשֶׁר הוֹצֵאתִי אוֹתָם מֵאֶרֶץ מִצְרָיִם. לֹא יִמָּכְרוּ מִמְכֶּרֶת עָבֶד.

# 20. LEVITICUS [11–26]

THE HOLINESS CODE:

YOU ARE A HOLY PEOPLE

AND THE LORD spoke to Moses, saying, "Speak to the whole congregation of the Children of Israel, and say to them: You shall be holy; for I, the Lord your God, am holy. [1] Every man shall fear his mother and his father, and you shall keep My Sabbaths; I am the Lord your God.

"Do not turn to the idols nor make molten gods; for I am the Lord your God.

---

[1] YOU SHALL BE HOLY: By imitating God, man can be holy. The Talmud points out those deeds of God which were holy. On the very first page of the Torah, for example, He clothes the naked—Adam. He feeds the hungry and cares for the orphans. He heals the sick and frees the captives. And on the last page we read that He buries Moses.

קְדוֹשִׁים תִּהְיוּ כִּי קָדוֹשׁ אֲנִי יְיָ אֱלֹהֵיכֶם.

"And when you reap the harvest of your land, you shall not wholly reap the corner of your field, neither shall you gather the gleaning of your harvest. And you shall not glean your vineyard, neither shall you gather the fallen fruit of your vineyard. You shall leave them for the poor and for the stranger; I am the Lord your God."

### BE RIGHTEOUS AND JUST

"YOU SHALL NOT steal; [2] neither shall you deal falsely nor lie one to another.

And you shall not swear by My name falsely, and so profane the name of your God; I am the Lord.

"You shall not oppress your neighbor, nor rob him.

"The wages of a hired laborer [3] are not to remain with you over night until morning.

"You shall not curse the deaf, nor put a stumbling block [4] before the blind, but you shall stand in awe before your God; I am the Lord.

"You shall do no unrighteousness in judgment; neither shall you favor the

[2] YOU SHALL NOT STEAL: "One may not steal, even if everyone else steals, nor even to reclaim one's own property, lest he seem a thief," said the *Sifra*. Anything that has the appearance of stealing is forbidden.

Not always recognized as robbery, but to be condemned nonetheless, is *g'nevat da'at*, the stealing of someone's reputation, whether by gossip or slander, or by false flattery.

[3] A HIRED LABORER: The Torah commands that a hired laborer be treated justly. The Talmud required an employer to give his helpers time to recite the *Sh'ma*, a respite for his meals, and a pause to say *Birkat ha-Mazon*, Grace After Meals.

[4] A STUMBLING BLOCK: "A stumbling block" can mean bad advice. Do not send a man on a useless journey, or advise him to sell his field for a pittance, or recommend a house you know is not well built.

[5] FAVOR NOT THE POOR: Our Rabbis were careful to maintain the purest justice. Therefore they specified that, just as one may not

לֹא תְקַלֵּל חֵרֵשׁ וְלִפְנֵי עִוֵּר לֹא תִתֵּן מִכְשֹׁל, וְיָרֵאתָ מֵאֱלֹהֶיךָ, אֲנִי יְיָ.

poor [5] nor defer to the mighty; in righteousness you shall judge your neighbor.

"You shall not go about as a talebearer among your people, neither shall you stand idly by the bloodshed of your neighbor; [6] I am the Lord.

"You shall not hate your brother in your heart. You shall not take vengeance, [7] nor bear any grudge against your

---

favor the rich, neither may he favor the poor. Justice must be free of all prejudice. Favoritism to the needy not only turns aside justice, but also humiliates the poor.

Similarly, a judge may not allow one person to sit and force the other to stand; or address one man kindly and be harsh to the other. "Justice, justice shall you pursue" (Deuteronomy 16:20).

[6] YOU SHALL NOT STAND IDLY BY: This verse warns against the sin of indifference, said the Rabbis. Whoever does not come to the aid of one who is drowning, pursued by a wild beast, or attacked by a robber, is himself guilty. His idleness allowed another to perish.

The verse ends, "I am the Lord," to tell man that God knows of his indifference and weighs it as a sin.

[7] YOU SHALL NOT TAKE VENGEANCE: Vengeance means the paying of evil with evil. It is the Jewish way to fight evil, rather than the evildoer. This philosophy was illustrated by Samuel ibn Nagrela, the Spanish-Jewish poet of the eleventh century, who was vizier to the king of Granada.

One day, Samuel was cursed by an enemy in the presence of the king. The irate king ordered him to have the man's tongue cut out. Samuel, however, did not take vengeance, but treated the man so kindly that he became a warm friend.

When the king observed that the man had not been mutilated, he expressed surprise. Samuel replied, "Your majesty, I have taken away his evil tongue and given him a kind one."

The Rabbis say, therefore, "Who is mighty? He who makes his enemy his friend."

בְּצֶדֶק תִּשְׁפֹּט עֲמִיתֶךָ.

people, [8] but *you shall love your neighbor as yourself*; [9] I am the Lord.

"You shall not eat anything with its blood; neither shall you practice divination nor soothsaying.

"You shall rise up before the hoary head, and honor the face of the old.

"And if a stranger resides with you in your land, you shall not do him wrong. The stranger that sojourns with you shall be to you as the native-born among you, and you shall love him as yourself; for you were strangers in the land of Egypt; I am the Lord your God.

"You shall do no injustice in weight or in measures. Just balances, just weights, a just *ephah,* and a just *hin,* shall you have; I am the Lord your God who brought you out of the land of Egypt. And you shall observe all My statutes and all My ordinances, and do them; I am the Lord.

"And you shall not follow the customs of the nation which I am casting out be-

fore you; for it was because they did all these things that I abhorred them. Therefore, sanctify yourselves and be holy; for I am the Lord your God, who sanctifies you."

### A SEPARATE PEOPLE

"YOU SHALL THEREFORE keep all My statutes and all My ordinances, so that the land to which I bring you to dwell shall not spew you out. I am the Lord your God who has set you apart from the peoples. You shall therefore distinguish between the clean beast and the unclean, and between the unclean fowl and the clean.

"And you shall be holy to Me; for I, the Lord, am holy, and have set you apart from the peoples to be Mine."

### ANIMALS, CLEAN AND UNCLEAN

"THESE ARE THE creatures which you

---

*❧* [8] AGAINST YOUR PEOPLE: Our Rabbis explain this verse with a parable: If a man cut his hand with a knife, shall he avenge himself by cutting his other hand which held the knife?

*❧* [9] YOU SHALL LOVE! Rabbi Akiba considered this the greatest verse of the Torah. Ben Azai, however, did not deem it sufficient only to love one's neighbor. The greatest verse is, "These are the generations of Adam" (Genesis 5:1), said he, "because it teaches that we are all children of the same father."

וְאָהַבְתָּ לְרֵעֲךָ כָּמוֹךָ.

may eat among all the beasts that are on the earth. Any with a cloven hoof, completely divided, and that chews its cud, you may eat. But those that only chew their cud, or those that have only a cloven hoof, you shall not eat. The camel, though it chews its cud, does not have a cloven hoof; it is unclean to you. And the pig, though it has a cloven hoof, does not chew its cud; it is unclean to you."

### FISHES, CLEAN AND UNCLEAN

"THESE YOU MAY eat of all that live in the water: whatever has fins and scales in the water, in the seas and in the rivers, you may eat. But all that do not have fins and scales, they are detestable to you."

### BIRDS AND INSECTS

"ALL BIRDS OF prey and every vulture are detestable; they shall not be eaten.

"All winged, swarming insects upon the earth are detestable to you.

"Whatever crawls on its belly, and whatever goes upon four legs, or whatever has many legs; any swarming insect on the earth, you shall not eat—they are detestable.

"For I am the Lord your God; sanctify yourselves therefore, and be holy, for I am holy. Therefore, you shall not defile yourself with any kind of swarming thing that crawls upon the earth."

### BLOOD

"ANYONE IN THE House of Israel, or of the strangers that reside among you, who eats any blood at all, I will set My face against him and will cut him off from among his people. For the life of a creature is the blood; therefore I said to the Children of Israel: No one among you shall eat blood, neither shall any stranger that resides among you eat blood."

### THE BLESSINGS

"IF YOU WILL observe My statutes, and keep My commands and do them, then I will give you rains in due season, and the land shall yield its produce, and the trees shall yield their fruit. And your threshing shall reach to the grape-gathering, and the grape-gathering shall reach to the sowing time. And you shall eat your bread until you have enough, and dwell in your land in safety.

"And I will give peace in the land, so that you shall lie down and none shall make you afraid. I will clear the land of wild beasts, and no sword shall pass through your land.

"I will turn My face toward you, and make you fruitful and multiply you; and I will maintain My Covenant with you. And you shall eat old grain long stored, and you shall clear out the old to make room for the new.

וְנָתַתִּי שָׁלוֹם בָּאָרֶץ וּשְׁכַבְתֶּם וְאֵין מַחֲרִיד.

"And I will set My Tabernacle among you. I will walk among you, and will be your God and you shall be My people. I am the Lord your God, who brought you forth out of the land of Egypt, out of slavery; and I have broken the bars of your yoke, and made you walk upright." [10]

### THE REPROOF

"BUT IF YOU will not listen to Me and will not observe all these commandments, and if you will reject My statutes, and if your soul will abhor My ordinances and you break My Covenant, then I will do this to you: I will appoint terror over you; and you will sow your seed in vain, for your enemies will eat it. And I will set My face against you, and you shall be defeated by your enemies; and you shall flee when no one pursues you.

"And if you will not listen to Me even after this, then I will punish you seven more times for your sins. And I will break the pride of your power, and I will make your heaven as iron and your earth as brass. And your strength shall be spent in vain; for your land shall not yield its produce, neither shall the trees of the land yield their fruit.

"And if you will not listen to Me in spite of these things, but will go contrary to Me, then I will act contrary to you in fury. And I will scatter you among the nations; and your land shall be a desolation and your cities shall be a waste.

"And those of you that are left, if they will confess their iniquity and the iniquity of their fathers, and their hearts will be humbled and they will make amends, then will I remember My covenant with Jacob, and with Isaac, and with Abraham; and I will remember the land.

"For, nonetheless, when they are in the land of their enemies, I will not reject them to destroy them utterly, and to break My covenant with them; for I am the Lord their God.

"I will remember the covenant I made with your ancestors, whom I brought forth out of Egypt in the sight of the nations that I might be their God; I am the Lord."

---

⋙ [10] AND MADE YOU WALK UPRIGHT: How do we walk upright before God? By performing His commandments proudly and gladly, not as slaves serve their masters, but with joy and a full heart.

וְאַף גַּם זֹאת בִּהְיוֹתָם בְּאֶרֶץ אוֹיְבֵיהֶם, לֹא מְאַסְתִּים וְלֹא גְעַלְתִּים לְכַלֹּתָם,
לְהָפֵר בְּרִיתִי אִתָּם.

# 21. NUMBERS [6–11]

### THE CLOUD AND THE FIRE OVER THE TABERNACLE IN THE DESERT

ON THE DAY that the Tabernacle was erected, the cloud covered the Tabernacle and the Tent of Meeting. And the appearance of fire was over the Tabernacle, from evening until morning. And whenever the cloud was lifted from over the Tent, all the Children of Israel journeyed; and wherever the cloud stopped, the Children of Israel camped. At the command of the Lord the Children of Israel journeyed, and at the command of the Lord they encamped.

At times the cloud would remain a few days upon the Tabernacle; and sometimes the cloud remained from evening till morning only. Whether it remained two days, or a month, or a year, as long as the cloud remained over the Tabernacle, the Children of Israel remained in camp and did not journey; only when it lifted did they set out. At the command of the Lord they encamped, and at the command of the Lord they journeyed.

### THE TWO SILVER TRUMPETS

AND THE LORD spoke to Moses, saying, "Make two trumpets of silver of beaten

וּלְפִי הֵעָלוֹת הֶעָנָן מֵעַל הָאֹהֶל וְאַחֲרֵי כֵן יִסְעוּ בְּנֵי יִשְׂרָאֵל, וּבִמְקוֹם אֲשֶׁר יִשְׁכָּן־ שָׁם הֶעָנָן שָׁם יַחֲנוּ בְּנֵי יִשְׂרָאֵל.

work, and they shall be for calling the congregation and for starting the camps on the journey. When they shall blow both of them, the whole congregation shall gather at the door of the Tent of Meeting. And if they blow only one, the princes, the heads of the clans of Israel, shall gather to you.

"And when you blow an alarm, the camps that lie on the east side shall set out on their journey. And when you blow a second alarm, the camps that lie on the south side shall set out.

"The sons of Aaron, the priests, shall blow the trumpets.

"And when you go to war in your land against an adversary that oppresses you, then you shall sound an alarm with the trumpets; and you shall be remembered before the Lord your God, and you shall be saved from your enemies.

"Also in the day of your gladness, and on your designated festivals, and on the first day of the month, you shall blow the trumpets."

THE JOURNEY BEGINS

AND IT CAME to pass in the second year, in the second month, on the twentieth day of the month, that the cloud was lifted from the Tabernacle of the Testimony, and the Children of Israel set out from the desert of Sinai. And they journeyed for three days, and the Ark of the Covenant of the Lord went before them to seek out a resting place for them.

And when the Ark set forward, Moses would say:

"Rise up, O Lord, [1] and let Thine enemies be scattered;
And let them who hate Thee flee from before Thee!" [2]

---

&⸇ [1] RISE UP, O LORD: These two verses still convey the thrill of the march into the wilderness. They are pronounced to this day in traditional synagogues at the opening and closing of the Ark, when the Torah is read. When the ancient Jews went into battle, the Levites would bear the Ark before them and the priests would cry out, "Rise up, O Lord!"

Today these words are still a call to battle—to the battle against evil.

&⸇ [2] LET THEM WHO HATE THEE: Why have the Jews been able to endure persecution? They have recognized that there are men who hate decency and righteousness. Since the Jewish people brought

קוּמָה יְיָ וְיָפֻצוּ אוֹיְבֶיךָ, וְיָנֻסוּ מְשַׂנְאֶיךָ מִפָּנֶיךָ.

And when the Ark would halt, he would say:

"Return, O Lord, unto the ten thousands of the clans of Israel."

THE PRIESTLY BLESSING

THE LORD SPOKE to Moses, saying, "Speak to Aaron and his sons, and say: This is how you shall bless the Children of Israel; [3] say to them:

The Lord bless you and guard you; [4]

The Lord make His face to shine upon you and be gracious to you;

---

God's word to mankind, those who hate His word must hate the Jews also. This realization has comforted the Jew in times of oppression.

Therefore, it is said that God is distressed whenever Jews suffer. It would be presumptuous to say that God suffers with the Jews, said Rabbi Akiba, if Scriptures did not record it: "You redeemed out of Egypt the nation and its God" (II Samuel 7:23). He Himself was in exile with the Hebrews.

✒ [3] YOU SHALL BLESS: Although Aaron has been told to bless Israel, the priestly blessing calls on God to bless them. Why? Moses understood that no man, priest though he be, can bless another. What he can do is ask God to bless.

Yet man, who cannot bless his fellow man, can bless God. This the Jew does every day in the b'raḥot, every one of which begins "Blessed art Thou, O Lord . . ." How can this be? Man is responding to the holiness of God.

✒ [4] THE LORD BLESS YOU: This blessing is called duchan, a name taken from the wooden platform on which the priests stood in the Temple courtyard when they pronounced these words.

Even today, in traditional synagogues on Holy Days and Festivals, the Kohanim, the descendants of the priests, assemble in front of the Ark, cover their heads with their Talétim, lift their hands high and invoke God's blessing on the congregation, while chanting the Biblical words in an age-old melody.

Tradition says that we may not look upon the Kohanim as they in-

יְבָרֶכְךָ יְיָ וְיִשְׁמְרֶךָ. יָאֵר יְיָ פָּנָיו אֵלֶיךָ וִיחֻנֶּךָ.

The Lord lift up His countenance upon you and give you peace. [5] So they shall put My Name upon the Children of Israel, and I will bless them."

### THE PEOPLE COMPLAIN

AND THE PEOPLE complained. The rabble among them had a craving; and the Children of Israel also wept, and said, "If only we were given meat to eat! We remember the fish that we ate without payment in Egypt; the cucumbers, and the melons, and the leeks, and the onions, and the garlic; but now our souls are dried away. We have nothing but this manna to look to."

Moses heard the people weeping, family by family, every man at the door of his tent. And Moses became displeased, [6] and said to the Lord, "Why hast Thou been so hard on Thy servant? And why have I not found favor in Thy sight, that Thou hast put the burden of all these people upon me? Have I conceived them that Thou shouldst say to me: Carry them in your bosom as a nurse carries an infant, to the land which Thou hast promised to their fathers? Where can I get meat to give to all these people? They weep on my

---

tone the ancient words, for if they are indeed holy and God-fearing men, the *Shechinah*, God's Presence, rests upon them; and, legend has it, we may be blinded by the radiance.

⋙ [5] AND GIVE YOU PEACE: Peace is perhaps the most important word in the Hebrew language. Because the wish for peace is so dear to us, we greet one another and take our leave with wishes for *shalom*. *Shalom* is even one of the great names of God.

Man can build a meaningful life only when there is peace: "Better a supper of herbs with love than a banquet with strife" (Proverbs 15:17).

The Midrash tells a story which shows that God seeks to keep peace in a household. Sarah overheard God tell Abraham that a son would be born to them, and she exclaimed, "How can I give birth to a child when I am old and my husband is old?" (Genesis 18:12). God repeated her remark to Abraham, but mentioned only her words, "When I am old" (18:13), lest Abraham be angered that Sarah had referred to him as old.

יִשָּׂא יְיָ פָּנָיו אֵלֶיךָ וְיָשֵׂם לְךָ שָׁלוֹם.

shoulders, saying, 'Give us meat to eat!' I am not able to carry all of this people alone, because it is too heavy for me. If this is the way Thou wouldst deal with me, kill me, I pray Thee, and let me not look upon my wretchedness!"

### THE SEVENTY ELDERS

AND THE LORD said to Moses, "Gather seventy of the elders of Israel, and bring them to the Tent of Meeting that they may stand there with you. And I will come down and speak with you there. And I will take of the spirit which is upon you and will put it upon them, that they may share the burden of the people with you, that you shall not bear it alone.

"And say to the people: Tomorrow you shall eat meat; for you have wept in the ears of the Lord, saying, 'If only we were given meat to eat, for it was well with us in Egypt;' therefore the Lord will give you meat to eat. You shall eat meat not one day, nor two days, nor five days, nor ten days, nor twenty days, but a whole month, until it comes out of your nostrils and becomes loathsome to you; because you have rejected the Lord who is among you, and have wept before Him, saying, 'Why did we ever leave Egypt?' "

And Moses said, "The people are six hundred thousand, and yet Thou hast said, 'I will give them meat to eat for a whole month.' Can enough flocks and herds be slaughtered to suffice them? Or if all the fish of the sea were gathered together, would they suffice them?" And the Lord answered, "Is there a limit to the Lord's power? Now you shall see whether My word shall come to pass or not."

And Moses went out, and he gathered seventy men of the elders of the people [7] and set them around the Tent. And the Lord came down in the cloud,

---

⊷ [6] MOSES BECAME DISPLEASED: Why was Moses so unhappy with the Children of Israel? Because he saw that small trials of the present loomed larger to them than the bitter oppression of the past. The Israelites had been slaves who labored the long day without pay, at the mercy of Egyptian masters who gave them barely enough food to keep them alive. All this they forgot, as they remembered only the taste of the fish.

⊷ [7] SEVENTY ELDERS: Moses was in a predicament because he could not evenly apportion seventy elders among twelve tribes. If he took

הֲיַד יְיָ תִּקְצָר? עַתָּה תִרְאֶה הֲיִקְרְךָ דְבָרִי אִם לֹא.

and took of the spirit that was upon Moses, and put it upon the seventy elders. [8] And when the spirit rested upon them, they prophesied, but not after that day.

### ELDAD AND MEDAD

NOW TWO MEN remained in the camp. The name of one was Eldad, and the name of the other Medad. They were among the seventy men recorded, but they had not gone to the Tent. And the spirit rested upon them, and they prophesied in the camp. [9]

A young man came running to Moses, and said, "Eldad and Medad are prophesying in the camp!"

---

five from each tribe, he would have only sixty elders; if he took six, he would have seventy-two. If he divided the honors unevenly, jealousy would result.

What did he do? He chose seventy-two worthy men, six from each tribe. He prepared seventy-two markers, two of which were blank. Each man chose a slip, and the two who had drawn blanks were not appointed.

[8] AND TOOK THE SPIRIT OF MOSES: Do not think, said the Rabbis, that when others prophesied, Moses' prophetic spirit was diminished. Prophecy may be compared to a candle. Many candles may be kindled from it, and though all will blaze into light, the original flame is not diminished.

[9] AND THEY PROPHESIED IN THE CAMP: What did Eldad and Medad prophesy? Our Rabbis declared that they prophesied, "Moses will die in the wilderness and Joshua will lead the Children of Israel into the Promised Land."

Joshua was shocked when he heard of this, and asked Moses for permission to arrest the men.

Moses answered, "God has put His spirit upon them, and they prophesy what He has put into their mouths. Why should they be punished?"

Throughout Jewish history, the Hebrew Prophets spoke the truth, despite any threat, despite any danger.

מֹשֶׁה מֵת, יְהוֹשֻׁעַ מַכְנִיס אֶת יִשְׂרָאֵל לָאָרֶץ.

And Joshua the son of Nun, who had served Moses from his youth, answered, "My lord Moses, shut them in!"

And Moses said to him, "Are you jealous for my sake? Would that all of the Lord's people were prophets, that the Lord would put His spirit on them!"

And Moses and the elders of Israel returned to the camp.

### THE QUAILS

THEN A WIND arose and brought quails from the sea, and let them fall near the camp, about a day's journey on each side, all around the camp, and about three feet high on the face of the earth. And all that day and all the night and all the next day, the people gathered the quail; he who gathered the least gathered ten heaps. And they spread them out for themselves all around the camp.

While the meat was still between their teeth, a great plague smote the people.

וּמִי יִתֵּן כָּל עַם יְיָ נְבִיאִים, כִּי יִתֵּן יְיָ אֶת רוּחוֹ עֲלֵיהֶם.

# 22. NUMBERS [12–22]

**MEN APPOINTED TO EXPLORE CANAAN**

THE CHILDREN OF ISRAEL camped in the wilderness of Paran. And the Lord spoke to Moses, saying, "Send men to spy out the land of Canaan, [1] which I am giving to the Children of Israel. Send one man from every tribe, every one a prince among them."

---

[1] SENDING THE SPIES: Why did God tell Moses to send spies who, He knew, would bring back a false report? The Rabbis declared that the Israelites had demanded that spies be sent to Canaan. They said to Moses, "Let us send men to search out the land, to see whether the land is good."

When Moses spoke of this to God, He answered, "These are people of little faith! Were I to forbid them to send scouts, they would say it is because the land is not good! Therefore, Moses, choose twelve men to spy out Canaan, although this people is not ready to inherit the land."

שְׁלַח־לְךָ אֲנָשִׁים וְיָתֻרוּ אֶת אֶרֶץ כְּנַעַן אֲשֶׁר אֲנִי נוֹתֵן לִבְנֵי יִשְׂרָאֵל.

And Moses sent twelve men, all of them heads of the Children of Israel. And Moses said to them, "Go up into the Negev and into the mountains; and see what the land is like, and the people who live there: are they strong or weak? Are they few or many? And see what the land is like; is it good or bad? And the kind of cities in which they live: are they open camps or fortified cities? Is the land fat or lean, wooded or not? And do your best to bring of the fruit of the land." [2] The season was that of the first ripe grapes.

So they went up and scouted the land, from the wilderness of Zin to Rehob. And they went into the Negev and came to Hebron. And they came to the valley of Eshcol, and cut a branch there with only one cluster of grapes, and they had to carry it upon a pole between two men. They also took some pomegranates and some figs.

They returned from scouting the land at the end of forty days. And they came to Moses and to Aaron and to all the congregation of Israel, in the wilderness of Paran at Kadesh, and showed them the fruit of the land. And they said, "We came to the land to which you sent us, and surely it flows with milk and honey; and this is its fruit. However, the people that live in the land are fierce, and the cities are fortified and very great; and besides, we saw the children of Anak [giants] there."

And Caleb, the head of the tribe of Judah, silenced them and said, "We should go up at once and possess it, for we can certainly overcome it."

But the men who had gone up with him said, "We are not able to go up against the people, for they are stronger than we." And they spread an evil report about the land which they had explored, saying, "The land through which we have passed is a land that devours its inhabitants; and all the people we saw

---

ﻬ [2] THE INSTRUCTION OF MOSES: Moses instructed the spies: "Surely God will protect you, but do not bring upon yourselves needless danger. When you come to a city, do not slink in, but walk in and say that you wish to buy grapes and pomegranates.

"Observe the people carefully. If you find them dwelling in open cities, know that they are mighty warriors, for they depend upon their own strength, and have no fear. If, however, they live in fortified cities, they are weak and need the protection of walls.

"Bring of the fruit of the land, that our people may see it with their own eyes, and judge it."

עֲלֹה נַעֲלֶה וְיָרַשְׁנוּ אֹתָהּ כִּי יָכוֹל נוּכַל לָהּ.

are men of great stature. And there we saw the Nephilim, the sons of Anak, and we seemed to ourselves as grasshoppers, [3] and looked the same to them."

Then all the congregation lifted up their voices and cried; and the people wept that night. [4] And all the Children of Israel murmured against Moses and against Aaron; and they said, "Would that we had died in the land of Egypt! Or would we had died in this wilderness! Why does the Lord bring us to this land to fall by the sword? Our wives and our little ones will be a prey; would it not be better for us to return into Egypt?" And they said to one another, "Let us choose a captain and return to Egypt!"

Then Joshua and Caleb, who were among those that had spied out the land, tore their clothes. And they said to all the congregation of the Children of Israel, "The land which we explored is a very good land, a land flowing with milk and honey. If the Lord is pleased with us, He will bring us into this land

---

&#8766; [3] WE WERE AS GRASSHOPPERS: Why did the spies return with an unfavorable report? They had carried back the largest, most luscious fruit any of them had ever seen, and God had promised them Canaan, a green and fertile land.

The answer is simply that they were afraid. Although Joshua was to conquer them in forty years, the inhabitants were many and strong, and their appearance was frightening to the timid ex-slaves.

The spies did not doubt the beauty or the fertility of the land; they doubted themselves, and the Hebrew people. Therefore, they made the Canaanites seem even bigger and fiercer than they were.

&#8766; [4] A NIGHT OF TEARS: The spies tried various tactics. They went to their tents, put on sackcloth and began to weep bitterly. When their children asked why they were mourning, each gave the answer, "Woe is me, my children! Know that we are all doomed to be slain by the Canaanites. And only by reason of Moses' obstinacy!"

At these words, all the household began to wail. The neighbors came, and heard what the spy had said. Soon, "all the congregation lifted up their voices and cried; and the people wept that night."

In the morning they demanded of Moses, "Let us choose a captain and return to Egypt."

הָאָרֶץ אֲשֶׁר עָבַרְנוּ בָהּ לָתוּר אוֹתָהּ טוֹבָה הָאָרֶץ מְאֹד מְאֹד, אֶרֶץ אֲשֶׁר הִיא זָבַת חָלָב וּדְבָשׁ.

and give it to us. Only do not rebel against the Lord, nor fear the people of the land; for they are bread for us. Their shadow has departed from them, [5] and the Lord is with us. Fear them not!"

But the whole congregation was ready to stone them, when the glory of the Lord appeared to all the Children of Israel in the Tent of Meeting.

And the Lord said to Moses, "How long will this people despise Me? And how long will they not believe in Me despite all the wonders which I have worked among them? I will smite them with pestilence and destroy them, but I will make of you a nation greater and mightier than they."

And Moses said to the Lord, "When the Egyptians shall hear that Thou shalt kill this people as one man, they will say: Because the Lord was not able to bring this people into the land which He promised them, therefore He has slain them in the wilderness. Now show Thy greatness, for Thou hast said: The Lord is slow to anger and full of lovingkindness, forgiving sins and wrongdoing. Pardon, I pray Thee, the sin of this people according to the greatness of Thy lovingkindness, as Thou hast forgiven this people since Thou didst bring them out of Egypt until now."

And the Lord said, "I have pardoned as you ask. But as surely as I live, and

---

◄§ [5] THEIR DEFENSE HAS DEPARTED: Jewish teaching has always stressed that Jews are not the only righteous. Noah is an outstanding example of a righteous non-Jew, and Job, the suffering servant of God, another.

Our Sages maintained that Job dwelt in Canaan, and that the spies were ordered to inquire if he was still alive. If not, the Israelites need not fear the Canaanites, as there was not among them one pious man whose merits might shield them. When the spies reached the land, they found that Job had just died, and there was no longer a righteous man to protect Canaan.

This echoes the Talmudic tale of the travelers who came to a town and asked for the *neturé karta,* the "protectors of the city." When they were taken to the armed watchmen, the travelers said, "This is not what we mean." At length they were shown the teachers and the children studying Torah. "These are the protectors of the city," the visitors said. "Unless the Lord guard the city, the watchman wakes but in vain" (Psalms 127:1).

וַיֹּאמֶר יְיָ: סָלַחְתִּי כִּדְבָרֶךָ.

as the whole earth shall be filled with the glory of the Lord, those men who have seen My glory and My wonders which I performed in Egypt and in the wilderness, and yet have not listened to Me, surely they shall not see the land which I promised to their fathers. All of you from twenty years up, you who have muttered against Me, surely you shall not enter the land in which I promised to settle you, except Caleb and Joshua.

"But your little ones, that you said would become prey, I will bring in, and they shall know the land which you have rejected. But as for you, your carcasses shall fall in this wilderness; and your children shall be wanderers in the wilderness for forty years."

And Moses told this to all the Children of Israel, and the people mourned greatly.

And the men whom Moses had sent to spy out the land, and who had spread an evil report, died by the plague. But Joshua and Caleb remained alive.

FRINGES

THE LORD SPOKE to Moses, saying, "Speak to the Children of Israel, and bid them to make fringes [6] on the corners of their garments throughout their generations, and they shall put a thread of blue [7] in the fringe at each corner.

"When you look at it you will remember all the commandments of the Lord and do them, and will not go astray by following the inclinations of your heart and your eyes. Thus may you remember and carry out all My commandments, and be holy to your God. I am the Lord your God, who brought you out of the land of Egypt to be your God; I am the Lord your God."

---

᭡ [6] FRINGES AND SLAVERY: What has Egypt to do with the fringes on garments? And why should fringes be worn?

Long garments with fringes, especially in the costly blue dye, were the garb of free men. Slaves wore short robes without ornaments that might interfere with their work.

When the Hebrews stood before God, they would stand as free men.

᭡ [7] THREAD OF BLUE: There is no longer a blue thread among the fringes of the *Talit*. The blue dye, which was derived from a mollusk found near the coast of Phoenicia, was rare and costly. The Rabbis agreed, therefore, that white wool thread alone would suffice.

וּרְאִיתֶם אֹתוֹ, וּזְכַרְתֶּם אֶת כָּל מִצְוֹת יְיָ וַעֲשִׂיתֶם אֹתָם, וְלֹא תָתוּרוּ אַחֲרֵי לְבַבְכֶם וְאַחֲרֵי עֵינֵיכֶם.

KORAH'S REBELLION

NOW KORAH, [8] of the tribe of Levi, with Dathan and Abiram and On, of the tribe of Reuben, [9] became rebellious, and they took with them two hundred and fifty men, leaders of the congregation. They assembled themselves together against Moses and against Aaron, and said to them, "You take too much authority! All the congregation are holy, [10] since the Lord is among them. Why do you raise yourselves above the assembly of the Lord?"

When Moses heard this he bowed low. [11] And he said to Korah and to all his company, "Hear, you sons of Levi: is it a small thing that the God of Israel has singled you out from the community of Israel, to do the service at the Tabernacle of the Lord, to stand before the congregation and minister to them, that you should seek priesthood also? For this you and all your company have

---

◦§ [8] KORAH: "And Korah took . . ." The Hebrew text does not immediately specify what Korah took. The Midrash Tanḥuma said that he took himself and separated himself from the congregation. In fact, the ancient Aramaic translation of the text renders the first words as, "And Korah separated himself."

◦§ [9] REUBEN: Why was the tribe of Reuben, and no other, implicated with Levi? They were encamped next to the tribe of Levi, and thus were influenced by them. As Rashi says (Numbers 16:1), "Woe to the wicked, woe to his neighbor."

◦§ [10] ALL ARE HOLY: Korah, like all who rebel with no cause, contradicts himself. First he maintains that Israel needs no leaders, since all Israel is holy and God is among them. Then we discover that Korah and his Levite followers wish to replace Aaron and the *Kohanim* in the Tabernacle worship. In effect, they say they wish no leaders but themselves.

◦§ [11] MOSES BOWED LOW: Why did Moses seem to give up when faced with Korah's rebellion? Moses had pleaded for the rebellious Hebrews three times before, but now he felt himself powerless.

This may be compared to the story of a prince who disobeyed his

אוֹי לָרָשָׁע וְאוֹי לִשְׁכֵנוֹ.

gathered together against the Lord? And what has Aaron done that you should grumble against him?"

And Moses sent for Dathan and Abiram, but they said, "We will not go up! [12] Is it not enough that you have brought us up out of a land flowing with milk and honey to kill us in the wilderness, but must you also make yourself a ruler over us? Moreover, you have not brought us into a land flowing with milk and honey, nor given us an inheritance of fields and vineyards. Are you trying to deceive these men? We will not come up!"

And Moses was angered, and said to the Lord, "Do not accept their offering. I have not taken a single donkey from them, neither have I done harm to any of them."

Korah assembled the whole congregation against Moses and Aaron at the door of the Tent of Meeting, and the glory of the Lord appeared.

And the Lord spoke to Moses and Aaron, saying, "Separate yourselves from this congregation that I may destroy them immediately!"

Then they fell upon their faces and said, "O God, the God of the spirits of all flesh, if one man sins, wilt Thou be angry with all the congregation?"

And the Lord spoke to Moses, saying, "Speak to the congregation, saying: Withdraw from the dwelling of Korah, Dathan, and Abiram!"

And Moses arose and went to Dathan and Abiram, and the elders of Israel followed him. And he spoke to the congregation, saying, "Depart, I pray you, from the tents of these wicked men and touch nothing of theirs, lest you be swept away because of their sins."

So they left the dwellings of Korah, Dathan and Abiram.

And Moses said, "By this shall you know that the Lord has sent me to do all these deeds, and that I have not done

---

father. A friend had pleaded with the angry king to forgive his son. Three times the king heeded the friend, but when the prince offended the fourth time, the friend felt himself powerless.

᪐ [12] WE WILL NOT GO UP: Moses asked Dathan and Abiram to come to him that they might discuss the situation. The two rebels took his request as a formal summons and replied, "We will not go up." They did not recognize him as their leader.

Moses was hurt that they would not so much as talk with him, so he himself went to them.

אַל תֵּפֶן אֶל מִנְחָתָם. לֹא חֲמוֹר אֶחָד מֵהֶם נָשָׂאתִי וְלֹא הֲרֵעֹתִי אֶת אַחַד מֵהֶם.

them of my own mind. If these men die as all men die, and suffer the fate of all men, then the Lord has not sent me. But if the Lord does something unheard-of, and the ground opens its mouth and swallows them up with all they possess, and they go down alive into the pit, then you shall know that these men despised the Lord."

As he finished saying these words, the ground under them split open. And the earth opened its mouth and swallowed them, with all the men who followed Korah, and all their goods. And the earth closed upon them, and they perished from the community.

And all Israel that were round about them fled, for they said, "The earth might swallow us!"

## AARON'S ROD BLOSSOMS

BUT ON THE next day the whole congregation of the Children of Israel grumbled against Moses and against Aaron, saying, "It is you who have slain the people of the Lord!" [13]

When the congregation assembled against Moses and Aaron, they looked toward the Tent of Meeting, and there was the cloud covering it, and the glory of the Lord appeared.

And the Lord spoke to Moses, saying, "Speak to the Children of Israel, and take a rod from each tribe, twelve rods in all. And you shall write every man's name upon his rod, and Aaron's name upon the rod of Levi. And you shall place them in the Tent of Meeting before the Ark, where I meet with you. And the rod of the man whom I choose shall blossom; [14] and thus will I stop the grumbling of the Children of Israel."

Moses spoke to the Children of Israel, and they gave him one rod for every one of their princes of their tribes, twelve rods in all; and Aaron's rod was among theirs.

---

[13] YOU HAVE SLAIN: "Moses and Aaron asked God to punish Korah and his followers because they felt personally insulted," the people said. They did not recognize that Korah's rebellion had threatened the whole structure of the Israelites, as well as their role as bearers of the Torah. If Korah had prevailed, Israel would have become obscure desert tribes with no purpose.

[14] HIS ROD SHALL BLOSSOM: The tribe whose rod blossoms will have within it the seed for the future flowering and fruit-bearing of all the people.

וַתִּפְתַּח הָאָרֶץ אֶת פִּיהָ וַתִּבְלַע אוֹתָם וְאֶת בָּתֵּיהֶם, וְאֶת כָּל הָאָדָם אֲשֶׁר לְקֹרַח וְאֶת כָּל הָרְכוּשׁ.

And Moses placed the rods before the Lord in the Tent of Meeting.

On the next day, when Moses entered the Tent, he found that the rod of Aaron for the tribe of Levi had budded, and bloomed blossoms, and bore ripe almonds. [15]

And Moses brought out all the rods from before the Lord to the Children of Israel; and they looked, and each man took his rod.

And the Lord said to Moses, "Put back the rod of Aaron before the Ark, to keep there as a sign for the rebellious men, that there may be made an end of their grumbling against Me, that they may not die."

And Moses did just as the Lord commanded him.

MOSES STRIKES THE ROCK

THE PEOPLE CAMPED in Kadesh; and Miriam died there and was buried there.

And there was no water for the congregation, and they assembled against Moses and against Aaron. And the people quarreled with Moses, saying, "Why have you brought the congregation of the Lord into this wilderness to die, we and our cattle? Why have you made us come up out of Egypt to this evil place? There is no grain, nor figs, nor vines, nor pomegranates; there is not even water to drink!"

And Moses and Aaron went from the congregation to the door of the Tent of Meeting, and fell upon their faces; and the glory of the Lord appeared to them.

And the Lord said to Moses, "Take the rod and assemble the congregation, you and Aaron your brother. Speak to the rock in the presence of all the congregation, so that it will give forth water; and you shall bring forth water out of the rock, so you shall give drink to the congregation and their cattle."

And Moses took the rod from its place before the Lord. Then Moses and Aaron assembled the congregation before the rock, and he said, "Hear, you rebels! Shall we bring water for you out of the rock?"

And Moses lifted up his hand and struck the rock with his rod twice; and

[15] WHY ALMONDS? The almond tree is the first to blossom and mature in the land of Israel. All the other trees soon follow. This indicates that Aaron and the Levites were not favored over the rest of the Israelites. They will merely lead the way, the others will follow them and attain the same spiritual level.

שִׁמְעוּ נָא הַמֹּרִים – הֲמִן הַסֶּלַע הַזֶּה נוֹצִיא לָכֶם מָיִם? וַיָּרֶם מֹשֶׁה אֶת יָדוֹ וַיַּךְ אֶת הַסֶּלַע בְּמַטֵּהוּ פַּעֲמָיִם.

water gushed out, and the congregation and their cattle drank.

And the Lord said to Moses and Aaron, "Because you did not believe in Me enough to sanctify Me in the eyes of the Children of Israel, therefore you shall not bring this congregation into the land which I have given them."

These are the Waters of Meribah: that is, the place where the Children of Israel quarreled with the Lord.

### ON THE BORDERS OF EDOM

THEN MOSES SENT messengers from Kadesh to the king of Edom: "Thus says your brother Israel: You know all the hardship that has befallen us; how our fathers went down into Egypt, and we dwelt there a long time; and the Egyptians treated us badly. And when we cried to the Lord, He heard our voice, and sent an angel, and brought us forth out of Egypt. Behold, we are in Kadesh, a city on your border. Let us pass, we pray you, through your land. We will not pass through field or through vineyard, neither will we drink the water of your wells. We will go along the king's highway, turning neither to the right nor to the left, until we have passed your border."

And Edom said to him, "You shall not pass through me, or I will come out with the sword against you."

And the Children of Israel said to him, "We will go up only by the highway; and if we drink of your water, we and our cattle, we will pay for it. Only let us pass through on foot; there is no harm in it."

But he said, "You shall not pass through." And Edom came out against them with many people and with a strong hand.

Thus Edom refused to give Israel passage through his border. Therefore Israel turned aside.

### AARON DIES AT MOUNT HOR

THEY JOURNEYED from Kadesh, and the whole congregation of Israel came to Mount Hor. And the Lord spoke to Moses and Aaron at Mount Hor, near the border of the land of Edom, saying, "Aaron shall be gathered to his people, for he shall not enter into the land which I have given to the Children of Israel, because you rebelled against My word at the Waters of Meribah. Take Aaron and Eleazar, his son, and bring them up to Mount Hor. And strip Aaron of his robes, and put them on Eleazar, his son; and Aaron shall be gathered to his people and shall die there."

Then Moses did as the Lord commanded, and they ascended Mount Hor before the eyes of the whole community. Moses stripped Aaron of his robes and

יַעַן לֹא הֶאֱמַנְתֶּם בִּי לְהַקְדִּישֵׁנִי לְעֵינֵי בְּנֵי יִשְׂרָאֵל, לָכֵן לֹא תָבִיאוּ אֶת הַקָּהָל הַזֶּה אֶל הָאָרֶץ אֲשֶׁר נָתַתִּי לָהֶם.

put them on Eleazar, his son; and Aaron
died there on the top of the mountain,
and Moses and Eleazar came down from
the mountain.

And when all the congregation saw
that Aaron was dead, the whole house
of Israel wept for Aaron thirty days. [16]

## THE WARS AGAINST SIHON AND OG

THEN ISRAEL SENT messengers to Sihon,
king of the Amorites, [17] saying, "Let
me pass through your land; we will not
turn aside into field or into vineyard; we
will not drink the water of your wells.

---

[16] THE WHOLE HOUSE OF ISRAEL WEPT: It is written that when
Moses died, "the Children of Israel wept for Moses." At Aaron's
death, however, "the whole house wept."

This shows, said our Sages, that only part of the people mourned
for Moses, whereas all wept for Aaron. Aaron was the peacemaker.
When he saw two people quarreling, he spoke to each separately.
saying, "You do not know how the man you quarreled with regrets
his action!" As a result, when the quarrelers met, they greeted each
other as friends.

When Aaron heard that someone was transgressing God's precepts,
he went out of his way to see him often. He greeted him cordially, and
talked to him as a friend. His kindliness led many evildoers to change
their ways; for if such a one was tempted to sin, he would think to
himself, "If I do this, how will I be able to talk with my friend Aaron
and not blush with shame?"

Many marriages were saved by Aaron. If he heard of discord between husband and wife, Aaron talked with each alone, and made
peace between them. The Israelites so revered him that no less than
eighty thousand boys bore the name Aaron, in honor of the High
Priest who valued peace above all else. He was known not only as
*Ohev Shalom* (Lover of Peace), but also as *Rodef Shalom* (Pursuer
of Peace).

But Moses was leader and lawgiver. It was he who forced the
Children of Israel to change their lives, to forgo the fleshpots of
Egypt, and to learn to live as a free people. He was the one who
judged the guilty; and in so doing he made enemies.

אוֹהֵב שָׁלוֹם וְרוֹדֵף שָׁלוֹם.

We will go by the king's highway until we have passed your border."

But Sihon did not permit Israel to pass through his border. Sihon gathered all his forces together and went out against Israel into the wilderness. And Israel smote him with the edge of the sword, and possessed his land from the Arnon to the Jabbok.

And they turned and went up by the way of Bashan; and Og, the king of Bashan, went out against them, he and all his people, to battle at Edrei.

Og, the king of Bashan, was the only one who remained of the Rephaim, the giants; behold, his bedstead was of iron, nine cubits long and four cubits wide!

And the Lord said to Moses, "Do not be afraid of him, for I have delivered him and all his people and all his land into your hand. You will do to him as you did to Sihon, king of the Amorites."

So the Children of Israel smote Og and his sons and all his people, and they possessed his land.

And the Children of Israel journeyed, and camped in the plains of Moab on the other side of the Jordan, near Jericho.

---

ᴇᴈ [17] MESSENGERS OF PEACE: At first God said to Moses, "I have given in your hand Sihon, the Amorite, and his land. Begin the conquest."

Moses, however, sent messengers of peace to Sihon, saying, "Let me pass through your land; we shall not turn aside."

God was pleased at this. "Though I told you to start the war immediately, you sent messengers of peace to Sihon. I will affirm your action in law. Therefore, write in the Torah: When you draw near a city to fight against it, you first shall offer it peace" (Deuteronomy 20:10).

This law had to be observed even toward the Canaanite nations whom God had commanded to be utterly destroyed. Our Sages say that Joshua wrote to all the inhabitants of Canaan, "Whosoever would migrate from here to another country, let him do so. Whosoever would make peace with us, with him we shall make peace. And whosoever would war on us, let him know that we are ready."

The Girgashites chose to leave Canaan, and God gave them in exchange a land as good. The Gibeonites offered peace, and the Children of Israel did not smite them. The other thirty-one kings of Canaan made war against Israel and were destroyed.

אַל תִּירָא אוֹתוֹ כִּי בְיָדְךָ נָתַתִּי אוֹתוֹ וְאֶת כָּל עַמּוֹ וְאֶת אַרְצוֹ.

# 23. NUMBERS [22-24]

## BALAAM

BALAK, THE KING of Moab, saw all that Israel had done to the Amorites. And Moab was in great fear of the Israelites because they were many. And Moab said to the elders of Midian, "Now this multitude will lick clean all that is round about us, as the ox licks up the grass of the field."

So Balak sent messengers to Balaam, [1] the son of Beor, at Pethor, by the Euphrates River, to call him, saying, "Behold, there is a people who have come out of Egypt! They cover the face of the earth and they are settled opposite me. Now come and curse this people for me, for they are too mighty for me. Perhaps I may be able to defeat them and drive them out of the land;

---

[1] BALAAM, A HEATHEN PROPHET: All humanity are God's children, and God has sent sages and prophets to all the nations.

Balaam was one of the pagan prophets, as were Job and Jethro. All were descendants of Abraham's brother, Nahor.

The Prophets of Israel felt compassion for all nations. Jeremiah

וְעַתָּה לְכָה נָּא אָרָה לִּי אֶת הָעָם הַזֶּה כִּי עָצוּם הוּא מִמֶּנִּי. אוּלַי אוּכַל נַכֶּה בּוֹ
וַאֲגָרְשֶׁנּוּ מִן הָאָרֶץ.

for I know that he whom you bless is blessed, and he whom you curse is cursed."

And the elders of Moab and of Midian departed, and came to Balaam and spoke to him the words of Balak. And he said to them, "Lodge here tonight, and I will give you an answer, as the Lord may speak to me." [2] So the princes of Moab stayed with Balaam.

And God came to Balaam and said, "Who are these men with you?"

And Balaam said to God, "Balak, king of Moab, has sent them to me, saying: Behold, the people that has come out of Egypt cover the face of the earth. Come now and curse them for me; perhaps I shall be able to fight against them and shall drive them out."

And God said to Balaam, "You shall not go with them; you shall not curse the people; for they are blessed."

So Balaam rose in the morning and said to the princes of Balak, "Go back to your land, [3] for the Lord bade me not to go with you."

Then the princes of Moab left, and came to Balak and said, "Balaam refuses to come with us."

And Balak sent princes again, more

---

said, "Therefore, I will wail for Moab; yea, I will cry out for all Moab" (48:31).

Ezekiel prophesied, "And you, son of man, take up a lamentation for Tyre" (27:2).

Balaam, however, was willing to curse a whole nation for his own gain.

ᕬᕒ [2] THE LORD MAY SPEAK TO ME: When the messengers came to Balaam, he was eager to accompany them, for he hoped to be richly rewarded. But God revealed Himself to him in a dream and said, "Do not go with them!"

"May I curse the Israelites from here?" Balaam inquired.

"You shall not curse them from here," God replied.

To curry favor with God, Balaam then asked, "Shall I bless them?"

"They need neither your honey nor your sting," was the reply.

ᕬᕒ [3] GO BACK TO YOUR LAND: Balaam did not tell the messengers that God had forbidden him to curse Israel. He reported only, "the Lord bade me not to go with you." Balak assumed that Balaam would not

לֹא תֵלֵךְ עִמָּהֶם; לֹא תָאֹר אֶת הָעָם כִּי בָרוּךְ הוּא.

in number and more distinguished than the others. And they came to Balaam and said, "Thus said Balak: Do not refuse to come to me, for I will reward you with very great honor, and whatever you say to me I will do; come and curse this people for me."

But Balaam answered, "If Balak would give me his house filled with silver and gold, I could not go against the word of the Lord, my God. But stay here this night, that I may know what else the Lord will speak to me."

And God came to Balaam at night and said, "If the men have come to call you, arise and go with them; but only the word which I speak to you shall you do."

### BALAAM'S DONKEY

SO BALAAM ROSE in the morning and saddled his donkey, and went with the princes of Moab. And God's anger was aroused because he went; and the angel of the Lord placed himself on the road to obstruct him. He rode on his donkey, and his two servants were with him.

Then the donkey saw the angel of the Lord standing on the road, with his drawn sword in his hand. And the donkey turned aside and went into the field; and Balaam struck the donkey to turn her back to the road.

Then the angel of the Lord stood in a narrow path between the vineyards. And the donkey saw the angel of the Lord and she pressed herself against the wall, and thrust Balaam's foot against the wall. And Balaam struck her again.

The angel of the Lord went further, and stood in a narrow place where there was no room to turn either right or left. When the donkey saw the angel of the Lord, she lay down under Balaam; and Balaam's anger was kindled and he struck the donkey with his staff.

---

accompany the messengers because they were not important enough, so he sent men of higher rank. To these, also, Balaam declared that he could not defy the Lord; yet he did not impart the full truth. The messengers gathered that he desired a greater reward. Balaam revealed his greed when he mentioned a house filled with silver.

In the night, God spoke once more to Balaam, "You wish to go to Moab because you expect to be rewarded. Go then, but speak only the words I say."

Man has free will. Our Sages say, "God permits man to go upon the road he chooses to travel."

אִם־יִתֶּן־לִי בָלָק מְלֹא בֵיתוֹ כֶּסֶף וְזָהָב לֹא אוּכַל לַעֲבֹר אֶת פִּי יְיָ אֱלֹהָי.

Then the Lord opened the mouth of the donkey and she said to Balaam, "What have I done to you that you have beaten me three times?"

And Balaam said to the donkey, "Because you have mocked me! If I had a sword in my hand now, I would kill you!"

And the donkey said to Balaam, "Am I not your donkey upon which you have ridden all your life long until this day? Was I disposed to act this way to you?" And Balaam said, "No."

Then the Lord opened Balaam's eyes, and he saw the angel of the Lord standing in the way, with his drawn sword in his hand; and he bowed his head and fell on his face.

And the angel of the Lord said to him, "Why have you struck your donkey three times? It was I who obstructed the road; and the donkey saw me and turned aside before me these three times. If she had not turned aside from me, I would have killed you but let her live."

And Balaam said to the angel of the Lord, "I have sinned; for I did not know that you stood in the way against me. Now, if it displeases you, I will go back."

But the angel of the Lord said to Balaam, "Go with the men; but only the word that I say to you shall you speak."

So Balaam went with the princes of Balak.

## BALAAM BLESSES THE CHILDREN OF ISRAEL

WHEN BALAK HEARD that Balaam had come, he went out to meet him. And Balak said to Balaam, "Did I not send for you urgently? Why did you not come to me? Did you think I am not able to honor you?"

And Balaam said, "See, I have come to you; but do I have power to speak anything? Only the word that God puts in my mouth shall I speak."

The next morning Balak took Balaam, and brought him up into Bamoth-baal, and from there he saw the border of the people [Israel]. And Balaam said to Balak, "Build me seven altars here, and prepare for me seven bullocks and seven rams."

And Balak did as Balaam said; and Balak and Balaam offered on each altar a bullock and a ram. Then Balaam said to Balak, "Stand here by your burnt-offering and I will go; perhaps the Lord will meet me, and whatever He reveals to me I will tell you."

So he went alone. And God met Balaam, and put a message in his mouth and said, "Return to Balak and thus you shall speak."

And Balaam returned and found Balak standing by his burnt-offering, with all the princes of Moab. And Balaam took up his message and said:

וַיִּפְתַּח יְיָ אֶת פִּי הָאָתוֹן וַתֹּאמֶר לְבִלְעָם: מֶה עָשִׂיתִי לְךָ כִּי הִכִּיתַנִי זֶה שָׁלשׁ רְגָלִים?

"From Aram Balak brings me,
The king of Moab, from the
    mountains of the East:
Come, curse Jacob for me,
Come, speak Israel's doom.


"How shall I curse whom God has
    not cursed?
How can I doom whom the Lord
    has not doomed?
From the top of the rocks I see him,
From the hills I behold him.
Behold, it is a people that
    dwell apart,
Not to be reckoned among the
    nations.


"Who can count the dust of Jacob,
Or number the stock of Israel?
May I die the death of the
    righteous,
And may my end be like his!"


And Balak said to Balaam, "What
have you done to me? I brought you to
curse my enemies, but you have blessed
them!"

And Balaam answered, "Must I not
take heed, to speak what the Lord puts
in my mouth?"

Then Balak said to him, "Come with
me to another place from which you
may see only part of them, and curse
them for me from there." And he took
him to the summit of Sedeh-zophim,

and built there seven altars, and offered
up a bullock and a ram on every altar.
Then Balaam said, "Stand here by your
burnt-offering, while I go to meet Him
yonder."

And the Lord met Balaam and put a
message in his mouth, and said, "Return
to Balak and thus you shall speak." So
he returned to Balak, who stood by his
burnt-offering with the princes of Moab.
And Balaam said:


"Arise, Balak, and hear!
Give ear to me, son of Zippor:
God is not a man, that
    He should lie,
Nor a human being, that He should
    change His mind.
What He has said, will He not do?
And when He has spoken, will He
    not fulfill?


"Behold, I am bidden to bless,
And when He has blessed, I cannot
    reverse it.
No one has seen iniquity in Jacob,
Neither has any one seen evil in
    Israel.
The Lord his God is with him,
And the acclaim of the King is
    among them."


Then Balak said to Balaam, "Neither
curse them nor bless them." But Balaam
answered and said, "Did I not say to

מַה אֶקֹּב לֹא קַבֹּה אֵל, וּמַה אֶזְעֹם לֹא זָעַם יְיָ?

you: All that the Lord speaks, that I must do?"

And Balak said to Balaam, "Come now, I will take you to another place; perhaps it will please God if you curse them for me from there."

And Balak took Balaam to the summit of Peor, that overlooks the wilderness. And Balaam said to Balak, "Build me seven altars here, and prepare for me seven bullocks and seven rams." So Balak did as Balaam said, and offered up a bullock and a ram on every altar.

When Balaam saw that it pleased the Lord to bless Israel, he turned his face toward the wilderness. And he saw Israel encamped tribe by tribe; and the spirit of God came upon him. And he lifted his voice, and said:

"The saying of Balaam, the son of
   Beor,
The saying of the man whose eye
   is opened,

The saying of one who hears the
   words of God,
Who sees the vision of the
   Almighty,
Prostrate, yet with opened eyes:
How goodly are your tents,
   O Jacob,
Your dwellings, O Israel! [4]

"As valleys stretched out,
As gardens by the riverside,
As aloes planted by the Lord,
As cedars beside the water;
Water shall flow from his branches,
And his seed shall be in many
   waters.

"He crouched, he lay down as a lion,
And as a lioness; who shall rouse
   him?
Blessed be those who bless you,
Cursed be those who curse you!"

Now Balak's anger blazed against

---

⤶ [4] BALAAM'S BLESSING: Balaam had intended to curse the Israelites, but when he saw their encampment stretched in orderly rows before him, the spirit of God came upon him, and he raised his voice in blessing.

So the Rabbis interpret Balaam's words, "your tents, O Jacob," to mean the synagogues; "your dwellings, O Israel," the houses of study. From this we learn that when Israel lives in peace, studying God's Torah and living by His teaching, even the greedy prophet must stand and praise.

מַה טֹּבוּ אֹהָלֶיךָ יַעֲקֹב, מִשְׁכְּנֹתֶיךָ יִשְׂרָאֵל !

Balaam, and he struck his fists together; and he said to Balaam, "I called you to curse my enemies, and you have blessed them three times. Therefore flee to your home! I had planned to honor you greatly, but the Lord has kept you back from honor."

And Balaam said to Balak, "Did I not tell your messengers whom you sent to me: If Balak were to give me his house full of silver and gold, I could not go beyond the word of the Lord to do either good or bad of my own mind. What the Lord speaks, that will I speak. And now, as I return to my people, let me tell you what this people will do to your people in days to come:

"I see them, but not as of now;
I behold them, but not in the near future;
A star shall step forth out of Jacob,
And a sceptre shall rise out of Israel,
And shall strike through the brow of Moab,
And break down all the sons of Seth.
And Edom shall become a possession,
But Israel will do valiantly,
And Jacob shall conquer his enemies."

Then Balaam arose and returned home. [5] And Balak also went his way.

---

⤴ [5] BALAAM'S ADVICE: Before Balaam returned to his home, the kings asked him how Israel could be destroyed.

Balaam answered, "Go to their synagogues. If you hear children's voices studying the Torah, you cannot destroy Israel. If the voices are silent, you may.

"For their patriarch Isaac said: 'The voice is the voice of Jacob, but the hands are the hands of Esau'" (Genesis 27:22). This means that so long as the sound of learning (the voice of Jacob) is heard, those who wish to destroy Israel (the hands of Esau) shall not succeed. Israel will perish when her children cease to study.

אֶרְאֶנּוּ וְלֹא עַתָּה, אֲשׁוּרֶנּוּ וְלֹא קָרוֹב; דָּרַךְ כּוֹכָב מִיַּעֲקֹב וְקָם שֵׁבֶט מִיִּשְׂרָאֵל.

# 24. NUMBERS [26–36]

### THE CENSUS AT THE END OF FORTY YEARS

AND THE LORD spoke to Moses and to Eleazar, the son of Aaron, saying, "Take a census of the whole congregation of Israel from twenty years old and upward, tribe by tribe, all who are able to go forth to war."

And the Children of Israel numbered six hundred and one thousand and seven hundred and thirty. But among them was not a man who was numbered by Moses and Aaron in the wilderness of Sinai. For the Lord had said of them,

"They shall surely die in the wilderness." So not one of them was left except Caleb, the son of Jephunneh, and Joshua, the son of Nun.

And the Lord said to Moses, "The land shall be divided as an inheritance according to the number of names. To the greater you shall give the larger inheritance, and to the fewer you shall give the lesser inheritance. The land shall be divided by lot; according to the names of the tribes of their fathers they shall inherit. So shall no inheritance pass from one tribe to another; for the Children of Israel shall keep each the inheritance of his own tribe."

לָאֵלֶּה תֵּחָלֵק הָאָרֶץ בְּנַחֲלָה בְּמִסְפַּר שֵׁמוֹת. לָרַב תַּרְבֶּה נַחֲלָתוֹ וְלַמְעַט תַּמְעִיט נַחֲלָתוֹ.

### DAUGHTERS, TOO, MAY INHERIT

THE DAUGHTERS OF Zelophehad, [1] of the families of Manasseh, drew near; and these are their names: Mahlah, Noah, Hoglah, Milcah, and Tirzah.

And they stood before Moses and before Eleazar the priest, and before the princes and all the congregation, at the door of the Tent of Meeting, and said, "Our father died in the wilderness, and he was not among those who gathered against the Lord; and he had no sons. Why should the name of our father be done away with in his own family just because he had no sons? Give us a possession among our father's brethren."

Moses brought their cause before the Lord. And the Lord said, "The daughters of Zelophehad speak rightly: you shall surely give them a possession of inheritance among their father's brothers. And you shall speak to the Children of Israel, saying: 'If a man dies without a son, then his inheritance shall pass to his daughter. And if he has no daughter, then you shall give his inheritance to his brothers. And it shall be a statute to the Children of Israel, as the Lord commanded Moses.' "

### A SUCCESSOR

AND THE LORD said to Moses, "Ascend this Mount Abarim [2] and behold the land which I have given to the Children of Israel. When you have seen it, you too shall be gathered to your people, as your brother Aaron was gathered."

And Moses spoke to the Lord, saying, "Let the Lord, the God of the spirits of all flesh, [3] appoint a man over the congregation who will lead them out and bring them in, so that the congregation of the Lord will not be as sheep without a shepherd."

---

⇜ [1] THE DAUGHTERS: From Israel's beginning, women were cherished and valued.

Protection of the daughter might come before the inheritance rights of the sons. If there was a son, married daughters received no share of an inheritance, but unmarried daughters received a portion. Provision for support of women was the first responsibility of the estate. If the property was small, the daughters received preference over the sons, who might get nothing.

⇜ [2] ASCEND MOUNT ABARIM: Why is Moses told in Numbers of his approaching death, although it does not occur until the end of Deu-

כֵּן בְּנוֹת צְלָפְחָד דֹּבְרֹת; נָתֹן תִּתֵּן לָהֶם אֲחֻזַּת נַחֲלָה בְּתוֹךְ אֲחֵי אֲבִיהֶם.

And the Lord said, "Take unto you Joshua, the son of Nun, a man of spirit, [4] and lay your hand upon him; and set him before Eleazar the priest, and before all the congregation, and commission him in their sight. And give him your authority, that all of the Children of Israel may obey. At his word shall they go out and at his word shall they come in, all the congregation."

And Moses did as the Lord commanded him. He took Joshua, and set him before Eleazar the priest, and before all the congregation. And he laid his hands upon him, [5] and charged him, as the Lord had spoken.

---

teronomy? The Midrash says that Moses already knew, after he had struck the rock at Meribah, that he would not be allowed to enter the Promised Land.

When God gave instructions on the dividing of the land among the tribes, He told Moses when he would die, so as not to raise false hopes within him.

[3] GOD OF THE SPIRITS OF ALL FLESH: Why does Moses use this unusual form of address to God? The phrase appears here, and also in Numbers 16:22, in both cases with the same meaning—that of the multitudes of people on this earth, each is an individual with a soul of his own.

[4] WHY JOSHUA? After the daughters of Zelophehad left, Moses asked, "If even daughters may inherit, why cannot my son inherit the leadership, as the son of Aaron inherited the priesthood?"

And God replied, "He that watches the fig tree shall eat its fruit. Your sons will not inherit your leadership because they concerned themselves not with the Torah. Joshua, however, served you with devotion and prepared himself for leadership. He has earned the right of succession."

[5] LAID HIS HANDS UPON HIM: God told Moses to lay his hand upon Joshua's head, to signify that he is leader. So great was Moses' concern for the man who was to succeed him, that he placed both his hands on Joshua's head.

קַח לְךָ אֶת יְהוֹשֻׁעַ בִּן־נוּן, אִישׁ אֲשֶׁר רוּחַ בּוֹ, וְסָמַכְתָּ אֶת יָדְךָ עָלָיו.

### THE TWO AND A HALF TRIBES

NOW THE TRIBE of Reuben and the tribe of Gad had a very great multitude of cattle. And when they saw that the land of Jazer and the land of Gilead were a suitable place for cattle, they came and spoke to Moses, saying, "This land which the Lord has conquered for the congregation of Israel is a land for cattle, and your servants have cattle. If we have found favor in your sight, let this land be given to your servants as a possession; do not take us across the Jordan."

And Moses said to the children of Gad and of Reuben, "Shall your brothers go to war and you sit here?"

And they came near him and said, "We will build sheepfolds here for our livestock, and cities for our little ones; but we ourselves will be armed and ready to go before the Children of Israel until we have brought them to their homes. We will not return to our own homes until the Children of Israel have each inherited his inheritance."

And Moses said, "If you will do this thing, if you will arm and go before the Lord into battle, and every armed man of you will cross the Jordan and fight until the land be subdued, then you will be clear before the Lord and before Israel, and this land shall be your possession. But if you will not do so, you will have sinned against the Lord, and be assured that your sin will find you out. So build your cities for your little ones and folds for your sheep, and keep your promise."

And Moses gave to the children of Gad and of Reuben, and to the half-tribe of Manasseh, the son of Joseph, the kingdom of Sihon, king of the Amorites, and the kingdom of Og, king of Bashan.

### CITIES OF REFUGE

AND THE LORD spoke to Moses, saying, "Speak to the Children of Israel, and say to them: When you cross the Jordan into the land of Canaan, you shall select cities to be cities of refuge [6] for you, so that a man who kills any person through error may flee there. These cities shall serve you as refuge from the avenger, that the slayer not die until he stand trial before the congregation.

---

&ъ [6] CITIES OF REFUGE: Why was Moses so interested in the cities of refuge? It is said that only he who has eaten a food knows its taste. Since Moses had unintentionally killed an Egyptian, he knew the feelings of a pursued man.

וַיֹּאמֶר מֹשֶׁה לִבְנֵי גָד וְלִבְנֵי רְאוּבֵן: הַאַחֵיכֶם יָבֹאוּ לַמִּלְחָמָה וְאַתֶּם תֵּשְׁבוּ פֹה?

"There shall be six cities of refuge, three cities beyond the Jordan, and three cities in the land of Canaan. These six cities shall serve as a refuge for the Children of Israel, and for the stranger and for the settler among them, so that anyone who kills a person through error may flee there.

"But if he struck him with an iron object, or with a stone, or with a weapon of wood so that he died, he is a murderer; the murderer shall be put to death. If he thrust him in hatred, or hurled something at him intentionally, or in enmity struck him with his hand so that he died, he is a murderer; he shall be put to death.

"But if he pushed him inadvertently, without enmity, or threw something at him unintentionally, or let a stone fall without seeing him, and he was not his enemy nor sought his harm, then the community shall judge between the slayer and the avenger of blood according to these regulations. And the community shall protect the manslayer from the avenger of blood; [7] and the community shall return him to his city of refuge to which he had fled, and he shall dwell in it.

---

~§ [7] AVENGER OF BLOOD: Avenging the death of a relative, even if his slaying was accidental, was required by custom, and even by law, in many supposedly civilized countries until very recently. In Arab lands to this day, a man who causes another's death, even by chance, is likely to be killed by the slain man's relatives. Every kinsman of the dead person is held responsible until the death is avenged.

Thousands of years ago our Scriptures legislated against senseless blood-letting, and forbade anyone to take the law into his own hands.

The statute on this was strict: the slayer had to flee to a special city of refuge, where the relatives could not touch him until after a trial. The court sent for the accused and tried him. If found guilty of willful murder, he was condemned; if not guilty, he was freed, and the avengers could not touch him without penalty of the law.

If the court decided that the slayer had killed unintentionally, he returned to the city of refuge, there to remain until the death of the High Priest. If he left it, the avengers could slay him without penalty.

Every city and town posted the locations of the refuge cities and the way to reach them.

וְהִצִּילוּ הָעֵדָה אֶת הָרוֹצֵחַ מִיַּד גּוֹאֵל הַדָּם, וְהֵשִׁיבוּ אוֹתוֹ הָעֵדָה אֶל עִיר מִקְלָטוֹ.

"But if the slayer ever goes beyond the bounds of his city of refuge to which he has fled, and the avenger of blood finds him outside and kills him, there shall be no blood-guilt for him. The slayer must remain in the city of refuge until the death of the High Priest.

"The testimony of a single witness shall not suffice for a death sentence.

"You shall accept no ransom for the life of a murderer who is guilty of murder; he shall surely be put to death. And you shall take no ransom in place of flight to the city of refuge. So you shall not pollute the land in which you are; for blood pollutes the land. And you shall not defile the land which you inhabit, in the midst of which I dwell; for I the Lord dwell in the midst of the Children of Israel."

וְעֵד אֶחָד לֹא יַעֲנֶה בְנֶפֶשׁ לָמוּת.

# 25. DEUTERONOMY [1-30]

**TAKE HEED LEST YOU FORGET**

THESE ARE THE words which Moses spoke to all Israel [1] beyond the Jordan. And it came to pass in the fortieth year, on the first day of the eleventh month, that Moses spoke to the Children of Israel all that the Lord had commanded him to say:

"And now, O Israel, heed the statutes and the ordinances which I teach you, to do them, that you may live and enter and possess the land which the Lord, the God of your fathers, gives you. For you who cleave to the Lord your God, are alive every one of you this day.

"I have taught you statutes and ordinances, as the Lord my God commanded

---

[1] TO ALL ISRAEL: The phrase "all Israel" in this case has special meaning. Why were "all" specified? The Israelites had been called together to hear a long discourse of exhortation and reproof. All had to attend so that no one should say, "I was not there. I cannot be held responsible."

וְאַתֶּם הַדְּבֵקִים בַּיָי אֱלֹהֵיכֶם חַיִּים כֻּלְּכֶם הַיּוֹם.

me. Observe and do them; [2] for this is your wisdom in the sight of the peoples, who when they hear all these statutes shall say: Surely this great nation is a wise and understanding people. For what great nation is there that has God so near to them as the Lord our God is whenever we call upon Him? And what great nation is there that has statutes and ordinances as righteous as all this Torah [3] which I give to you this day?

"Only take heed and watch most carefully that you do not forget the things which your eyes saw, [4] but make them known to your children and your children's children."

---

⤐ [2] OBSERVE AND DO THEM: Of all his subjects, only the Jews refused to worship Emperor Hadrian as a god. Therefore, he forbade the teaching of Judaism on pain of death. Nonetheless, Rabbi Akiba continued to teach the Torah. When his friend, Pappas, warned him of his peril, Akiba answered with a story.

It seems that a fox passed a stream and saw that the fish were greatly agitated. "We are trying to evade the fishermen's nets," they explained.

Said the wily fox, "Why not come up on dry land with me, and escape the fishermen?"

"If we are not safe in the water, which is our natural habitat," the fish replied, "how can we live on land?"

Akiba concluded with, "If we are not safe when we study the Torah, how can Judaism survive if we stop?"

⤐ [3] THIS TORAH: The Hebrew word "Torah" means "teaching" or "instruction." It is sometimes translated as "Law," a mistranslation which is unjust to the original. Torah comes from the root of the verb, "to aim at a target and hit it," just as the word ḥet (sin), comes from the root, "to aim at a target and miss it."

It was probably Philo, the Jewish sage of Alexandria of two thousand years ago, who used the term "Law" as translation for Torah. He meant to point out the logic of the Jewish religion as contrasted with Greek worship, in which there was neither order nor meaning.

וּשְׁמַרְתֶּם וַעֲשִׂיתֶם, כִּי הִיא חָכְמַתְכֶם וּבִינַתְכֶם לְעֵינֵי הָעַמִּים.

THE SH'MA—HEAR, O ISRAEL

"HEAR, O ISRAEL [5]— Sh'ma Yisrael—
the Lord is our God, the Lord is One!

"And you shall love [6] the Lord your
God with all your heart and with all
your soul [7] and with all your might.
And these words which I command you

---

ᴖᴕ [4] YOUR EYES SAW: Never before in human history had God revealed
Himself to an entire people. Every other revelation had been made
to an individual or to a few. At Sinai God revealed Himself to all
Israel, to make of them "a kingdom of priests and a holy people."

ᴖᴕ [5] HEAR, O ISRAEL: The Sh'ma, the essence of our faith, is recited
at every morning and evening prayer, as well as before retiring
at night.

It is so important that the Scribes set it apart from the rest of the
text with a large ayin in Sh'ma and a large dalet in Ehad. The dalet
is clearly distinguished so as not to be mistaken for a résh, which
would produce "the Lord is another," the very opposite of what is
intended. If the ayin in Sh'ma were misread as aleph, the word
would mean "perhaps." There is no "perhaps" in Israel's conviction
that "the Lord is our God, the Lord is One."

ᴖᴕ [6] AND YOU SHALL LOVE: The sage, the Ḥafetz Ḥayyim, observed
that when a child sits on his father's lap he first learns to know him,
then to love him, and at length to obey him. Similarly, we are told
first to acknowledge God, next to love Him, and finally to observe His
commandments.

ᴖᴕ [7] WITH ALL YOUR SOUL: The Romans seized Akiba and condemned him to death by torture. As his weeping pupils watched, the
old man's body was raked with iron combs. When the hour for the
evening prayer came, Akiba said, "All my life I loved God with all
my heart and all my might. Now, as I give up my soul to Him, I
know that I love Him with all my soul as well."

Then Rabbi Akiba recited the Sh'ma, and died.

שְׁמַע יִשְׂרָאֵל, יְיָ אֱלֹהֵינוּ, יְיָ אֶחָד.

this day [8] shall be upon your heart; and you shall teach them [9] diligently to your children, and shall talk of them when you sit in your house and when you walk by the way, and when you lie down and when you rise up. And you shall bind them [10] as a sign upon your hand, and they shall be as symbols be-tween your eyes. And you shall write them upon the doorposts [11] of your house and upon your gates."

### WHEN YOUR SON ASKS YOU

"WHEN YOUR SON asks [12] you in time to come: 'What is the meaning of the

---

◆§ [8] THIS DAY: The Hebrew word for "this day," can also mean "to-day." The Rabbis saw that both meanings applied to its use in the *Sh'ma*. Its teachings are never old or out of fashion, they pointed out, but are freshly commanded to us each day, and remain as vital and as significant as at first.

◆§ [9] TEACH THEM: The Hebrew word, *shinantam*, means "you shall cut them in," almost as though we were to chisel the teachings onto our children. It tells us that these ideas are not remote and unrealistic classroom lessons, but the very fabric of life and living.

In Judaism, the teaching of the word of God is considered the greatest *mitzvah* (commandment or "good deed"). The Jew does not worship because he fears God, but because he reveres the holiness, the goodness and the beauty of Judaism. "Know before whom you stand!" says the Talmud.

◆§ [10] BIND THEM: Traditional Jews take these words as an injunction to wear *T'fillin* (phylacteries).

◆§ [11] ON YOUR DOORPOSTS: This refers to the *M'zuzah*, a small parch-ment scroll (bearing the Sh'ma plus 11:13-21 of Deuteronomy), en-closed in a protective case. The *M'zuzah* is placed on the right door-post of the Jewish home.

The word *Shaddai*, the Almighty, which is written on the reverse of the parchment, is visible through a tiny window in the case. The

וְשִׁנַּנְתָּם לְבָנֶיךָ וְדִבַּרְתָּ בָּם, בְּשִׁבְתְּךָ בְּבֵיתֶךָ וּבְלֶכְתְּךָ בַדֶּרֶךְ וּבְשָׁכְבְּךָ וּבְקוּמֶךָ.

laws, the statutes, and the ordinances which the Lord our God has commanded you?' then you shall say to your son: 'We were Pharaoh's slaves in Egypt; [13] and the Lord showed signs and wonders, great and terrible, upon Egypt, and upon Pharaoh. <u>And He brought us out from there that He might bring us into the land which He promised to our fathers.</u> And the Lord commanded us to observe all these laws, to fear the Lord our God, for our good always, that He might keep us alive, as it is this day.

And we shall be righteous to the Lord our God if we observe all His commandments.' "

### WHY ISRAEL?

"WHEN THE LORD your God brings you into the land which you go to possess, He shall cast out many nations before you. Then you shall make no covenant with them; neither shall you marry with them: [14] you shall not give your daughter to his son, nor take his daugh-

---

M'zuzah is a symbol of God's watchful care. It serves to remind us, when we enter or leave, that our home is dedicated to the spirit of Judaism.

⤸ [12] WHEN YOUR SON ASKS: The *Pesaḥ Seder* is a fulfillment of the command to answer one's son properly. To make certain that the boy asks the question, the *Mah Nishtanah,* or Four Questions, is recited at the *Seder.*

The *Seder* is enlivened by songs. The search for the *Aphikoman* also serves to keep the children interested, so that the Biblical command may be fulfilled.

⤸ [13] SLAVES IN EGYPT: Spiritually we are all descendants of Pharaoh's slaves, even those of us who were converted to Judaism after the Exodus. Converts are considered children of Abraham, whose descendants were enslaved in Egypt. "Every Jew should regard himself as though he himself came forth from Egypt," the *Haggadah* tells us.

⤸ [14] YOU SHALL NOT MARRY THEM: To a small nation surrounded by different peoples, intermarriage was a grave threat. When an Israelite

וְאוֹתָנוּ הוֹצִיא מִשָּׁם לְמַעַן הָבִיא אוֹתָנוּ לָתֶת לָנוּ אֶת הָאָרֶץ אֲשֶׁר נִשְׁבַּע לַאֲבוֹתֵינוּ.

ter for your son. For they will turn away your children from following Me to serve other gods.

"But you shall break down their altars, and dash into pieces their gods. For you are a holy people to the Lord your God: the Lord your God has chosen you to be His own treasure, [15] from all peoples upon the earth. The Lord did not set His love upon you nor choose you because you were more numerous than any people, for you were the smallest of any people; [16] but because the Lord loved you, and because He would keep the oath which He swore to your fathers.

"Know, therefore, that the Lord your God, He is God; the faithful God who keeps covenant and mercy to a thousand generations with those who love Him and keep His commandments."

### AND YOU SHALL REMEMBER

"YOU SHALL OBSERVE all the commandments that I command you today, so that you may live and multiply, and enter and possess the land which the Lord promised to your fathers. And you shall remember the way the Lord your God has led you these forty years in the wilderness. And He afflicted you and allowed you to hunger, then fed you

---

married a heathen, he often was lost to Judaism, for he might be turned away from the worship of the One God. A marriage between a Jew and a convert to Judaism is not considered an intermarriage, however; it is a marriage of two Jews.

⋙ [15] HIS OWN TREASURE: The fact that Israel was chosen by God does not imply that other peoples are inferior. Every nation has its role to play in human history. The role of Judaism is to bring mankind closer to God and, therefore, to righteous ways. God's closeness is always linked with holiness; only as we are holy are we close to God. As the *Kiddush* says: "For You have chosen us and sanctified us from all the nations."

⋙ [16] SMALLEST OF ANY PEOPLE: The role of the Jewish people does not depend on its numbers. This is reflected in the words of the prophet Zechariah, "Not by might, nor by power, but by My spirit, says the Lord of hosts" (4:6).

לֹא מֵרֻבְּכֶם מִכָּל הָעַמִּים חָשַׁק יְיָ בָּכֶם וַיִּבְחַר בָּכֶם, כִּי אַתֶּם הַמְעַט מִכָּל הָעַמִּים.

with manna which was strange to you, so that you might know that man does not live by bread alone, but by everything that is uttered by the Lord.

"Your clothes did not wear out, nor did your feet swell, these forty years. So you shall understand in your heart that as a man disciplines his son, so the Lord your God disciplines you.

"And you shall keep the commandments of the Lord your God, to walk in His ways, and to fear Him. For the Lord your God brings you to a good land, a land of brooks of water, of fountains and underground springs, bursting forth in valleys and hills; a land of wheat and barley, and vines and fig trees and pomegranates; a land of olive trees and honey; a land where you shall eat bread without scarcity—you shall not lack anything in it; a land whose stones are iron and out of whose hills you may dig copper. And you shall eat and be satisfied, and bless the Lord your God [17] for the good land which He has given you."

### IT IS NOT YOUR POWER

"BEWARE LEST YOU forget the Lord your God by not keeping His commandments; lest when you have eaten and are satisfied, and have built fine houses and dwell in them, and your herds and your flocks multiply, and your silver and gold have increased, that your heart does not become haughty and you forget the Lord your God. And lest you say in your heart, 'My power and the might of my hand have gotten me this wealth.' But you shall remember the Lord your God, for it is He who gives you power to get wealth, that He may establish His Covenant which He swore to your fathers."

### HE IS YOUR GLORY

"AND NOW, ISRAEL, what does the Lord your God require of you, [18] but to fear the Lord your God, to walk in all His ways, and to love Him; and to serve the Lord your God with all your heart

---

ᴇᏅ [17] AND BLESS THE LORD: The Talmud says: "Whoever enjoys a thing without blessing the Giver, commits a theft against God."

The Rabbis held that every meal must be followed by blessings of gratitude. "A loaf of bread on the table is a greater miracle than the parting of the Sea," they said.

ᴇᏅ [18] REQUIRE OF YOU: God asks nothing that is beyond man's abilities: only love, reverence, service and the fufillment of the *mitzvot*,

אֶרֶץ חִטָּה וּשְׂעוֹרָה וְגֶפֶן וּתְאֵנָה וְרִמּוֹן, אֶרֶץ זֵית שֶׁמֶן וּדְבָשׁ.

and with all your soul; to keep for your good the commandments of the Lord and His statutes, which I command you this day.

"For to the Lord your God belongs the heaven and the heaven of heavens, the earth with all there is on it. Only the Lord delighted in your fathers to love them, and He chose their children after them, even you, above all peoples. The Lord your God, He is God of gods and Lord of lords, the mighty and the awe-inspiring, who does not show partiality nor seek reward. [19] He upholds justice for the orphan and widow, [20] and loves the stranger, giving him food and clothing. Therefore, you shall love the stranger, for you were strangers in the land of Egypt. You shall fear the Lord your God. He is your glory and He is your God, who has done these tremendous things for you. Your fathers went down into Egypt with seventy persons; and now the Lord your God has made you as the stars of heaven for multitude."

## BEWARE OF STRANGE GODS

"WHEN THE LORD your God cuts off the nations before you, and you take their

---

His commandments. So long as we remember that it is God who created the beauties and wonders of life, not only may we partake of them, we are commanded to do so.

As illustration, a Nazarite was required to atone for a sin. What was his sin? That he had denied himself full enjoyment of God's world.

 [19] NOR SEEK REWARD: Worship, sacrifice, or even charity—all are of no value if they are attempts to reward or to "bribe" God. There are those who would change God's will without changing their own hearts. One must right the wrong he has done before he can come to God in prayer.

 [20] JUSTICE FOR THE ORPHAN AND WIDOW: It might seem, at first glance, that justice for all people should be indicated. The orphan and the widow, however, are given extra protection because they are helpless.

וַאֲהַבְתֶּם אֶת הַגֵּר כִּי גֵרִים הֱיִיתֶם בְּאֶרֶץ מִצְרָיִם.

place and dwell in their land, take care that you are not lured into following their ways. Do not inquire about their gods, and ask: 'How did these nations serve their gods? for I would like to do likewise.' You shall not do so to the Lord your God; for they have done every abomination which the Lord hates; for even their own sons and daughters do they burn in fire to their gods.

"You shall observe all this which I command you; you shall not add to it nor diminish it.

"If a prophet or a dreamer of dreams arises in your midst and he gives you a sign or a wonder, and the sign or the wonder comes to pass, and he says: 'Let us go after other gods which you have not known, and let us serve them,' you shall not listen to the words of that prophet or of that dreamer. For the Lord your God is testing you, to know whether you love the Lord your God with all your heart and with all your soul. After the Lord your God you shall walk, and Him you shall fear, and His commandments you shall keep, and you shall listen to His voice, and serve Him and cleave to Him."

### CHOOSE LIFE

"YOU ARE STANDING this day, all of you, before the Lord your God: your leaders, your tribes, your elders, and your officers, even all the men of Israel; your little ones, your wives, and the stranger that is in your camp, from the hewer of your wood to the drawer of your water. You are entering into a Covenant, sealed by an oath, which the Lord your God makes with you this day, that He may make you this day His own people and that He may be your God, as He has spoken to you and as He swore to your fathers, to Abraham, to Isaac, and to Jacob. Not with you alone do I make this Covenant and this oath, but with him that stands here with us this day before the Lord our God, and also with him who is not here with us this day.

"For this commandment which I command you this day is not too hard for you, neither is it far off. It is not in heaven, that you should say: 'Who shall go up to heaven, and bring it to us, and make us understand it, so that we may do it?' Neither is it beyond the sea, that you should say: 'Who will go across the sea for us and bring it to us, and make us understand it, so that we may do it?' But the word is very near to you, in your mouth and in your heart, that you may do it.

"See, I have set before you this day life and good, and death and evil, for I command you this day to love the Lord your God, to walk in His ways, and to keep His commandments, so that you

כִּי קָרוֹב אֵלֶיךָ הַדָּבָר מְאֹד, בְּפִיךָ וּבִלְבָבְךָ לַעֲשׂוֹתוֹ.

shall live, and the Lord your God shall bless you in the land which you go to possess. But if your heart turns away and you will not heed, but shall worship other gods and serve them, I declare to you this day that you shall surely perish.

"I call heaven and earth to witness against you this day, that I have set before you life and death, the blessing and the curse! Therefore, choose life that you may live, you and your children; that you may love the Lord your God, and heed His voice, and cleave to Him; for that is your life and the length of your days; that you may dwell in the land which the Lord promised to your fathers, to Abraham, to Isaac, and to Jacob."

הַחַיִּים וְהַמָּוֶת נָתַתִּי לְפָנֶיךָ, הַבְּרָכָה וְהַקְּלָלָה. וּבָחַרְתָּ בַּחַיִּים, לְמַעַן תִּחְיֶה אַתָּה וְזַרְעֶךָ.

# 26. DEUTERONOMY [16-31]

### MOSES WRITES THE TORAH

AND MOSES WROTE the Torah and delivered it to the priests, the sons of Levi, who carried the Ark of the Covenant of the Lord, and to all the elders of Israel. And Moses commanded them, saying:

### JUSTICE

"JUDGES AND OFFICERS shall you appoint in all your gates, which the Lord your God will give you, tribe by tribe, and they shall judge the people with righteous judgment. [1]

---

[1] RIGHTEOUS JUDGMENT: Why was God so concerned about justice? Because God's own honor was at stake. A judge's decision could destroy a person's livelihood, if not his life; could strip him of pride and honor. Because his responsibility was so great, a judge must be both wise and impartial. Since he sat as religious arbitrator, the honor of Judaism, and even of God, was involved.

שׁוֹפְטִים וְשׁוֹטְרִים תִּתֶּן לְךָ בְּכָל שְׁעָרֶיךָ אֲשֶׁר יְיָ אֱלֹהֶיךָ נֹתֵן לְךָ לִשְׁבָטֶיךָ, וְשָׁפְטוּ אֶת הָעָם מִשְׁפַּט צֶדֶק.

"You shall not pervert justice. [2]

"You shall not show favoritism; neither shall you take a gift, for a gift blinds the eyes of the wise, and perverts the words of the righteous.

"Justice, justice, [3] shall you pursue, that you may live and inherit the land which the Lord your God gives you.

"You shall not pervert the justice due to a stranger or to an orphan; nor take a widow's garment in pledge. And you shall remember that you were once a slave in Egypt, and that the Lord your God redeemed you from there, therefore I command you to do this thing.

"The fathers shall not be put to death for the children, neither shall the children be put to death for the fathers; only for his own sin [4] shall anyone be put to death. [5]

"And if a man has committed a sin deserving of death, and he is put to death, you shall then hang him on a tree. But his body shall not remain all night upon the tree; you shall bury him the same day; for he who is hanged is a reproach to God.

"You shall not oppress a hired servant who is poor and needy, whether he is one of your brethren or a stranger resid-

---

✒ [2] PERVERT JUSTICE: The Rabbis maintained that bribery or favoritism was only one type of misuse of justice. Any extra favor to one party (such as addressing him in a kinder tone, or allowing him to sit while the other stands), is forbidden. Acceptance of the slightest favor by a judge is also barred, even though he may assure himself that it will not affect his decision. He might be inclined against the donor, and again justice would not be served.

✒ [3] JUSTICE, JUSTICE: Certain Rabbis held that "justice" is repeated to indicate that an accused person who has been found innocent cannot be tried a second time for the same crime. This is comparable to present-day law forbidding double jeopardy.

A person who has been judged guilty can be retried if his innocence may thus be established.

Other Rabbis pointed out that justice is linked with living in the land of Israel. If there is no justice, the land cannot exist. *Sifri*, an ancient legal book, declares: "The appointment of honest judges is sufficient merit to keep Israel alive and secure on their land."

לֹא יוּמְתוּ אָבוֹת עַל בָּנִים וּבָנִים לֹא יוּמְתוּ עַל אָבוֹת. אִישׁ בְּחֶטְאוֹ יוּמָתוּ.

ing in your land. In the same day you shall give him his pay, before the sun goes down, because he is poor and awaits it urgently."

### LOANS AND PLEDGES

"YOU SHALL NOT take interest [6] for what you lend to your brother: interest of money, of food, or of anything else that is lent upon interest.

"When you do lend your neighbor any kind of loan, you shall not go into his house to take his pledge. You shall wait outside, and the man to whom you are making the loan shall bring the

---

&ら [4] ONLY FOR HIS OWN SIN: This ordinance seems to contradict the statement in Exodus that the descendants of an evildoer will suffer to the fourth generation.

The line in Exodus teaches a different moral lesson: that the influence of a bad home life is likely to persist for several generations.

The teaching here, that man is punished judicially only for his own sins, is to make certain that no one is punished for the sins of his parents or of other members of his race, nationality or religion. In its era, this idea was a break with tradition. Until very recently, if a man committed certain crimes, his whole family was punished; their property was confiscated, and they all might be driven into exile, or even put to death.

&ら [5] PUT TO DEATH: In the time of the Second Temple, the Rabbis had almost completely dispensed with capital punishment. They so interpreted the Biblical laws that an execution was rare. A Sanhedrin, Jewish court, that condemned one man to death in seventy years is called a "murderous" Sanhedrin by the Talmud. Rabbis Tarphon and Akiba commented, "If we had been members of that Sanhedrin, no man would have been condemned to death."

Only God can give life; only He should be able to take it. A candle which cannot be rekindled should not be extinguished.

&ら [6] YOU SHALL NOT TAKE INTEREST: Lending to a needy fellow-Jew became an important matter for the Jewish community. Charity, no

אִלּוּ הָיִינוּ בְּסַנְהֶדְרִין – לֹא נֶהֱרַג אָדָם מֵעוֹלָם.

pledge outside to you. And if he is a poor man and you take his garment in pledge, you shall return it to him by sunset that he may sleep in his garment and bless you.

"No man shall take a handmill or an upper millstone [7] in pledge, for he is taking a man's life in pledge."

### SLAVES

"IF YOUR BROTHER, a Hebrew man or a Hebrew woman, be sold to you, he shall serve you six years; and in the seventh year you shall let him go free. And when you let him go free, you shall not let him go empty-handed; you shall provide for him liberally [8] from your flock and from your threshing-floor, and from your winepress, and from all with which God has blessed you. And you shall remember that you were a slave in the land of Egypt, and the Lord your God redeemed you, therefore I command you to do this thing.

"And you must not begrudge it when you let him free; for he has served you six years at half the wage of a hired worker; and the Lord your God will bless you in all that you do.

"You shall not deliver to his master a slave who has escaped to you. He shall live with you, within your community, wherever he chooses to dwell; you shall not wrong him.

"If a man is caught kidnapping any

---

matter how kindly, damages the pride of him who receives it; but a loan without interest helps him re-establish himself. As a result, Hebrew Free Loan Societies, which exist to this day, have helped many get back on their feet without loss of self-respect.

A proverb says, "If you give a man a fish, you have fed him for one day; if you teach him to fish you have fed him all his days."

ᴄ§ [7] A HANDMILL OR MILLSTONE: A handmill or millstone could not be taken by a debtor as a pledge, lest his whole family go hungry. The Rabbis also forbade the taking in pledge of a man's tools, for without them the borrower could not earn a living.

ᴄ§ [8] PROVIDE FOR HIM LIBERALLY: When a Hebrew slave went free, his master had to provide for him liberally, so that he might have a fresh start in life. If the freed man left empty-handed, he would be

כִּי יִמָּכֵר לְךָ אָחִיךָ הָעִבְרִי אוֹ הָעִבְרִיָּה וַעֲבָדְךָ שֵׁשׁ שָׁנִים, וּבַשָּׁנָה הַשְּׁבִיעִת תְּשַׁלְּחֶנּוּ חָפְשִׁי מֵעִמָּךְ.

of his fellow Israelites, [9] and he treats him as a slave, or sells him, the thief shall die; so shall you put away the evil from your midst."

### GOING TO BATTLE

"WHEN YOU GO forth to battle against your enemies, and see horses and chariots and forces greater than yours, you shall not be afraid of them; for the Lord your God, who brought you up out of Egypt, is with you.

"And before the battle, the officers shall speak to the people, saying: If there is a man who has built a new house and has not dedicated it, let him return to his house, lest he die in the battle and another man dedicate it.

"If there is a man who has planted a vineyard and has not used its ripened fruit, let him return to his house, lest he die in the battle and another man enjoy its fruit.

"And if there is a man who has betrothed a wife but has not married her, let him return to his house, lest he die in the battle and another man marry her.

"And the officers shall speak further to the people: If there is a man who is fearful and faint-hearted, let him return to his house, lest his brethren's hearts melt as does his.

"And when the officers have finished speaking to the people, the army captains shall be placed at the head of the people."

---

unable to earn a livelihood, and might soon be forced to sell himself into bondage again. For this reason, the Rabbis required that he be given animals that bear young (a mule would not do), so that he might have a chance to prosper in his new freedom.

Contrast this with the too-long delayed freedom for slaves in Western countries. In many, the masters were compensated for loss of their slaves, but the slave received neither payment for his years of labor nor a sum to help him get started.

*⧉* [9] THE KIDNAPPER: Why was there a death penalty for kidnapping?

A man's freedom is so precious in Judaism that he who steals a human being to sell him as a slave is condemned.

When the Babylonian Code of Hammurabi decreed death for stealing a slave, it was out of concern for the property rights of the owner, even when the property was a human being.

מִי הָאִישׁ אֲשֶׁר בָּנָה בַיִת חָדָשׁ וְלֹא חֲנָכוֹ, יֵלֵךְ וְיָשֹׁב לְבֵיתוֹ, פֶּן יָמוּת בַּמִּלְחָמָה וְאִישׁ אַחֵר יַחְנְכֶנּוּ.

## ATTACKING A CITY

"WHEN YOU DRAW near a city to fight against it, [10] you shall offer it peace. If it accepts peace and opens its gates to you, then all the people in it shall pay tribute to you and shall serve you. If it will not make peace with you, but will make war against you, then you shall besiege it.

"When you besiege a city, you shall not destroy its trees by wielding an ax against them; you may eat their fruit, but you shall not cut them down; for the tree of the field [11] is not men, to be besieged by you. Only those trees which you know are not fruit-bearing may you destroy and cut down, in order to build a siege-work against the city that makes war against you, until it falls."

## THE KING

"WHEN YOU COME into the land which the Lord your God has given you, and shall say, 'I will set a king over me, like all the nations that are around me,' you shall set over you only a king whom the Lord your God shall choose: only one from your brethren shall you make king over you; you may not put over you a foreigner who is not your kinsman.

"He shall not acquire for himself many horses, [12] nor cause the people

---

&#8667; [10] TO FIGHT AGAINST A CITY: The Israelites might fight against a city, our Rabbis said, but not starve it out, or cut off its water supply, or afflict it with pestilence.

A city may be conquered, but not destroyed, said the *Sifri*.

&#8667; [11] TREE OF THE FIELD: The Rabbis further declared that wanton destruction was hateful. Anything of value was created for use, and its destruction was considered a sin. The destruction of food in a world that still hungers is criminal.

&#8667; [12] TOO MANY HORSES: The reference to "many horses" could have only one meaning: the build-up of cavalry for war. Egypt was noted for its horses. The Rabbis said that the king may acquire horses and chariots for his private use only. If he acquires many chariots he puts his faith in weapons of destruction instead of in God, and this will lead to war.

כִּי תִקְרַב אֶל עִיר לְהִלָּחֵם עָלֶיהָ, וְקָרָאתָ אֵלֶיהָ לְשָׁלוֹם.

to return to Egypt so that he may get horses, because the Lord has said to you: You shall return no more that way. Neither shall he take many wives, [13] that his heart be not turned away; neither shall he acquire too much silver or too much gold.

"And it shall be, when he sits upon the throne of his kingdom, that he shall have a copy of this Torah written for him in a book which is before the priests, the Levites. And he shall keep it with him and he shall read in it all the days of his life, that he may learn to keep all the words of this Torah and these statutes, to do them. He shall not become proud, nor turn aside from the commandment to the right or to the left; so that he may prolong his days in his kingdom, he and his children, in the midst of Israel."

## FIELDS AND VINEYARDS

"WHEN YOU COME into your neighbor's vineyard, [14] you may eat your fill; but you shall not put any in your vessel.

"When you come into your neighbor's standing corn, you may pluck ears with your hand; but you shall not use a sickle on your neighbor's standing corn.

"When you reap your harvest in your field and have forgotten a sheaf in the field, you shall not go back to fetch it; it shall be for the stranger, for the fatherless, and for the widow.

"When you beat your olive tree, you shall not go over the branches a second time; it shall be for the stranger, for the fatherless, and for the widow.

"When you gather the grapes of your vineyard, you shall not glean it afterward; it shall be for the stranger, for

---

&ε [13] TOO MANY WIVES: Solomon, who was famous for his thousand wives, is an example of what happened when a king disobeyed the law against multiplying wives. He taxed his citizens ruinously so that he might support his wives in luxury, while his people became impoverished and embittered. On his death his kingdom fell apart.

&ε [14] YOUR NEIGHBOR'S VINEYARD: The Rabbis limited this rule. They said that if every passerby took just one cluster of grapes or one piece of fruit, the farmer would be left with empty boughs. They limited this right to the hired men who worked the farm.

The Talmud warns, however, "Do not be a glutton, or you will not be hired again."

וְהָיְתָה עִמּוֹ וְקָרָא בוֹ כָּל יְמֵי חַיָּיו, לְמַעַן יִלְמַד לְיִרְאָה אֶת יְיָ אֱלֹהָיו לִשְׁמֹר אֶת כָּל דִּבְרֵי הַתּוֹרָה הַזֹּאת.

the fatherless, and for the widow. For you shall remember that you were a slave in the land of Egypt, therefore I command you to do this.

"You shall not muzzle the ox when he treads out the grain. [15]

"At the end of every three years, you shall take a full tenth of your produce and shall lay it within your gates. And the Levite, because he has no portion nor inheritance in your land, and the stranger, and the fatherless, and the widow shall come and eat their fill."

### PILGRIMAGES

"THREE TIMES A year shall all your males appear before the Lord your God, in the place which He shall choose; on the Festival of Unleavened Bread, and on the Festival of Weeks, and on the Festival of Booths. And they shall not appear before the Lord empty-handed; every man shall give as he is able, according to the blessing of the Lord your God which He has given you."

### THE OFFERING OF THE FIRST-FRUIT

"AND WHEN YOU come into the land which the Lord your God gives you as an inheritance, and you possess it and dwell in it, you shall take the first of all the soil's produce that you harvest from the land; and you shall put it in a basket and shall go to the place in which the Lord your God chooses that His name dwell. And you shall come to

---

[15] THE OX: "A righteous man regards the life of his beast," says the Book of Proverbs (12:10). He cares for the animal's needs and respects its feelings. He must feed his animals before he feeds himself. Consideration for animals is part of Jewish belief, in marked contrast to almost all other early civilizations.

The Romans pitted maddened animals against one another in the arenas. This is not surprising, since they did the same with human beings. When gladiators fought and killed each other, the Romans considered it a holiday.

"Blood sport" is the name given to hunting for sport, in which hundreds of birds or small animals might be slaughtered for amusement. The Bible despises Esau for the very reason that he was a hunter.

שָׁלֹשׁ פְּעָמִים בַּשָּׁנָה יֵרָאֶה כָל זְכוּרְךָ אֶת פְּנֵי יְיָ אֱלֹהֶיךָ בַּמָּקוֹם אֲשֶׁר יִבְחָר:
בְּחַג הַמַּצּוֹת וּבְחַג הַשָּׁבוּעוֹת וּבְחַג הַסֻּכּוֹת.

the priest who will be at that time, and say: I give thanks to the Lord your God that I came to the land which the Lord promised to our fathers to give us.

"And the priest shall take the basket from your hand, and place it before the altar of the Lord your God. And you shall declare before the Lord your God: 'A wandering Aramean was my father, and he went down into Egypt and sojourned there, few in number; and he became there a great nation, mighty and numerous. And the Egyptians treated us harshly and oppressed us, and laid upon us hard bondage. And we cried to the Lord, the God of our fathers, and the Lord heard our voice, and saw our affliction and our toil and our oppression. And the Lord brought us forth out of Egypt with a mighty hand and with an outstretched arm, and with great terror, and with signs and with wonders. And He has brought us to this place and has given us this land, a land flowing with milk and honey. And now, behold, I

have brought the first-fruit of the land, which Thou, O Lord, hast given me.'

"And you shall set it down before the Lord your God, and worship before the Lord your God. And you shall rejoice in all the good fortune which the Lord your God has given to you and to your house, and the Levite and the stranger in your midst."

### FOR ALL TO SEE

THEN MOSES AND the elders of Israel commanded the people, saying, "Keep all the commandments which I command you this day.

"And on the day when you pass over the Jordan to the land which the Lord your God gives you, you shall raise up great stones and plaster them over. And you shall write upon them all the words of this Torah, so that you may go into the land which the Lord your God gives you, a land flowing with milk and honey."

אֲרַמִּי אוֹבֵד אָבִי וַיֵּרֶד מִצְרַיְמָה, וַיָּגָר שָׁם בִּמְתֵי מְעָט, וַיְהִי שָׁם לְגוֹי גָּדוֹל עָצוּם וָרָב.

# 27. DEUTERONOMY [27–32]

**THE GREAT DOOMS**

THEN MOSES AND the priests, the Levites, spoke to all Israel, saying, "Keep silence and hear, O Israel: this day you are become a people [1] to the Lord your God. You shall therefore hearken to the voice of the Lord your God, and observe His commandments and His statutes, which I command you this day."

And Moses charged the people that day, saying, "These shall stand on Mount Gerizim to bless the people, when you have passed over the Jordan:

---

[1] YOU ARE BECOME A PEOPLE: It was fully forty years after the Exodus that Moses said to Israel, "This day you are become a people to the Lord." Had this not happened at the Exodus or at Sinai?

The Rabbis recognized that a new generation had arisen in the wilderness. Their fathers had experienced the Exodus and the revelation at Sinai, not this generation. Each generation must confirm for itself its relationship to God.

Therefore, Israel was asked to reaffirm the Covenant. They would

הַסְכֵּת וּשְׁמַע, יִשְׂרָאֵל: הַיּוֹם הַזֶּה נִהְיֵיתָ לְעָם לַיָי אֱלֹהֶיךָ.

Simeon, and Levi, and Judah, and Issachar, and Joseph, and Benjamin; and
these shall stand on Mount Ebal for the
dooms: Reuben, Gad, and Asher, and
Zebulun, Dan, and Naphtali.

"And the Levites shall speak and say
to all the men of Israel with a loud voice:

"Cursed be he [2] who makes a graven
or molten image, an abomination to the
Lord, and sets it up in secret. And all
the people shall answer: Amen.

"Cursed be he who dishonors his
father or his mother. And all the people
shall say: Amen.

"Cursed be he who removes his neighbor's landmark. And all the people shall
say: Amen.

"Cursed be he who makes the blind
go astray. And all the people shall say:
Amen.

"Cursed be he who perverts the justice
due to the stranger, fatherless, and
widow. And all the people shall say:
Amen.

"Cursed be he who strikes his neighbor in secret. And all the people shall
say: Amen.

"Cursed be he who does not uphold
the words of this Torah to do them. And
all the people shall say: Amen."

### THE GREAT BLESSINGS

"AND IT SHALL come to pass, if you
hearken diligently to the voice of the
Lord your God, to observe all His commandments, that the Lord your God will
set you high above all the nations of the
earth. And all these blessings shall come
upon you and overtake you, [3] if you
will listen to the voice of the Lord your
God.

"Blessed shall you be in the city, and
blessed shall you be in the field.

---

do so again after they had crossed the Jordan and taken possession
of the Promised Land.

⁊ [2] CURSED BE HE: These commandments are concerned with sins
which might be committed privately, without anyone else's knowledge. What one does in the privacy of his home is as important as
that which is visible to all.

The Rabbis illustrate this with the story of a man who began to
bore a hole under his seat in a boat. When the other passengers
complained, he retorted, "It's none of your business! The hole is
under my seat!" They answered, "Yes, but the water will enter and
drown us all."

בָּרוּךְ אַתָּה בָּעִיר וּבָרוּךְ אַתָּה בַּשָּׂדֶה.

"Blessed shall be the fruit of your body, and the fruit of your land, and the fruit of your cattle.

"Blessed shall be your basket and your kneading trough.

"Blessed shall you be when you come in, and blessed shall you be when you go out.

"The Lord will ordain blessing to you in your barns, and in all that you undertake; and He will bless you in the land which the Lord your God gives you.

"The Lord will establish you as a holy people unto Himself, as He has sworn to you, if you keep His commandments and walk in His ways. And all the peoples of the earth shall see that the name of the Lord is upon you.

"The Lord will open to you His goodly treasure, the heaven, to give the rain of your land in its season, and to bless all the work of your hand; and you shall lend to many nations, but you shall not borrow. And the Lord will make you the head and not the tail, if you hearken to the commandments of the Lord your God, which I command you this day to do."

BE STRONG AND OF GOOD COURAGE!

THEN MOSES WENT and spoke these words to all Israel: "I am one hundred and twenty years old this day; I can no longer come and go; and the Lord has said to me, 'You shall not go over the Jordan.' The Lord your God, He will go over before you; He will destroy these nations before you, and you shall take their place. And Joshua shall be at your head, as the Lord has spoken. Be strong and of good courage! Do not be afraid nor fear them; for the Lord your God goes with you! He will not fail you nor forsake you."

And Moses called Joshua and said to him before all Israel, "Be strong and of good courage; for you shall go with this people into the land which the Lord has promised to their fathers to give them; and you will enable them to inherit it."

And the Lord said to Moses, "The time is near when you must die. Call Joshua and present yourselves in the Tent of Meeting, that I may instruct him."

---

ᵉᵍ [3] THE BLESSINGS SHALL OVERTAKE YOU: These blessings, like the curses, seem almost like living things which will pursue one who does good or one who performs evil. He will earn more than the blessing or the curse: it is as though his deeds will give birth to more deeds, to make his life wonderful or hideous, as he has chosen.

חֲזַק וֶאֱמָץ, כִּי אַתָּה תָּבוֹא אֶת הָעָם הַזֶּה אֶל הָאָרֶץ אֲשֶׁר נִשְׁבַּע יְיָ לַאֲבוֹתָם לָתֵת לָהֶם, וְאַתָּה תַּנְחִילֶנָּה אוֹתָם.

So Moses and Joshua went to the Tent of Meeting. And the Lord appeared in a pillar of cloud in the Tent. And the Lord said to Moses, "Behold, you are soon to sleep with your fathers; and this people will rise up and go astray after the foreign gods of the land to which they go, and will forsake Me and break My Covenant which I have made with them. Now, therefore, write this song for you, [4] and teach it to the Children of Israel; then, when many evils and troubles have come upon them, this song shall confront them as a witness."

MOSES' SONG OF GOD

SO MOSES WROTE this song the same day;

and he commanded the Levites, "Assemble all the elders of your tribes and your officers, that I may speak these words in their ears, and call heaven and earth to witness against them."

And Moses spoke in the ears of all the assembly of Israel the words of this song:

"Give ear, you heavens, [5] and I
   will speak;
And let the earth hear the words of
   my mouth.
May my teaching drop as the rain,
My speech fall as the dew;
As a gentle rain upon the tender
   grass,
And as the showers upon the herb.

---

◦§ [4] WRITE THIS SONG FOR YOU: Since the command to write the song is put in the plural, the Rabbis understood that both Moses and Joshua were to write it.

Abraham ibn Ezra, the great Spanish-Jewish Biblical commentator, held that the plural form instructs each Israelite that he must write for himself a copy of the Torah. Since few men are capable of this, the custom arose that during the celebration which is held when a scribe is finishing a scroll, each man present is given the honor of filling in one of the final letters in order that he may fulfill his obligation.

◦§ [5] GIVE EAR, YOU HEAVENS: Moses calls on the heavens and earth to witness that God has made a Covenant with the Israelites, for no treaty is legal without witnesses. The only eternal witnesses—for this Covenant is everlasting—are heaven and earth.

הַאֲזִינוּ הַשָּׁמַיִם וַאֲדַבֵּרָה, וְתִשְׁמַע הָאָרֶץ אִמְרֵי פִי.

For I will proclaim the name of the
    Lord;
Give greatness to our God.

"The Rock, His work is perfect;
For all His ways are justice;
A faithful God, [6] without
    iniquity;
He is just and upright.

"Remember the days of old,
Consider the years of many
    generations;
Ask your father, and he will in-
    form you,
Your elders, and they will tell you.
When the Most High gave the
    nations their inheritance,

When He separated the children
    of men,
He fixed the borders of the peoples
According to the number of the
    Children of Israel.
For the portion of the Lord is His
    people,
Jacob the share of His inheritance.

"He found him in a desert land,
In the waste of the howling
    wilderness;
He surrounded him, He cared for
    him,
He kept him as the apple of His
    eye.
As an eagle that stirs up her nest,
Hovers over her young,

---

[6] A FAITHFUL GOD: Why should God be faithful to man? God is faithful not for His own gain, but so that man will follow His goodness.

Dama ben Netaniah had a precious stone which he hid for safe-keeping under his bed. A merchant offered him a large sum for the gem, but when he went to get the stone, he found his father asleep on the bed. He reported that he could not sell the gem at that time. The merchant thought that he was bargaining, and offered him a higher price. Dama still refused.

After a while his father awoke, whereupon Dama gave the gem to the merchant. The buyer expected to pay the larger sum, but Dama refused it.

"Your first price was sufficient," he said. "My father was sleeping and the gem was under his bed. I do not wish to be rewarded for obeying God's command. As God is faithful to man, so do I wish to be faithful to God, for His sake, and not for reward."

כַּנֶּשֶׁר יָעִיר קִנּוֹ, עַל גּוֹזָלָיו יְרַחֵף ...

Spreads out her wings, takes them,
Carries them on her wings—
The Lord alone did lead him,
And there was no strange god with
   Him.

"He made him ride on the high
   places of the earth,
And he ate the fruit of the field;
And he sucked honey out of the
   crag, [7]
And oil out of the flinty rock;
Curd of cows, and milk of sheep,
With fat of lambs,
And rams of the herds of Bashan,
   and he-goats;
And from the blood of grape you
   drank foaming wine.

"But Yeshurun grew fat, [8] and
   kicked—
You grew fat, you grew thick, gross
   with food—

And he forsook God who made
   him,
And scoffed at the Rock of his
   salvation.

"And He said: I will hide My face
   from them,
I shall see what their end shall be;
For they are a very perverse
   generation,
Children in whom there is no
   faithfulness.
They angered Me with a no-god;
I will anger them with a no-people.

"And the teeth of beasts will I send
   upon them,
With the poison of crawling things
   of the dust.
The sword shall bring death outside, as shall the terror within;
Slaying both young man and
   maiden,

---

   [7] HONEY OUT OF THE CRAG: Bees often make their hives in the clefts of rocks or in hollow trees, from which the honey oozes. A wandering shepherd is able to suck honey from a crag or from the side of a tree.

     Oil does come from flinty rock. The farmers deliberately plant their olive trees among limestone rocks. Fed by the minerals, the trees flourish and grow heavy with fruit.

   [8] YESHURUN GREW FAT: "Yeshurun," a poetic name for the people of Israel, comes from the word *yashar*, upright. Even the upright man, however, may become complacent if he is too prosperous.

...יִפְרֹשׂ כְּנָפָיו יִקָּחֵהוּ, יִשָּׂאֵהוּ עַל אֶבְרָתוֹ.

The infant as well as the man of
gray hairs.
Vengeance is Mine, [9] and
recompense,
For the time when their foot shall
slip.
But the Lord will vindicate His
people
And He will take compassion on
His servants.

"See now that I, I am He,
And there is no god besides Me;

I deal death, and I bring to life;
I have wounded, and I heal;
And there is none that can deliver
out of My hand.

"Sing aloud, O you nations, of His
people;
For He avenges the blood of His
servants,
And renders vengeance to His
enemies,
And clears guilt from the land of
His people."

---

[9] VENGEANCE IS MINE: When Israel sins, he will be punished, for
he is failing to live up to the Covenant, said the Rabbis.

They also derived a second meaning from this verse: man must
never take revenge, for this is God's privilege alone. In taking vengeance, man sins anew. His revenge is a fresh crime which may in
itself call forth vengeance.

הַרְנִינוּ גוֹיִם עַמּוֹ, כִּי דַם עֲבָדָיו יִקּוֹם, וְנָקָם יָשִׁיב לְצָרָיו וְכִפֶּר אַדְמָתוֹ עַמּוֹ.

# 28. DEUTERONOMY [32–34]

IT IS YOUR LIFE

AND WHEN MOSES finished speaking the words of this song to all Israel, he and Hoshea [Joshua], [1] the son of Nun, he said to them, "Take to heart all the things of which I warn you today, that you may instruct your children to observe all the words of this Torah. For it is not an empty thing [2] for you, because it is your life; [3] and through this you shall lengthen your days upon the land which you go to possess."

[1] WHY IS JOSHUA CALLED HOSHEA? Our Sages explain that Hoshea was Joshua's childhood name and this serves to clarify Joshua's relationship to Moses. Although Joshua was now leader of his people and a man of stature and position, he still gave Moses the same respect he gave him when a youth.

[1] HE AND HOSHEA: At the beginning of the great song, Moses alone is speaking, but at its close, both Moses and Joshua speak. The Tal-

כִּי לֹא דָבָר רֵק הוּא מִכֶּם, כִּי הוּא חַיֵּיכֶם וּבַדָּבָר הַזֶּה תַּאֲרִיכוּ יָמִים.

MOUNT NEBO

AND THE LORD said to Moses that selfsame day, [4] "Ascend Mount Nebo,
which is in the land of Moab facing
Jericho; and view the land of Canaan
which I am giving to the Children of
Israel as a possession. And you will die

---

mud considers this the occasion when Moses transferred his authority
to Joshua. He chose to establish Joshua as leader in his own lifetime,
so that none might say that this was not Moses' choice.

[2] IT IS NOT AN EMPTY THING: Moses was careful to point out that
his words were more than poetry or sermonizing. They are law; and
as man lives by it or fails to live by it, his life is affected.

Rashi puns on the phrase, "an empty thing," making it read, "an
empty word." There is not an empty word in the whole Torah, he
says. One may not decide to obey this Torah regulation, but not
that; for there is not one word in the Torah which, if properly interpreted, will not prove to be of profound value.

Rashi's point of view was in keeping with the Rabbis' teachings
that all wisdom could be found in the Torah, if one searched wisely.
"Turn it, turn it, for all is in it," they said.

[3] IT IS YOUR LIFE: An aged woman asked a rabbi, "I am too old to
live, but cannot die. How can I find death?"

The rabbi asked how she had reached her advanced years. "My
father trained me in the Torah," she replied, "and I study in it every
day. Moreover, no matter what the day holds, I pray in the synagogue
regularly."

"Do not study and do not pray for three days," said the rabbi. The
old woman obeyed; she refrained from study and prayer. On the
third day she died.

The old woman symbolizes the community of Israel, which lives
only because of the Torah and the Synagogue. Should Israel abandon
Torah and prayer, she will find a speedy death.

וּרְאֵה אֶת אֶרֶץ כְּנַעַן אֲשֶׁר אֲנִי נוֹתֵן לִבְנֵי יִשְׂרָאֵל לַאֲחֻזָּה.

on the mountain and be gathered to your people, as Aaron your brother died on Mount Hor. Because you broke faith with Me among the Children of Israel at the waters of Meribath-kadesh, in the wilderness of Zin; because you did not sanctify Me among the Children of Israel. For you shall see the land afar off, but you shall not go into the land which I am giving the Children of Israel!" [5]

### THE BLESSING OF MOSES

AND THIS IS the blessing with which

---

◄§ [4] THAT SELFSAME DAY: The Rabbis interpreted this phrase to mean, "in the middle of the day," and taking place before the eyes of all. The expression, "the selfsame day," occurs only three times in the Bible.

Three great events recorded in the Pentateuch had to take place before the eyes of all the people: the Flood, which teaches that only a righteous humanity can survive; the Exodus, which teaches that man must be free; and Moses' death, from which we learn that even the Prophet chosen of God must die, and that the people must rely on no one man.

In the first case, Noah's warnings of the coming flood had been in vain. The scoffers even threatened to prevent him from entering the ark. Hence, God did not command Noah to embark at night, when he might climb aboard unseen, but in broad daylight. Noah and his family braved the mob, and calmly went aboard at noontime.

In the second instance, the departure from Egypt, the Hebrews' former masters awoke as from a stupor, and cried, "Our slaves are leaving! Let us take our whips, and drive them back to their labors!" The Hebrews might have waited for night to slip out of Egypt, but they marched out at noon.

Third, when Moses was commanded to ascend Mount Nebo, the Children of Israel realized that he was leaving them forever. They cried out in anguish for their beloved leader not to leave them. Moses did not wait for night: at midday he turned his steps toward the peak; and not a hand could be raised to restrain him, though every eye saw him go.

כִּי מִנֶּגֶד תִּרְאֶה אֶת הָאָרֶץ וְשָׁמָּה לֹא תָבוֹא, אֶל הָאָרֶץ אֲשֶׁר אֲנִי נוֹתֵן לִבְנֵי יִשְׂרָאֵל.

Moses, the man of God, blessed the
Children of Israel before his death:
   "The Lord came from Sinai,
   And rose from Seir to them;
   He shone from Mount Paran,
   And He came from the holy
      myriads,
   At His right hand lightning flashed
      for them.

   "Yea, He loves the peoples;
   All His holy ones—they are in Thy
      hand;
   And they sit down at Thy feet,
   Receiving Thy words.

Moses commanded us the Torah,
A heritage for the congregation of
Jacob.

   "There is none like God,
      O Yeshurun,
   Who rides upon the heavens as
      your help,
   And in His grandeur on the skies.
   The eternal God is a dwelling-
      place,
   And underneath are the everlast-
      ing arms;
   And He thrust out the enemy from
      before you.

---

[5] YOU SHALL NOT GO: According to legend, Moses was grief-stricken that he could not enter the Promised Land. "Let me enter the land," he begged. "Have I not served You these years in the wilderness?"

"The giving of the Torah was accomplished," God answered, "and the time for conquest and settlement has come. Therefore, Joshua must take over."

"Let Joshua be the leader and I will serve him," Moses pleaded. The next morning he rose early to prepare Joshua's garments, and to sweep the Tabernacle. Joshua was startled to see Moses acting as his servant. "Only by serving you," Moses explained, "can I enter the Promised Land."

As Joshua stood in the Tabernacle, the voice of God spoke to him. As the new leader stood, silent and awed, Moses asked the reason. "God is speaking to me," Joshua replied. "Do you not hear His voice?"

A wave of envy came over Moses, for he had not heard. And then he prayed to God, "I forgo the privilege of entering Canaan. Better I die, than live in envy."

תּוֹרָה צִוָּה לָנוּ מֹשֶׁה, מוֹרָשָׁה קְהִלַּת יַעֲקֹב.

"And Israel dwells in safety,
The fountain of Jacob apart,
In a land of corn and wine;
And His heavens drop down dew.
Happy are you, O Israel! Who is
like you?
A people saved by the Lord."

### THE DEATH OF MOSES

AND MOSES WENT up from the plains of Moab to Mount Nebo, to the summit, which faces Jericho. And the Lord showed him all the land, even Gilead as far as Dan.

And the Lord said to him, "This is the land which I promised to Abraham, to Isaac, and to Jacob, saying: 'I will give it to your children.' I have let you look upon it, but you shall not go over there."

So Moses, the servant of the Lord, died there [6] by command of the Lord.

And he was buried in the valley of the land of Moab; and to this day no one knows his burial place.

And Moses was a hundred and twenty years old when he died: neither were his eyes dimmed nor his vigor lessened.

And the Children of Israel wept thirty days for Moses in the plains of Moab. And Joshua, the son of Nun, was full of the spirit of wisdom, for Moses had laid his hands upon him; and the Children of Israel obeyed him and did as the Lord had commanded Moses.

And there has not arisen a prophet since in Israel like unto Moses, whom the Lord knew face to face; in all the signs and the wonders which the Lord sent him to do in Egypt, to Pharaoh, and to all his servants and to all his land; and in all the mighty hand and in all the wonders, which Moses wrought in the sight of all Israel.

---

⁊ [6] MOSES DIED THERE: The Rabbis maintained that Moses wrote the entire Pentateuch. How could he have written of his own death? Some Rabbis said that Joshua wrote these lines, others that God had dictated the last verses to Moses, whose final act on earth was to write them down, his eyes blurred with tears. This done, he calmly climbed Mount Nebo.

ḤAZAK, ḤAZAK, V'NIT-ḤAZEK

וּלְכֹל הַיָּד הַחֲזָקָה וּלְכֹל הַמּוֹרָא הַגָּדוֹל אֲשֶׁר עָשָׂה מֹשֶׁה לְעֵינֵי כָּל יִשְׂרָאֵל.

# SOURCES

All references to the tractates of the Talmud are from the Babylonian Talmud unless otherwise indicated.

The references listed in the sources are from the following editions:

M'chilta d'Rabbi Ishmael, Meir Ish Shalom, editor, Vina, 5630 (1870)

Midrash Rabbah, Epstein edition, Warsaw

Midrash Tanḥuma, Rosen edition, Warsaw

Pirké d'Rabbi Eliezer ha-Gadol, Bamberg edition, Warsaw, 5612 (1852)

Sifra, Schlosberg edition, Vienna, 5622 (1862)

Sifri, Meir Ish Shalom, editor, Vina, 5624 (1864)

Tana D'vé Eliyahu Rabbah and Zuta, Tzinkes edition, Warsaw 1883

Zohar, Rom edition (3 vol.), Vilna, 5642 (1882)

## CHAPTER ONE

1. Genesis Rabbah (Gen. R.) 1:2; Tanḥuma (Tan.) B'reshit 1
2. Gen. R. 3:9; Zohar I 24b
3. Gen. R. 12:15
4. Gen. R. 3:1, 4; 11:2
5. Gen. R. 5:10
6. Sanhedrin 38a
7. Sanhedrin 38a, 37a
8. Gen. R. 10:12
9. Yalkut Shim'oni (Yalkut) I §13
10. Sanhedrin 38a
11. Ginzberg, Legends of the Jews (Ginzberg, Legends), I, p. 70
12. Gen. R. 8:15; 18:2
13. Gen. R. 19:1, 4

## CHAPTER TWO

1. Gen. R. 22:8, 16, 17
2. Gen. R. 22:22; Tan. B'reshit 7
3. Gen. R. 22:21
4. Sanhedrin 56b
5. Tan. B'reshit 11
6. Tan. Noaḥ 5, 18
7. Gen. R. 33:9

8. Pirké d'Rabbi Eliezer, Chap. 24
9. Sefer ha-Yashar, p. 25

## CHAPTER THREE

1. Sefer ha-Yashar, pp. 21–24
1. A. Jellenik, Bet ha-Midrasch, Ma'aseh Avraham Vol. II, pp. 118–119
1. Gen. R. 38:18
1. Gen. R. 38:18
2. Gen. R. 39:2
3. Gen. R. 39:21, 43:8
4. Gen. R. 39:10
5. Gen. R. 41:6
6. Gen. R. 41:13; Yalkut I §71
7. Da'at Z'kénim mi-Ba'alé ha-Tosephot (Da'at Z'kénim), Gen. 15:12; Naḥmanides, Gen. 15:12

## CHAPTER FOUR

1. Gen. R. 43:8; N. Krochmal, Moreh N'vuché ha-Z'man, S. Ravidowitz, editor, p. 455
2. Tan. Noaḥ 18

3. Gen. R. 119:10; Sanhedrin 109b; Pirké d'Rabbi Eliezer, Chap. 25
4. Folklore

## CHAPTER FIVE

1. Yalkut I §101; Tan. Vayera 22, 23
2. M. J. Berditchevsky Mi-m'kor Yisrael, Vol. II, p. 135
3. Gen. R. 55:11
4. Sanhedrin 89b
5. Tan. Vayera 23

## CHAPTER SIX

1. Zohar I 131b
2. Pirké d'Rabbi Eliezer, Chap. 16; I. B. Levner, Kol Aggadot Yisrael (Levner, Aggadot) I, pp. 107–108; Gen. R. 57:1
3. Levner, Aggadot I, pp. 107–108
4. Gen. R. 60:12
5. Gen. R. 60:15

## CHAPTER SEVEN

1. Gen. R. 63:6; Tan. Ki Tetze 4

2. Gen. R. 63:14
3. Gen. R. 63:15
4. Yalkut I §110; Gen. R. 63:15
5. Gen. R. 63:16, 18
6. Gen. R. 63:19
7. Yalkut I §115; Gen. R. 65:11
8. Gen. R. 65:15
9. Gen. R. 63:18

CHAPTER EIGHT
1. Gen. R. 68:7
2. Sforno, Gen. 28:11
3. Ibn Ezra, Gen. 28:12
4. Gen. R. 69:2
5. Gen. R. 68:13; Pirké d'Rabbi Eliezer, Chap. 35
6. K'tubot 50a
7. Gen. R. 70:8
8. Gen. R. 68:13; Shabbat 146a
9. Homiletics

CHAPTER NINE
1. Gen. R. 84:4, 6
2. Gen. R. 84:8
3 & 4. Rashbam, Gen. 37:28
5. Sefer ha-Yashar, p. 118
6. Tan. (Buber) Numbers 22b
7. Gen. R. 87:3
8. Midrash Lekkaḥ Tov (Buber), Gen. 40:21
9. Tradition; Homiletics
10. Gen. R. 89:7; Oraḥ Ḥayyim 41:33

CHAPTER TEN
1. Levner, Aggadot I, p. 227, based on Gen. R. 91:5
2. Gen. R. 91:6
3. Tradition
4. Gen. R. 91:4
5. Gen. R. 91
6. Gen. R. 91:10
7. Gen. R. 91:12
8. Gen. R. 91:13
9. Gen. R. 93:5, 9

CHAPTER ELEVEN
1. Yalkut I §152; Gen. R. 94:3, 4
2. Sefer ha-Yashar, p. 157
3. Yalkut I §152; Gen. R. 94:8
4. Ginzberg, Legends, II, p. 137

5. Gen. R. 98:4
6. Gen. R. 82:11; Yalkut I §126

CHAPTER TWELVE
1. Exodus Rabbah (Ex. R.) 1:10; Tan. Sh'mot 5
2. Yalkut I §163; Sotah 11b; Ex. R. 1:15; Tan. Vayetze 9; Midrash T'hillim (Buber) Psalm 114
3. Ex. R. 1:16; Sotah 11b
4. Ex. R. 1:19
5. Ex. R. 1:31; Yalkut I §166
6. Ex. R. 1:32; Sefer ha-Yashar, p. 191
7. Ex. R. 2:2
8. Ex. R. 2:9, 10
9. Ex. R. 3:16; 5:2, 3
10. Ex. R. 4:2; Yalkut I §174; Ex. R. 4:4; Rashi, Ex. 18:2

CHAPTER THIRTEEN
1. Ex. R. 5:17; Tan. Sh'mot 24
2. Sefer ha-Yashar, p. 205; Ex. R. 5:18
3. Ex. R. 5:23
4. Ex. R. 5:26
5. Ex. R. 9:12

CHAPTER FOURTEEN
1. Sanhedrin 91a
2. Tan. (Buber) Numbers 30b
3. Ex. R. 20:10
4. M'chilta d'Rabbi Ishmael (M'chilta) Bo 15b
5. Ex. R. 20:2, 3
6. M'chilta B'shalaḥ 28b, 31b; Sotah 37a; Ex. R. 21:7; Bialik & Ravnitzky, Midrashim K'tannim, Vol. I, p. 62
7. Ex. R. 21:9
8. Ex. R. 21:9; Bialik & Ravnitzky, Midrashim K'tannim, Vol. I, p. 61
9. Yalkut I §225
10. Ex. R. 20:9

CHAPTER FIFTEEN
1. M'chilta B'shalaḥ 44b
2. Sifri, Numbers §89; Yoma 76a
3. Tan. (Buber) Exodus 34a; Ex. R. 25:3

5.
6.
7. M
8. Ginz
   65
9. B'rachot
10. Yalkut I
    Eliyahu Zu.

CHAPTER SIXTEE
1. Ex. R. 28:2
2. Sifri, Deuteronomy M'chilta Yitro 67
3. Bialik & Ravnitzky, Midrashim K'tannim, Vol. I, p. 74
4. Ex. R. 29:1
5. Ex. R. 29:9
6. Yalkut I §286
7. Shabbat 88b, 89a
8. Yalkut I §286
9. Baba Kamma 83b
10. M'chilta Yitro 62a

CHAPTER SEVENTEEN
1 & 2. Yalkut I §391
3. Ex. R. 42:6; B'rachot 32a; Ex. R. 43:7, 8
4. Ex. R. 42:3
5. Yalkut I §391; Avot d'Rabbi Natan 2:3; Tan. Ki Tissa 30
6. Yalkut I §392
7. B'rachot 63b; Yalkut I §394
8. Tan. T'rumah 8

CHAPTER EIGHTEEN
1. Tan. (Buber) Exodus 58b; Tan. Ki Tissa 27
2. Tan. Ki Tissa 10; Hertz Pentateuch (Hertz)
3. Tan. Ki Tissa 10; Ex. R. 34:1
4. Yoma 72b
5. Ex. R. 51:4

CHAPTER NINETEEN
1 & 2. Hertz
3. Sifra Vayikra, Chap. 2, p. 4b
4. Ḥullin 5a (see Rashi); Hertz
5. Sifra Vayikra, Chap. 22, p. 27b
6. Yerushalmi, Pe'ah, V:5; Ḥullin 131b

...ah 16a
M'chilta 16a
Shabbat 119a
10. Yoma 35b
11. M'chilta Mishpatim 101
12. P'saḥim 36a
13. Hertz
14. Yoma 74b
15. Folklore
16. Naḥmanides, Lev. 23:43
17. Sanhedrin 26a
18. Yerushalmi, Rosh Hashanah, I:2; Hertz
19. Sforno, Lev. 25:42

CHAPTER TWENTY
1. Sotah 14a
2. Sifra K'doshim, Chap. 3, p. 88b; Baba M'tzia 61b
3. B'rachot 16a
4. Yalkut I §609
5. Sifra K'doshim Chap. 4, p. 89a
6. Sanhedrin 73a
7. Folklore
8. Yerushalmi, N'darim, IX:4
9. Ibid. (See commentary "Korban Edah")
10. Homiletics

CHAPTER TWENTY-ONE
1. Hertz
2. Yalkut I §730, 210
3. Ḥullin 49a; Homiletics
4. Tradition
5. Numbers (Num.) R. 11:16
6. Sifri, Numbers §85–87
7–9. Num. R. 15:15

CHAPTER TWENTY-TWO
1. Num. R. 16:6
2. Yalkut I §742; Num. R. 16:9
3. Num. R. 16:8
4. Yalkut I §743
5. Sotah 35a; Yerushalmi, Ḥagigah, I:7

6. M'naḥot 43b (see Rashi and Tosefot)
7. M'naḥot 43b, 44a, 38a
8. Tan. Korah 2
9. Num. R. 18:4
10. Num. R. 18:9
11. Num. R. 18:5
12. Num. R. 18:8
13 & 14. Samson Raphael Hirsch
15. Homiletics
16. Yalkut I §764
17. Deuteronomy (Deut.) R. 5:13

CHAPTER TWENTY-THREE
1. Num. R. 20:1
2. Num. R. 20:9
3. Num. R. 20:11
4. Sanhedrin 105b; Homiletics
5. Échah Rabbati P'siḥta 2

CHAPTER TWENTY-FOUR
1. Ḥoshen Mishpat, Halachah 276
2 & 3. Yalkut I §776
4. Num. R. 21:15
5. Num. R. 21:16
6. Deut. R. 2:20
7. Tan. Massé 11

CHAPTER TWENTY-FIVE
1. Sifri, Deuteronomy 1
2. B'rachot 61b
3. Philo; R. Travers Herford, Pharisees, p. 54
4. Homiletics
5. Lev. R. 19:2; Hertz
6. Folklore
7. B'rachot 61b
8. Sifri, Deuteronomy 33
9. Kiddushin 30a; Homiletics
10. Naḥmanides, Deut. 6:8
11. Tradition; Homiletics
12 & 13. Tradition
14. Homiletics
15. Hertz
16. Homiletics

17. B'rachot 35b; P'saḥim 118a
18. N'darim 10a
19. Homiletics
20. M'chilta Mishpatim 95b

CHAPTER TWENTY-SIX
1. Midrash T'hillim (Buber) Psalm 82
2. Sifri, Deuteronomy 17, 144
3. Sifri, Deuteronomy 144; Yalkut I §907
4. Ibn Ezra, Deut. 24:16; Ex. 20:5
5. Makkot 7a
6. Folklore
7. Sifri, Deuteronomy 272
8. Sifri, Deuteronomy 119
9. Homiletics
10. Sifri, Deuteronomy 203
11. Shabbat 105b
12. Sanhedrin 21b
13. I Kings, 11:1–8
14. Baba M'tzia 92a (see Rashi)
15. Gittin 62a

CHAPTER TWENTY-SEVEN
1. Homiletics
2. Da'at Z'kénim, Deut. 27:15; Lev. R. 4:6
3. Ibn Ezra, Deut. 28:2
4. Ibn Ezra, Deut. 31:19
5. Rashi, Deut. 32:1
6. Kiddushin 31a
7. Yerushalmi, Pe'ah, VII:3
8. Hertz
9. Sifri, Deuteronomy 325

CHAPTER TWENTY-EIGHT
1. Sifri, Deuteronomy 334
1. Sotah 13a; Rashi, Deut. 32:44
2. Rashi, Deut. 32:47; Pirké Avot 5:25
3. Yalkut II on Proverbs 8, §943
4. Yalkut I §948
5. Deut. R. 9:5
6. Baba Batra 15a